understanding **Marxism**

understanding **Marxism**

Geoff Boucher

ACUMEN

First published in 2012 by Acumen

Acumen Publishing Limited

4 Saddler Street
Durham
DH1 3NP, UK

ISD, 70 Enterprise Drive
Bristol
CT 06010, USA

www.acumenpublishing.com

ISBN: 978-1-84465-520-5 (hardcover)
ISBN: 978-1-84465-521-2 (paperback)

British Library Cataloguing-in-Publication Data
A catalogue record for this book is available from the British Library.

Typeset in Minion Pro.
Printed in the UK by MPG Books Group.

Contents

Acknowledgements

I wish to thank Deakin University for its grant under the Outside Studies Placement scheme, which made possible six months of research for this book. I also wish to thank the Department of Philosophy at Macquarie University for generously hosting me during this period. I could not have wished for better discussion partners than Nicholas Smith and Heikki Ikaheimo during this time; special thanks are due to Jean-Philippe Deranty, whose accurate political instincts on theoretical questions and committed materialism make him an ideal interlocutor, and to Robert Sinnerbrink, whose breadth of engagement with radical theory and voracious appetite for philosophical dialogue mean that no coffee break is ever wasted. Early drafts of some chapters of this book have appeared as background notes and occasional papers for the Melbourne Hegel Summer School, and some material from my *The Charmed Circle of Ideology* has been substantially reworked here. Dialogues with Jeff Sparrow and Matthew Sharpe have enabled me to clarify the positions expressed here in a multitude of ways. Jeremy Moss is another friend who has generously shared his knowledge of political philosophy; the remaining mistakes are obviously the result of my incorrigibility. Christine McMahon prepared the figures in the text, for which, thanks. Andy Blunden is, in addition to being a great friend, a wonderful interlocutor. He is also one of the editors of the Marxist Internet Archive: all hail the MIA! The work that has gone into its database is staggering, and I am personally deeply grateful to its editorial collective. What on earth did we do before that searchable archive? Frauke Hoffmann read parts of the manuscript and lived through much more; for her love and support, my astonished gratitude.

Abbreviations

MESW   Karl Marx & Friedrich Engels, *Selected Works in One Volume* (seventh edition) (Moscow: Progress Publishers, 1986).

MECW3   Karl Marx & Friedrich Engels, *Collected Works Volume 3* (of 50) (New York: International Publishers, 1976) (contains "Economic and Philosophical Manuscripts of 1844").

MECW5   Karl Marx & Friedrich Engels, *Collected Works Volume 5* (of 50) (New York: International Publishers, 1976) (contains "The German Ideology").

MECW6   Karl Marx & Friedrich Engels, *Collected Works Volume 6* (of 50) (New York: International Publishers, 1976) (contains "The Poverty of Philosophy").

C1–3   Karl Marx, *Capital: A Critique of Political Economy* in 3 volumes (Moscow: Foreign Languages Publishing House, 1959–61).

TSV1–3   Karl Marx, *Theories of Surplus Value* in 3 volumes (Moscow: Progress Publishers, 1963–66).

introduction

Marx and Marxism

Today, radical thinking about social alternatives stands under prohibition. According to defenders of the neoliberal transformation of every facet of human existence into a market, Marxism has failed. The catastrophe of historical Communism – the human rights abuses and totalitarian repression characteristic of the so-called "socialist states" of the former Soviet Union and contemporary China – is adduced as the proof. Anything that goes beyond the advocacy of human rights, it is claimed, necessarily ends in disaster. Parliamentary democracy is the final horizon of good government; capitalism is the ultimate form of the just society; Marx is supposed to be directly responsible for the atrocities of Stalin and Mao; and Marxism, benevolent as it might seem, is said to result in totalitarian dictatorship. Anybody who dares to question this is promptly arraigned on charges of moral and political irresponsibility.

Not so long ago, a philosopher in the pay of a multinational think tank linked to the US State Department triumphantly announced that radical free-market capitalism was the "end of history". Such voices have muted somewhat of late, in light of unprecedented financial crises and continuing foreign wars. They have had little to say in the face of the persistence of untold millions in the slums of this planet, whose quiet misery silently refutes the great lie of our time, that the market is the best and fairest way to deliver prosperity and justice to all. But the apologists for the status quo rise to a great crescendo whenever the unquiet ghost of Marx is invoked. Marx is dead; Marxism is finished – *and it must stay that way!*

The aim of this book is to defy that prohibition on radical thinking about social alternatives. Marxism as an intellectual movement has been one of the most important and fertile contributions to twentieth-century thought. The influence of Marxism has been felt in every discipline in the social sciences and interpretive humanities, from philosophy, through sociology and history, to literature. The emancipatory social movements of the future will draw their inspiration from Marx, and Marxism, among others. This is because Marxism is a politics of mass struggle and popular mobilization in the name of a social alternative to the profit system, and this is likely to remain a feature of political life in the future.

Announcements of the death of Marxism are seriously premature. Indeed, no social theory in the twenty-first century that retains an emancipatory intent can be taken seriously unless it enters a dialogue not just with the legacy of Marx, but also with the innovations and questions that spring from the movement that he sparked, Marxism. For Marxism – this book will argue – has two characteristics that mean that engagement with it is a must for any resolutely modern thought:

1. Marxism is the most serious normative social-theoretical challenge to liberal forms of freedom that does not at the same time reject the modern world.
2. Marxism is the most sustained effort so far to think the present historically and to reflexively grasp thought itself within its socio-historical context.

("Normative" here has the philosophical meaning of tending to establish a value, that is a standard of correctness, by prescription of rules that are evaluative rather than descriptive. A normative social theory states how society should be, as well as how things are now. It should not be confused with "normalized", meaning statistically regular and conforming to the normal distribution, or "bell-shaped curve".)

Accordingly, Marx and Marxism claim to burst the horizon of modernity through a progressive radicalization of its premises, rather than a reactionary repudiation of the modern world's distinctive historical consciousness and practical freedom.

Firmly convinced that Marxism matters, and will continue to matter in the future, this book seeks to understand the greatness and limitations of Marx and of Marxism. Marx is a controversial figure whose work is sometimes rightly criticized, but more often simply misrepresented, even demonized. Expressions such as "the dictatorship of the proletariat", which in its context very clearly meant a radically new form of participatory democracy, lend themselves to the facile equation between Marx and totalitarianism. Marx was not a totalitarian. The "socialist" states run by Stalin and Mao (for instance) bear no resemblance whatsoever to Marx's description of socialism. But this book advocates intellectual autonomy, not political conversion: it is not a defence and vindication of Marx, but a clear-headed effort to *understand* and to *explain* Marxism. In the right place, I will explain how limitations in Marx's position left the door open for a form of politics that is the direct opposite of the emancipatory intention that frames historical materialism.

If Karl Marx (1818–83) is a controversial figure, Marx*ism* is an absolute commotion of dissent. The fierce debates begin with the development of Marx's own thought. Because of the radically historical character of Marx's thinking, Marx was "the philosopher of eternal new beginnings, leaving behind him *many* incomplete drafts and projects" (Balibar 1995: 6). Accordingly, some distinguish between the philosophical "young Marx" (1843–58) and the scientific "mature Marx" (1859–83). What is the relationship between them? Transcendence of youthful naivety or betrayal of an original insight? In this book, I reject the fiction of an iron wall between youth and maturity, along with the idea that Marx had a watertight system. Marx's thought is characterized by unresolved tension as well as by an astonishing power of synthesis and integration.

Then there is the lifelong collaboration between Karl Marx and Friedrich Engels (1820–95). Is Engels an independent thinker, the first Marxist, or the first distorter of Marx's thought? It is all too convenient to celebrate Marx as an unsystematic genius in possession of a radical anti-philosophy, in order to place a dunce's cap on Engels and parade him around as responsible for the disasters produced under the banner of Marxism. In this book, I treat Engels as an independent thinker who influenced Marx, and who in turn systematized Marx's research into party educational material while making original contributions to historical materialism. There is, however, a tension within Marxism, between social philosophy and "scientific socialism". Historical materialism as a social philosophy makes normative claims. Scientific socialism is a non-philosophical research programme that uses the methodologies of the natural sciences in sociology and politics. Marx described the working class as the key to universal human emancipation, while Engels invented the term "scientific socialism". But although this opposition helps describe the difference between Marx and Engels, it is also internal to the thought of the mature Marx.

Finally, there are the differences between various sorts of Marxism. There is theoretical Marxism and there is the practical activity of the communist movement. There is "Western Marxism" and Soviet Marxism, and there is the Marxism of the intellectuals and the Marxist theory of the party leaders. What, then, does "Marxism" mean? First, we can speak about the century of Marxism in terms of the communist movement (1890–1990). This is the hundred years of mass parties whose programmes were based exclusively on the work of a single Marxist figure, for instance Lenin or Mao, as the "authentic" interpretation of Marx. The history of the communist movement is essential to an understanding of Marxism, but it is not the central focus of this book. Accordingly, although I will discuss Lenin, Trotsky, Luxemburg, Gramsci, Stalin and Mao, some of the most fascinating non-canonical theoretical writings of other party leaders must be merely mentioned in passing. Related to this decision, second, the Marxist theory of the party leaders that I do discuss is not the centre of this book. Soviet Marxism, and more generally historical materialism as scientific socialism, is treated as less important than Marxism as a social philosophy. What that effectively means is that this book seeks to understand the Marxism of the intellectuals, especially so-called "Western Marxism".

There is a compelling reason for this decision. Within the Marxism of the intellectuals, we can distinguish (somewhat schematically) between the social-scientific and the normative social-theoretical approaches. Historical materialism as an approach in the social sciences is all about the role of economic factors, regarded as involving a relation between classes and production, in historical explanations. This is Marx's most important contribution to contemporary social scientific research. No body of thought can be considered to be a form of Marxism if it does not include central reference to the idea (explained in Chapter 1) of a class-based understanding of "economic determination in the final instance" (MESW: 682–3). Indeed, the majority of Marx's research was aimed at formulating a scientific theory of social systems and a science of history capable of explaining how societies emerge, mature and decay. On the basis of scientific analysis of the contradictions of capitalism's political economy, Marx predicted that the system was headed for deep crisis and long-term stagnation. He maintained that capitalism would be overthrown by the exploited class of that system, the working class, or "proletariat", in a socialist revolution that would lay the foundation for a radically new form of society, communism. The social scientific side of Marxism is concerned with the revision and correction of these hypotheses and predictions, in light of economic developments, political history and sociological data.

But that is not why Marx is a controversial figure, and it is not the main reason why Marxism will remain relevant in the future. Marx was also a political activist whose allegiance to the oppressed sections of the population led him to participate in the foundation of international parties with communist politics. The partisan side of Marx's work is expressed in his theoretical writings through a keen interest in political strategy and moral condemnation of what he described as capitalist exploitation. In the *Communist Manifesto*, Marx and Engels do not only claim that history can be explained through class struggle – they also advocate taking the side of the proletariat in the forthcoming revolution. Marx memorably declared that "the proletarians have nothing to lose but their chains", and encouraged the international unity of the working class in winning the world for communism (MESW: 63). Historical materialism as a normative social theory is a philosophy of liberation. It makes a series of striking claims that the social scientific historical research is intended to support, not to establish. These claims involve ideas about what human existence through creative labour ought to be, how the working class embodies moral universality, the roots of social inequality in the exploitation of labour, and the material interests represented by the capitalist state. They mandate the realization of freedom in a new society. In other words, Marxism justifies revolution. *That* is controversial – extremely so. It is the fundamental reason why Marx has been accused of totalitarianism. It is also the reason why the encounter with Marx is transformative, not only of the way people think, but of their lives as well. Marxism is a distinctively historical theory that normatively challenges liberalism in a way no other modern theory does. This side of Marxism, then, can be defined as the series of efforts to update and correct Marx's outline of a modern social philosophy that is based on an emancipatory practical intention to change the world.

Historical materialism

At the heart of the Marxist vision is the idea that proletarian struggles potentially represent a new ethical basis for human society beyond capitalism. But we cannot understand this political commitment in isolation from the social scientific aspect of Marx's theory, which, among other things, is supposed to determine what is realistically possible. To formulate the historical materialist position on society, Marx used dialectical philosophy (explained in Chapter 1), to bring together three threads. These are an understanding of the historical process as driven by class struggle to attain higher and higher forms of society, a theory of the terrain of the class struggle in terms of how social structure is shaped by economic factors, and a concept of the roots of class struggle as located in the fundamental relation between humanity and nature, the labour process. According to Marx and Engels's *Communist Manifesto*:

> The history of all hitherto existing society is the history of class struggles. Freeman and slave, patrician and plebeian, lord and serf, guild-master and journeyman – in a word, oppressor and oppressed – stood in constant opposition to one another, carried on an uninterrupted, now hidden, now open, fight, a fight that, each time, ended either in a revolutionary reconstitution of society at large, or in the common ruin of the contending classes.
> (MESW: 35–6)

For Marx, the social classes involved in historically decisive struggles are defined through antagonistic relations in economic production. In the celebrated "1859 Preface" to *A Contribution to the Critique of Political Economy*, Marx summed up his conception of the connections between class, production, society and history. He also mapped out the central categories of historical materialism and thereby defined the major parameters of what would become Marxism. Few summaries can match it for concision and accessibility; it is well worth reading it slowly through in its entirety.

> The general conclusion at which I arrived and which, once reached, became the guiding principle of my studies can be summarised as follows. In the social production of their existence, men inevitably enter into definite relations, which are independent of their will, namely relations of production appropriate to a given stage in the development of their material forces of production. The totality of these relations of production constitutes the economic structure of society, the real foundation, on which arises a legal and political superstructure and to which correspond definite forms of social consciousness. The mode of production of material life conditions the general process of social, political and intellectual life. It is not the consciousness of men that determines their existence, but their social existence that determines their consciousness. At

a certain stage of development, the material productive forces of society come into conflict with the existing relations of production or – this merely expresses the same thing in legal terms – with the property relations within the framework of which they have operated hitherto. From forms of development of the productive forces these relations turn into their fetters. Then begins an era of social revolution. The changes in the economic foundation lead sooner or later to the transformation of the whole immense superstructure. In studying such transformations it is always necessary to distinguish between the material transformation of the economic conditions of production, which can be determined with the precision of natural science, and the legal, political, religious, artistic or philosophic – in short, ideological forms in which men become conscious of this conflict and fight it out. … No social order is ever destroyed before all the productive forces for which it is sufficient have been developed, and new superior relations of production never replace older ones before the material conditions for their existence have matured within the framework of the old society. … In broad outline, the Asiatic, ancient, feudal and modern bourgeois modes of production may be designated as epochs marking progress in the economic development of society. The bourgeois mode of production is the last antagonistic form of the social process of production … but the productive forces developing within bourgeois society create also the material conditions for a solution of this antagonism. The prehistory of human society accordingly closes with this social formation. (MESW: 181–2)

What Marx does in the "1859 Preface" is to set up a relationship between three major terms: production, structure and history.

Marx concentrates on production because, for him, "praxis", the active transformation of the natural environment, human nature and the social world, is centred on the social labour involved in the "production of material existence". In other words, Marx holds a production-centred theory of praxis (for present purposes, social practice) that is modelled on the labour process. The labour process is accordingly not only the kernel of economic practice, but also the model for non-economic (that is, political, juridical and ideological) practices.

Marx defines the forces of production as the sum of the means of production (technological capacity, plant and equipment, instruments of labour, raw materials) and labour power (human energy to perform work, including knowledge of technique). Marx, impressed by the connection between technological development and social progress, once quipped that "*the hand-mill gives you* society with the feudal lord; the steam-mill, society with the industrial capitalist" (MECW 6: 166). That sounds like technological determinism, the idea that social development is caused by technological advances. But the centrality of the social relations of production, defined as the ownership of the means of production and consequently the ability to exploit labour, demonstrates that Marx is not a technological determinist. It is the relations of production, or property relations, that foster, correspond with and then retard the advance of the productive forces.

Structure, the resulting totality of material institutions and social relations, can in turn be divided into economic infrastructure, and political, juridical and ideological superstructure. Marx's "base-and-superstructure" model in the "1859 Preface" can helpfully be represented in a diagram (Figure 1).

Marx's conception of structure in the "1859 Preface" involves the idea that the economic foundation sets limits of variation to the superstructural levels. Marx holds that the economic foundation has particular laws of motion, necessary laws of economic development specific to the mode of production in question, which account for its emergence, operation and degeneration. By contrast, developments in the superstructural levels depend on the interplay of economic factors with a multitude of other factors. Accordingly, in abstract and formal terms, the economic foundation is the space of logical necessity, while the superstructures are a space of historically contingent variation. Accordingly, in the "1859 Preface" the progression of society through a series of

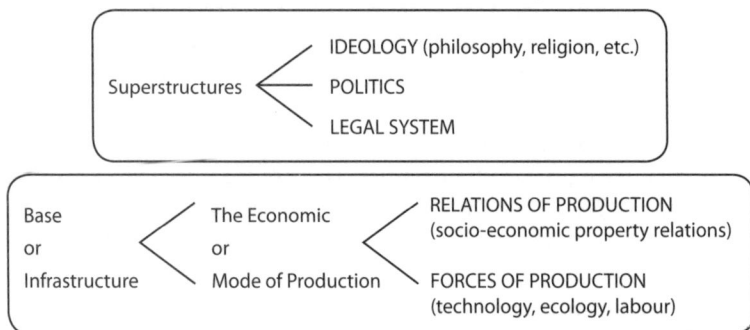

Figure 1 Marx's base-and-superstructure model (based on Jameson 1981: 32).

modes of production (Asiatic, ancient, feudal and bourgeois) represents an upwards ascent in humanity's productive forces, from scarcity to the threshold of abundance, unfolding with historical necessity through the lawful evolution of the economic infrastructures. Political revolutions, juridical transformations and ideological struggles execute (or seek to retard) this historical necessity, under conditions where, as Engels clarifies, "the economic movement finally asserts itself as necessary" (MESW: 682). By contrast with the blind process of pre-communist revolutions, however, the communist revolution will involve a conscious transformation of society, first into socialism (eradication of residual inequalities), then communism (full material abundance and the withering away of the state). Although communism represents the logically necessary conclusion of class history, conscious political, juridical and ideological struggle is essential to the realization of the historical potentials released by capitalism. By seizing the state as the lever of social transformation in a revolutionary insurrection, the communists set about the planned and deliberate renovation of society. Humanity, under the flag of communism, although it does not make history under circumstances of its own selection, nonetheless becomes fully the author and agent of its own destiny.

From Marx ... to Marxism

This book's central thesis, then, is that that there are three threads in Marx: history, structure and praxis. Against the background of the influence of Hegel's dialectical philosophy, Marx succeeded in producing a synthesis of these elements that provided a compelling normative vision of a liberated humanity, reconciled to the natural world. He also produced a social scientific research programme, outlined in the "1859 Preface", that provided a powerful explanatory framework for grasping historical change. This was intended to situate his normative vision within the limits of political realism, as opposed to utopian speculation.

For Marx, historical materialism as a comprehensive social theory represented the end of philosophy. Philosophical systems had interpreted the world and indicated the potential for the actualization of reason in society. But the achievement of a rational society could only happen through political action guided by enlightened consciousness. Philosophy, with its contemplative stance and its treatment of the historically developed world as a social fact, stood condemned as little more than an apology for alienated social conditions. Yet, paradoxically,

Marx's synthesis of the potentially disparate elements of history, structure and praxis in fact represented a new social philosophy, integrated through a materialist interpretation of the Hegelian dialectic. As social and political conditions changed and new intellectual challenges to Marx's social philosophy arose, the Marxist theorists sought to update his social theory, rectify the sociological positions of historical materialism and respond to philosophy with a Marxist reply. Their interrogation of philosophy remains one of the most morally serious and intellectually comprehensive challenges of the last hundred years, and the result is Marxism as an intellectual current in twentieth-century thought.

After a concise explanation of Marx's theory (Chapter 1), I turn to the development of Marxism for the bulk of the book. While paying attention to the complexity of Marxism as a movement, I intend to adapt a schema initially developed by the neo-Marxist philosopher Jürgen Habermas as an interpretive device (Habermas 1979a: 130–77). (I deal with Habermas in the chapter on Critical Theory.) My intention is to provide the book with a strong narrative that explains how and why Marx's original synthesis broke up and to clarify why Marxism today is necessarily a dispersion of Marx's original theoretical unity. The idea is that the evolution of a research programme happens through stages of "restoration", "renaissance" and "reconstruction". Restoration means the recovery of an original doctrine from its subsequent distortion, which happens when the connection between praxis, structure and history is reasserted. Renaissance means opening up new directions through a variation of an argument's premises; in this case through taking any two of praxis, structure and history, and varying the third. Restoration means complete redesign of an argument to fit its goals to new premises; in other words rethinking praxis, structure and history, and their connection, from the ground up. Habermas proposes this as a theoretical description of the Marxist field without discussing the empirical complexity of the movement and the many variants of the Marxist renaissance and efforts towards its reconstruction, as I shall do.

The relevant developments are:

- The attempted *restoration* of Marx's doctrine in the classical, or "orthodox", Marxism of the Second, Third and Fourth Internationals (Chapter 2). Marx had integrated praxis, structure and history through dialectical philosophy. These thinkers and leaders responded to new conditions which seemed to invalidate Marx's synthesis and, for them, called for the re-integration of history, structure and praxis through the procedures of the natural sciences.

- The *renaissance* in historical materialism sought by the Western Marxists, who selectively highlighted elements of Marx's combination and brought in fresh philosophical ideas, to integrate the parts in a new synthesis. In the context of a return to the Hegelian roots of Marxism, the Hegelian Marxists highlighted praxis and history in Marx, which enabled a novel conceptualization of structure (Chapter 3). By contrast, the Frankfurt School was most interested in the relation between structure and history, which soon led to a radical interrogation of praxis itself, with startling results (Chapter 4). Structural Marxism entirely rejected the teleological implications of Marx's conception of history, generating a rich research programme in the relation between practices and structure that made possible a striking reconceptualization of the historical process (Chapter 5).
- Although this strategy produced impressive results, it ultimately ran its course and ceded place to efforts to *reconstruct* Marx's insights into social alienation and political liberation around new concepts of history, structure and practice. Although Analytical Marxism has posed significant challenges to central parts of Marx's synthesis, instead of turning aside from Marxism, it has sought to reconstruct historical materialism from the perspective of methodological individualism and using the methods of contemporary philosophical research (Chapter 6). The efforts of the successors to the Frankfurt School in Critical Theory, and centrally Jürgen Habermas, have sought to generate a "critical theory of society with an emancipatory intent" by engaging with a wide variety of non-Marxist sources in a highly critical reconstruction of historical materialism (Chapter 7). Finally, the post-Marxism arising initially from a critical reconstruction of Structural Marxism is examined, to illustrate the potentials of encounters between post-structuralism and the Marxist renaissance for future research (Chapter 8).

Throughout, the aim is to position the reader to grasp the stakes in many current debates and the essential conceptual background to some of the most exciting and important contemporary thinkers. To achieve these aims, it has been necessary to restrict the scope of the treatment. Although I aim to integrate social history, theoretical development and philosophical arguments into a concise and accessible analysis of historical materialism, I have not been able to discuss every thinker or the broader history of the socialist movement. Concentrating on Marxism as a contribution to the intellectual project of modern thought, I have been forced to neglect the detailed geographical and historical treatment of socialist politics in the twentieth century. Likewise, there are many important contributions to Marxist historiography, sociology and anthropology, political science and philosophy of science that I have had to pass over in silence. Several important thinkers in twentieth-century Marxism, such as the Praxis Group, the Austro-Marxists, Jean-Paul Sartre and Maurice Merleau-Ponty, Ernst Bloch and Walter Benjamin, Giovanni Della Volpe and Lucio Colletti, have been neglected in the interests of precision of exposition and clarity of explanation. Finally, I have not been able to cover contemporary classical Marxism, although I do suggest further reading in my conclusion.

In its exposition of Marx and Marxism, the book highlights a series of key social-theoretical and philosophical topics that have been at the core of debate in the twentieth century. The Marxist theory of history, its thesis of the primacy of economic determinations, the concepts of ideology and social class, Marxist theory of the state and the emancipatory vision of Marxism are introduced, and then the progressive revision of these ideas is explained as each school of thought is discussed. Each chapter is relatively free-standing, with a survey of the movement in question's position on the major topics of Marxist social philosophy. Although I thereby introduce the major schools of Marxist social thought and critically assess their strengths and weaknesses, this is not a partisan argument designed to evaluate which part of the tradition is the most authentic or correct. Instead, it seeks to understand how and why Marxism developed as it did and to position readers to draw their own conclusions about Marxism's advantages and limitations.

one

Marx before Marxism

Marx's social philosophy is a theory of freedom in the spirit of the Enlightenment, which holds that only the rational society makes the good life possible. By linking moral independence and individual fulfilment to rational conduct and reasoned debate, the Enlightenment inaugurated critical social theory, the study of the degree to which the social conditions necessary for rational living have been achieved. Marx's innovation in this programme is to have seen that the achievement of reason in society means that social theory must issue in political strategy if it is not to become an apology for the unreasonable conditions it detects (Marcuse 1999: 252–7). Marx's social philosophy accordingly developed a theory of the historical sequence of modes of production, which matured through several phases, as his research turned from practical politics to political economy and back again. Throughout, it is the relation between praxis, structure and history that guides Marx's conception of social struggles and political freedom.

This chapter explores the central ideas of Marx – alienation, the labour theory of value, the contradictions of capitalism, the state and ideology, classes and revolution – as the essential background to understanding Marxism. I trace Marx's development from the materialist inversion of Hegelian philosophy of the "young Marx" to the more scientific theory of the "mature Marx", indicating breaks and continuities between the "two Marxes". I close with an extended reflection on the tension between descriptive–explanatory and normative–evaluative accounts in Marx. I propose that these are crucial for grasping the impact of historical experiences and intellectual challenges that arose after Marx.

Dialectical philosophy

The dialectical philosophy of G. W. F. Hegel (1770–1831) was a major intellectual inspiration for Marx. The most important descriptive meaning of "dialectics" is that Hegel's philosophy focuses on the idea of historical development through social and intellectual contradictions, where the contradiction between antagonistic forces is eventually resolved by means of revolutionary change. The basic schema operating in Hegel's model of history is that social evolution begins from a primordial unity, then divides and becomes alienated, opposing individuals to the society, before finally reconciling the individual to society. Every stage of development involves both increasing antagonism between the individual and society, and expanded possibilities for individual self-realization. The final social form retains the individuality that alienation made possible but resolves the contradictory divisions which generated alienation. Because for Hegel freedom means the ability of individuals to self-realize under conditions of moral autonomy, he describes the historical process as a series of stages of progress in the consciousness of freedom (Hegel 1956: 19). History, from Hegel's perspective, has an underlying built-in goal (or "teleology"), which operates independently of individual intentions, consisting of a final stage of history in a free and rational society. For Hegel, capitalism is the "end of history" (Hegel 1956: 103, 442), which mandates the reform of capitalism rather than anti-capitalist revolution.

Although the complexity of Hegelian philosophy means that it defies quick summary (see Sinnerbrink 2007, also in this series), its normative core can be economically stated. Hegel thinks that the social conditions necessary for moral autonomy and individual self-realization, which together he calls freedom, have developed historically. The Enlightenment philosopher Immanuel Kant (1724–1804) defined moral autonomy as individual self-determination through rational reflection on norms of action. Refusing to be dictated to by authorities, the morally autonomous individual would test practical actions for their universality, and in this way become a rationally self-legislating person guided only by universal principles. This Enlightenment ideal is crucial to the liberal vision of a social contract involving "negative liberty", that is protection of the freedom of autonomous individuals from interference and representative government.

Although there is no doubt that Hegel was a sort of liberal, he found Kant's philosophical execution of this programme extremely disappointing. Hegel argued that Kant's idea of the autonomous subject failed to understand its social and historical conditions (Hegel 1977: 355–74). Further, socio-historical alienation is still present in the Kantian picture. Notoriously, Kant's *Critique of Pure Reason* (theory), *Critique of Pure Practical Reason* (practice or morality) and *Critique of Judgment* (art) have significant tensions between them. For Kant, theoretical reasoning about the natural environment regards the world as determined by natural laws, while practical (moral) reasoning about social action considers the world as an arena for free self-determination. Kant's aesthetics, intended to resolve the potential contradiction between freedom (practical reason) and determinism (theoretical reason), only demonstrated that the idea of teleology provided a possible way out of the impasse, but went no further. Furthermore, at the heart of Kantian moral autonomy lurks a split between virtue and happiness, between doing one's universal duty and satisfying the basic human end of attaining wellbeing. That undermines the motivations of the self-legislating rational agent supposed to support the social contract and representative government. Unless it could be shown that general prosperity resulted from the same conditions as those that mandated action according to universal principles, Hegel reasoned, many would conclude that the road to human happiness lay through irrational and immoral behaviour (for example exploiting others).

Against this intellectual background, it is perhaps not surprising that Hegel hit upon the idea of a historical teleology, one that generated a series of social stages in the evolution of freedom and whose final result would be the reunification of social prosperity (i.e. human happiness) with universal principles (i.e. moral autonomy). The core driver of this process is the evolution of the social conditions for moral autonomy and social prosperity in what Hegel called "mutual recognition", the ability of each individual to recognize the other as free and to rationally consent to the liberty of each as the condition for the freedom of all. Hegel insisted that this was not an intellectual process alone, but was instead institutionally embedded in the social structures of "ethical life", the normatively rich arrangement of the family, civil society (meaning economic organizations and civic associations) and the state. Struggles for recognition by individuals seeking the full realization of their moral autonomy and human happiness were shaped by their institutional location in the alienated social structures of ethical life. These structures matured through a series of historical changes expressing an increasing consciousness of freedom, until finally a society emerged that self-consciously represented a de-alienated condition. In *The Philosophy of Right* (1821), Hegel described capitalism as such a society: rational, free and universal.

Hegel's synthesis of the social practices of mutual recognition, the social structures of ethical life and a historical teleology of the realization of freedom influenced Marx tremendously. Yet from the beginning, Marx detected a tension in Hegel's philosophy, which Engels later spelt out in terms of a contradiction between system and method (MESW: 591). On the one side was its character as a finished system, announcing such baroque achievements as "absolute knowledge" of the "rationality of the real" in capitalism as the "end of history". On the other side was its relentlessly historical character, as an effort to think through ever-changing social contradictions. Hegel regarded social antagonisms as a "unity of opposites", that is as a contradiction between opposed forces, generated by the historical limitations of the situation of conflict. The dialectical method proposed that the resolution of these contradictions happened through the "determinate negation" of current limitations. Intellectually, this means the process of holistically specifying the causal determinants of isolated phenomena and abstract ideas, thereby locating them in their social and historical context. Practically, it describes the emergence and actualization of latent potentials for expanded freedom from the very core of the existing conflict situation, through concrete historical processes of struggle that formed an ascending series of higher and higher stages in the liberation of humanity. In Hegel's philosophy, the methodology is harnessed to the system through the figure of the "negation of the negation", the idea that the sequence of determinate negations that constitute the stages of history have a teleological goal in a final, positive society lacking all contradictions. Controversially, Marx retained the basic schema of a series of determinate negations as upwards progress towards a society free from contradiction, but insisted that because he had no blueprint for the future society, this was not a historical teleology.

Marx's inversion of Hegel

The death of Hegel resulted in a political split among his followers into conservative "Right Hegelians" and progressive "Left Hegelians". Among the Left Hegelians was a young Doctor Marx, who had just finished a thesis on Greek materialist philosophy. After graduating, Marx became involved with Left Hegelian and pro-democratic journals, but following important early involvement in Germany with the *Rheinische Zeitung*, he was forced by police censorship to shift to Paris to work on the *Deutsche-Französische Jahrbücher* in 1843. In left-wing France, Marx came into contact not only with other progressive exiles, but also with the French working-class socialist movement, which had developed as a result of the social conditions created by the industrial revolution. Here, Marx began to diverge from the Left Hegelians on two decisive points.

First, consistent with their idealist assumption that history was the progressive development of rational freedom, the Left Hegelians argued for an intellectual revolution as the key to "true democracy" (i.e. a parliamentary system of representative government). They considered religion, still used in the 1800s to justify the rule of princes, the main obstacle to democracy. The Left Hegelians' proposals, however, went beyond Enlightenment denunciations of religious superstition in one crucial respect. They considered the core of religious ideals to be a legitimate, but distorted, expression of human solidarity. Marx adopted these ideas in his famous "Theses on Feuerbach", but he criticized the idea that a purely intellectual grasp of what he was soon to call "ideology" was the key. The new philosophy must provide a materialist interpretation of distorted ideas about the human essence – such as religious beliefs and idealist philosophies. That meant it must concentrate on social practices in relation to the natural environment, especially material production. As Marx later wrote, this would enable a recovery of Hegelian philosophy for materialist ends: "the mystification which dialectic suffers in Hegel's hands by no means prevents him from ... present[ing] its general form ... [but] it must be turned right side up again, if you would discover the rational kernel within the mystical shell" (C1: 20).

Second, the Left Hegelians followed Hegel in maintaining that the state is (or should be) a neutral universal arbiter standing above society and representing the public interest. From their intellectual revolution, the Left Hegelians proposed, would flow the reform of the state, so that the state could finally achieve its philosophical goal in the representation of universal human interests. But through contact with the French socialist movement, Marx began to fully realize the limitations of the Left Hegelians. In his *Contribution to the Critique of Hegel's "Philosophy of Law"* (1844), Marx contested the neutrality and universality of the capitalist state. Moral reform through an intellectual revolution was unlikely to succeed when the state defended private property.

Political revolutions patterned on the French Revolution created private individuals "separated from the community", Marx proposed, whereas a social revolution that abolished private property would achieve "human emancipation" (MECW3: 164, 168). He proposed that the social revolution in Germany must be undertaken by the proletariat, because this is the social movement with "radical chains" whose emancipation entails the complete restructuring of society (*ibid.*: 186). The new philosophy is to lead this "passive element" so that "the *head* of this emancipation is *philosophy*, its *heart* is the *proletariat*" (*ibid.*: 187). In a decisive encounter in 1844, Marx met Friedrich Engels and read his *The Condition of the English Working Class* (1843), beginning a lifelong intellectual collaboration.

By 1844, then, Marx had become a communist. Unlike the Left Hegelians, Marx's political commitments did not remain armchair convictions but formed the basis for intense organizational work that led, with Engels, to the *Communist Manifesto* in 1848. The defeat of the revolutions of 1848 and the subsequent political reaction confirmed the main thesis of the *Manifesto* that history was the result of class struggles. This radical position meant that Marx was forced into another exile, this time in England, and an extended period of further research into political economy.

Ironically, in turning to political economy to understand revolutionary failure, Marx followed Hegel, whose "dialectic of lordship and bondage" (i.e. master–slave dialectic) is based on a reading of classical political economists Adam Smith and David Ricardo (Lukács 1975: 301–466). Not knowing this history, Marx saw this as a radical break with Hegel, claiming that:

> My dialectical method is not only different from the Hegelian, but its direct opposite. To Hegel … the process of thinking, which under the name of "the Idea" he even transforms into an independent subject, is the demiurgos of the real world, and the real world is only the external, phenomenal form of "the Idea". With me, on the contrary, the ideal is nothing else than the material world reflected by the human mind and translated into forms of thought. (C1: 19)

There is considerable evidence that the materialist content of Marx's critique of political economy is expressed within dialectical forms directly derived from Hegel's philosophy (Rosdolsky 1977). Marx's preparatory work for *Capital*, the *Grundrisse*, employs a dialectical schema taken from Hegel's *Logic* (Uchida 1988), and *Capital* itself is best reconstructed through dialectical forms (Smith 1989). That is not surprising, because, as Marx says, his methodology is formally Hegelian, and his conception of "science" is based on Hegel's idea of a dialectical reconstruction of the results of natural and social sciences (Zeleny 1980). Marx's break with Hegel is also a return to Hegel.

Species being and creative praxis

Many brief introductions to Marx scarcely mention Ludwig Feuerbach (1804–72), the radical philosopher who inspired Marx (and Engels) to turn to materialism. In *The Essence of Christianity* (1841), Feuerbach inverted Hegel by using the dialectical method together with a material-ist anthropology. Instead of studying historical forms of consciousness, Feuerbach regarded "the subject" as the human animal in the natural environment. As Engels afterwards summarized, Feuerbach maintains that "nothing exists outside of nature and man, and the higher beings our religious fantasies have created are only the fantastic reflection of our own essence" (MESW: 592). The human animal projects its natural capacities onto abstract ideas and an imaginary being: divine love and Christian morality are really humanity's capacity for natural affection and social solidarity. Christ is the "species being" of humanity in an alienated, inverted form.

According to Feuerbach's reading, then, idealist philosophy turned out to be an alienated expression of social capacities grounded in human nature. Consequently, Feuerbach called for a radical "new philosophy [that] makes human beings (including nature, as the basis for human beings) into the sole, the universal, and the highest object of philosophy. It therefore makes anthropology, including physiology, into the univer-sal science" (Schmidt 1971: 25, Feuerbach cited). In Feuerbach's concept of species being, Marx found the inspiration for a new philosophy. What Feuerbach lacked, though, according to Marx, was the relentlessly *historical* approach of Hegel. The idealist philosopher had grasped the his-torical development of the human essence, but failed to understand this in terms of humanity's natural species being. Feuerbach's materialism had understood humanity's natural species being, but he had imagined that this was something static and ahistorical (MESW: 29).

For Marx, the idea that human beings are natural animals, who must satisfy basic needs through the collective transformation of the natural environment in order to generate their material conditions of exist-ence, has revolutionary implications. The human being is a labouring animal, whose species being consists in the social transformation of the natural world (MECW3: 277), so that "*labour* [is] the *essence* of man" (*ibid.*: 333). The human being, Marx went on to claim, is a "universal animal" who, because it is conscious, can imitate the transformations of nature performed by any other animal and, indeed, can imaginatively transcend the instinct-driven "work" of the animal kingdom. Labour, though, is historical: as the implements and methods of labour vary, human beings alter the expression of their essence. The consequence is that labour is both generated by human species being and in turn forms that species being as a historical product. Furthermore, labour is collective and therefore social:

> The human being is in the most literal sense a *zoon politikon* [a socio-political animal], not merely a gregarious animal, but an animal which can individuate itself only in the midst of society. Production by an isolated individual outside society ... is as much an absurdity as is the development of language without human beings living *together*.   (Marx 1973: 84)

To summarize, social labour by this universal animal transforms the natural environment into the material conditions of human society, and at the same time transforms the historical expression of the labourers' essence through the actualisation of human potentials.

Marx's materialism has been described as "non-ontological" (Schmidt 1971). That description is intended to highlight something important about Marx's idea of human nature. Marx most definitely has a theory of human nature, but, as Norman Geras (1983) points out, it is the Greek concept of *physis* (potential powers) rather than the Roman idea of *natura naturans* (fixed nature). Marx is proposing a shifting equilibrium between the natural environment and human society, in which the "retreat of the natural boundary", that is the gradual transcendence of natural necessity by creative labour, shapes humanity as it forms society and transforms nature. History means the development of human nature, that is, of human powers, capacities and needs (Sayers 1998: 164). This is the fundamental meaning of Marx's famous dictum that "human nature is ... the ensemble of social relations" (MESW: 29).

Marx's insistence that social labour is creative self-transformation, at the same time as it is the transformation of nature and the production of society, informs the normative conception of "praxis" that guides Marxism. For Marx, praxis is not only a material activity, but also represents an intellectual synthesis of theory, practice and art. Praxis as the completely free, creative transformation of nature, society and humanity can only happen in a social condition of material abundance, Marx thinks. Marx therefore often contrasts praxis, as a normative standard, with labour, as the historical reality of brutal drudgery under conditions of semi-starvation and social domination.

Marx's materialist inversion of Hegel, a prolongation of Feuerbach's breakthrough, leads him to concentrate on the history of labour as the key to human history. The history of labour, undertaken through an investigation of political economy, especially the works of Adam Smith and David Ricardo, discloses the extent to which praxis, as the potential of human nature, has been realized in actual societies.

Against the background of his social and political concerns, Marx understood that the historical development of the labour process was both beneficial and destructive. Following the political economists, Marx holds that the division of labour – the social practice of specialized work, beginning with the splits between domestic and public labour, and then the division between mental and manual labour – is the key to productivity increases, and therefore to social prosperity. The labour process develops historically only through increasing specialization within the social division of labour. This is crucial for creating a situation of material abundance, freedom from want, said to release human creative potentials. But at the same time, unlike the political economists, Marx holds that the division of labour is also the key to generating a class society. The polarization of wealth observed by Marx and Engels during the Industrial Revolution had, they both argued, historical roots lying in the development of the division of labour. This went right back to the development in pre-historical socities of a labour-based split between men and women. On this foundation, they argued, class society emerged from the division between manual and mental labour, with the creation of a group specialized in attending to the affairs of society as a whole.

Alienated labour

In the *Economic and Philosophical Manuscripts of 1844*, Marx frames the historical and materialist version of the "new philosophy" as a reflection on the "alienation" of praxis into labour. For Hegel, alienation describes the way that an idea, once externalized in an object, can appear as something estranged from the subject. In particular, society is generated from the idea of freedom by humanity as a collective subject, but because of historical limitations in the development of liberty, society appears to the individual as an alien, coercive reality. Significantly, when Hegel formulated this idea, he was also engaged in research into political economy (Lukács 1975). But unlike Hegel, Marx supposes that this condition of alienation is grounded in material conditions, not just in historical ideas. Accordingly, Marx's term "alienation" must not be confused with psychological suffering and the individual's personal feeling of anomie (lack of integration into society).

For Marx, alienation is caused by the link between the social division of labour and the institution of private property in capitalist society. The institution of private property appears as the "product, result and inevitable consequence of the alienated mode of labour" and derives from the mechanisms of the social division of labour, within which "each man has a particular, exclusive sphere of activity, which is forced upon him and from which he cannot escape" (MECW5: 47). In Adam Smith's famous example of the pin factory, breaking down the entire (skilled) labour process into detail tasks, and assigning individual workers to these repetitive and unskilled routines, yields tremendous efficiencies and vast profits. In fact, the general principle of the division of labour operates across entire economies, with major divisions between agriculture, manufacture and trade, and ramifying distinctions between specialized industries. From the perspective of those individuals condemned within the division of labour to unskilled, manual work, capitalism involves loss of control over the labour process and material impoverishment. But from the standpoint of the "collective worker", of the society as a whole, the opposite is true: there is massive expansion in material wealth, immense increase in technological sophistication, intellectual and cultural revolutions unprecedented in human history, and an impressive new raft of rights and institutions, pointing the way to self-government. When it is not simply tragic, history, regarded through this lens, is a paradox, an enigma.

To solve the "riddle of history", Marx conceptualizes alienated labour as an existential condition, rooted in the mutilation of praxis caused by the division of labour. According to Marx, alienation has four aspects (MECW3: 275–7):

1. from the product of labour (which, as social wealth, contributes only to the worker's impoverishment);
2. from the natural world (which appears only as raw materials);
3. from the other person (human beings' mutual relations are mediated by commodities); and
4. from themselves (the worker's animal functions become the refuge of their humanity, while their human creativity is bestialized in labour).

In alienated labour, the worker "does not affirm but contradicts his essence" – "instead of developing his free physical and mental energies, he mortifies his body and ruins his mind" (*ibid.*: 274). This means that "the more the worker toils, the more powerful becomes the alien world of objects he produces to oppose him, and the poorer he himself becomes" (*ibid.*: 272).

The alienation of labour, the mutilation of praxis caused by the division of labour and private property, is a negation of the labourer's self-realization as a free and creative individual. As Herbert Marcuse points out (Marcuse 1999: 282), this provides a powerful insight into Marx's version of the dialectical method, and in particular into the otherwise arcane terms the "unity of opposites" and the "negation of the negation". The opposition between labour and capital is one in which capital "negates" labour. But this is a unity of opposites, because both poles of the opposition spring from the contradictory nature of capitalism. But, Marx adds, the negation of labour by capital will itself be negated with the abolition of alienated labour, through the elimination of the institution of private property and its enforced division of labour (MECW3: 342).

Now, there is something important to notice about all of this. Until the 1850s, Marx thinks that the problem with capitalism is alienated labour, which leads to maldistribution of economic wealth and the existential mutilation of the working class. Consequently, Marx claims that the proletariat is:

> *a class with radical chains* … which has a universal character by its universal suffering and claims no *particular right* because no *particular wrong*, but *wrong generally*, is perpetuated against it; which can invoke no *historical*, but only *human*, title; … which … is the *complete loss* of man and hence can win itself only through the *complete re-winning of man*.   (*ibid.*: 186)

Accordingly, many things might be said of capitalism – it is unnatural, immoral and oppressive. The fact of classes, arising from the division of labour and private property, transforms freedom into an empty abstraction. *What Marx does not say is that it is exploitative.* Marx thinks that commodity production, under a system of free competition and waged labour, means that the labour contract represents an equal exchange: money wages in return for commodities produced.

During the 1850s, as Marx's research into political economy deepened, Marx realized that the wage contract involved economic exploitation and not just alienated labour conditions. This shift was catalysed by historical developments, for in the European revolutions of 1848, the bourgeoisie shifted decisively to the side of anti-liberal aristocracies, breaking its alliance with the emergent proletariat by abandoning the barricades. The bourgeoisie had achieved economic dominance and, more frightened of proletarian insurrection than aristocratic reaction, became a conservative class. This momentous change triggered a major transition in Marx, from the materialist inversion of Hegel to a properly historical materialism, and it profoundly altered his conception of the relation between practice, structure and history.

Marx's insight into capitalist exploitation is based on a critical reading of David Ricardo's *Principles of Political Economy* (1817). In many respects, however, Marx now breaks with the normatively rich theory of alienation, moving in the direction of descriptive social science. For where the young Marx had thought that alienation was a moral wrong, perhaps surprisingly the mature Marx maintains that exploitation is "a natural consequence of the relations of production" (C3: 333). Nonetheless, the idea of exploitation relies on what Marx described as his most important contribution to the critique of political economy in the first volume of *Capital* (1867). This was Marx's philosophical analysis of the oppositions between use-value and exchange-value, concrete and abstract labour, paid labour time and unpaid labour time. These oppositions, explained in a moment, effectively recast, in the terms of political economy, the opposition between praxis and labour that was central to the idea of alienation. The result is contradictory. On the one hand, Marx rejects moral language in describing exploitation. On the other hand, because exploitation recasts alienation in terms of political economy, the whole idea relies on the normatively rich philosophical anthropology of Marx's early work. The mature Marx both has and does not have a theory of human nature with moral implications.

The labour theory of value

Marx's critique of Ricardo is crucial to the difference between Hegel and Marx, for Hegel had uncritically adopted Ricardo's results. Ricardo recasts the political economy of Adam Smith in two decisive ways. First, he regards the source of wealth for capitalists, labourers and landowners as arising from different things (profits, wages and rent), breaking Smith's undifferentiated connection between the entire population and the "wealth of nations" into three component parts. The implication is that capitalism is a *class society* where different groups have distinct material interests, rather than society being just a national aggregate of roles in the total social production process. And second, Ricardo rejects as absurd Smith's idea that commodities have a natural value, expressed as a monetary price, which is based on supply and demand. According to Ricardo, the natural value of a commodity is the socially average ("necessary") labour time that went into the manufacture of the item.

According to Ricardo, capitalism is fair because although labour is the source of value, proportionality is retained. The labourers are paid the equivalent in monetary wages of the value of the commodities that they produce (minus costs and rent). But then what is profit? Brilliant as it is, Ricardo's theory has a major hole in it: if labour is the source of value, and profit is a surplus beyond the recovery of the capitalist's costs and the expense on wages, then profit must be *surplus value extracted from labour* beyond the share of the total product that wages, rent and the capitalist's expense represent. Profit must ultimately come from *labour performed for free*. This is the germ of the specifically Marxist version of the labour theory of value.

To explain this insight theoretically, Marx had to develop a philosophical analysis of the commodity form of the social product and relate this to the ability, or power, of the labourer to perform socially useful work. Commodities are items that satisfy socially defined human needs and which are produced under two special conditions: the units of production are not communal but mutually separated ("private property"), and the exchange generally happens through the medium of money. Thus the definition of a commodity as "a utility made by private producers for sale on the market" implies a conceptual division in the object between its ability to satisfy a socially determined human need (its *use value*, or utility for the consumer) and the end for which it was produced (its *exchange value*, or tradable worth). Money, as "the embodiment of social labour" (TSV3: 130), is a special commodity that reflects the exchange value of other commodities by functioning as a universal equivalent, that is a medium for the representation of value, as well as being something that is bought and sold on the market.

The separation of the units of production and the integration of their products through the exchange process means that capitalism is paradoxically both more and less social than other modes of production. Labour is a social process not only because individuals must cooperate in a workplace, but because in a capitalist society with an extensive division of labour, the satisfaction of the totality of needs in the community requires a vast collaboration by the entire society. Yet this collaboration is accomplished through the blind mechanism of the market and is accompanied by the private appropriation of the surplus social product. Although capitalism goes beyond communal production and barter systems in its socialization of labour, it is at the same time deeply anarchic and individualistic in its organization of production and distribution, respectively.

The difference between use and exchange mirrors another distinction, between concrete and abstract labour. *Concrete labour* is the expenditure of human effort by a specific individual in the production of a determinate item with a socially defined use value, whereas *abstract labour* is the socially necessary labour time required by an average individual, which determines the exchange value of the item. Significantly modifying Ricardo, Marx argues that the exchange value of a commodity reflects the socially necessary labour time required for its production *at the moment of exchange*. Thus, according to the labour theory of value, advances in production techniques actually devalue existing commodities. With the distinction between abstract and concrete labour in mind, what Marx means by "socially necessary" is the average labour time required by a worker of median skill under the generally obtaining conditions in the industry in question to produce the thing in question (C1: 44–5). What Marx calls "real abstraction" is the social dominance of abstract labour over concrete labour:

> All labour is, speaking physiologically, an expenditure of human labour power, and in its character of identical abstract human labour, it creates and forms the value of commodities. On the other hand, all labour is the expenditure of human labour power in a special form and with a definite aim, and in this, its character of concrete useful labour, it produces use values. (C1: 46)

Following the twofold character of labour and the difference between use and exchange, Marx introduces a further distinction within the notion of labour. The exchange value of the commodity labour power, reflected in the wage, is the amount required to sustain the workers and their dependents (that is the value needed to reproduce labour power). The use value of labour power is labour itself, the transformation of nature into items of utility. The implication is that for part of the day the labourer reproduces their labour power. For the rest of the day, they perform labour for the capitalist. The value produced by the worker therefore consists of two parts: the paid labour that is reflected in wages, and *unpaid labour* or *surplus value*, appropriated by the employer as profit, in the uniquely capitalist form of the extraction of the social surplus product:

> [A] false appearance distinguishes waged labour from other historical forms of labour. On the basis of the wages system even the unpaid labour seems to be paid labour. With the

slave, on the contrary, even that part of his labour which is paid appears to be unpaid. Of course, in order to work the slave must live, and one part of his working day goes to replace the value of his own maintenance. But since no bargain is struck between him and his master, and no acts of selling and buying are going on between the two parties, all his labour seems to be given away for nothing. Take, on the other hand, the peasant serf ... This peasant worked, for example, three days for himself on his own field or the field allotted to him, and the three subsequent days he performed compulsory and gratuitous labour on the estate of his lord. Here, then, the paid and unpaid parts of labour were sensibly separated, separated in time and space ... In point of fact, however, whether a man works three days of the week for himself on his own field and three days for nothing on the estate of his lord, or whether he works in the factory or the workshop six hours daily for himself and six for his employer, comes to the same, although in the latter case the paid and unpaid portions of labour are inseparably mixed up with each other, and the nature of the whole transaction is completely masked by the intervention of a contract and the pay received at the end of the week. The gratuitous labour appears to be voluntarily given in the one instance, and to be compulsory in the other. That makes all the difference. (MESW: 211)

The commodity form of labour power – the workers' capacity to perform multiples of socially average labour time – depends on their freedom. This means both their freedom from extra-economic coercion, unlike the slave and the serf, but also their "freedom" from possession of the means of production. Finally, the value of the wage, the value of the commodity labour power, reflects a dynamic equilibrium. There is a tendency to decrease because of advances in techniques for producing workers' necessities. There is also a tendency to increase because of what Marx called a "historical and moral element", that is improvements in education and training resulting from high-tech production and gains that reflect successful union struggles.

Capital accumulation and historical decline

The details of Marx's discussion of labour power and the commodity form are crucial to understanding Marxism. By contrast, when we turn to the other volumes of *Capital*, only the results of Marx's investigation of the accumulation of capital and the crisis tendencies of the system are important for present purposes. It is beyond the scope of this book to examine Marx's formulae or to consider questions of the transformation of values into prices, the mathematical form of the falling rate of profit tendency or other specialized issues.

That is not to imply that Marxian economics is unimportant. Alongside the development of Marx's social philosophy, of course, Marxian economics is now a completely mathematical and highly specialized field whose predictive capacity and sophisticated modelling rivals neo-classical economics. Highlights include Pierro Sraffa's neo-Ricardian reconstruction of Marxian economics (Sraffa 1975), Makoto Itō's mathematical consideration of Marxian economics (Itō 1988), Michel Aglietta's analysis of post-war American capitalism (Aglietta 1979), Samir Amin's examination of the world economy (Amin 1974) and Giovanni Arrighi's study of finance capitalism in the twentieth century (Arrighi 1994).

Marx's "general law of capitalist accumulation" describes the replacement of variable capital, or "living labour", in the production process by constant capital, or "dead labour". Marx proposes that although *absolute surplus value* can be generated by increasing the duration and intensity of labour, the specifically capitalist form of exploitation is the generation of *relative surplus value*, through improving the productivity of labour (C1: 508–18). Through the introduction of new machinery, capitalism stimulates technological innovation, but "like every other instrument for increasing the productivity of labour, machinery is intended to cheapen commodities, and, by shortening the part of the working day in which the worker works for himself, to lengthen the part he gives the capitalist for nothing" (*ibid.*: 371). The drive to technological innovation, whose mechanism is exploitation through the production of surplus value, increases labour productivity (new techniques, improved machinery) and reduces the value of labour power (cheap goods, weakened unions). The major philosophical point is that class struggle and the exploitation of labour are therefore the same thing as the accumulation of capital and the expansion of value. Capitalist exploitation is driven by the "world spirit" of money, that is, by the dynamic of accumulation and the logic of value. "Accumulate, accumulate!" Marx writes: "Accumulation for accumulation's sake, production for production's sake: by this formula [is] expressed the historical mission of the bourgeoisie" (*ibid.*: 595).

Marx devotes the second volume of *Capital* to the complex process of expanded reproduction, which involves a dynamic equilibrium between different economic sectors that he divides, for simplicity, into Department I (means of production) and Department II (consumer goods). In the third volume of *Capital*, Marx introduces competition and brings two aspects of accumulation – the generation of relative surplus value through technological innovation and the cannibalization of firms in competition – together. The "concentration and centralization of capital" means the concentration of means of production through technological innovation and the centralization of many capitals into vast corporations.

Marx demonstrates is that there is a relationship between market competition and the class dimension of exploitation, because competition enforces capitalist discipline on "individual capitals", who then "must conduct themselves as capital" (Marx 1973: 657). Although competition imposes capitalism's inherent tendencies on individual entrepreneurs, the main mechanism generating the concentration and centralization of capital is the periodic crises that beset the system. According to Marx, periodic crises of the over-production of commodities happen as a natural consequence of the anarchy of capitalist production, thanks to the tendency of capital to migrate in the direction of higher rates of profit, combined with the inability to rationally plan the capitalist economy. When this happens, an economic "bust" or crisis is triggered following a spectacular boom, with the result that many firms are made bankrupt and cannibalized by the survivors. "The violent destruction of capital", he writes in the *Grundrisse*, "not by relations external to it, but rather as a condition of its self-preservation, is the most striking form in which it is given to it to be gone and to give room to a higher state of social production" (*ibid.*: 749–50).

Periodic crises result in a temporary increase in the general rate of profit as a consequence of the destruction of some capitals (plus sometimes a lowering of wages because of high unemployment). The process precipitates a new round of technological innovation together with the concentration and centralization of capital, until a point is reached where capitalism has eliminated backward areas. Then the remaining firms are so huge that their failure, catalysed by over-production but fundamentally caused by declining profits, would imply the complete collapse of the economy. Once this happens, the dynamism of capitalism is lost. For Marx, therefore, the periodic crises of capitalism culminate in a long-term historical tendency to stagnation in the capitalist mode of production.

To explain this, Marx develops an analysis of the tendency of capital to migrate away from advanced economic sectors, industries and countries to backward sectors, industries and countries, in search of higher rates of profit. Marx believes that he can demonstrate a tendency for investment costs to rise with technological innovation. When combined with an equilibrium rate of profit generalized across the entire economy, this means a general tendency of the rate of profit to fall (Tendency of the Falling Rate of Profit: TFRP). Marx stated that "this is in every respect the most important law of political economy, and the most essential for understanding the most difficult relations. It is the most important law from the historical standpoint" (*ibid.*: 748).

The implication of the TFRP is historical in the Hegelian sense that it indicates the epochal rise and fall of capitalism. Because the dynamics of capitalism lead to the migration of capital to under-developed sectors, this industrialization spreads nationally and then internationally, but ultimately, "beyond a certain point, the development of the forces of production becomes a barrier for capital; hence the capital-relation a barrier for the development of the productive powers of labour" (*ibid.*: 749). This barrier has the phenomenal appearance of the TFRP, whose consequence is generalized stagnation, in the capitalist version of the long crisis of feudalism. To explain why this had not already transpired, Marx hypothesized that several counter-tendencies to the TFRP existed, which prolonged the life-expectancy of capitalism through temporarily raising profits. Probably the most important of these from the historical perspective is foreign investment and colonial exploitation, since these provide potentially vast opportunities for generating superprofits.

Marx and Engels both anticipated the collapse of capitalism within their lifetimes. Volume 1 of *Capital* closes on exactly this note of expectation: "the [death] knell of capitalist property sounds; the expropriators are expropriated!" (C1: 763). Many Marxists have continued this tradition, with every generation bringing forth a new prediction of the imminent end of exploitation in a catastrophe scenario.

Social classes

The intention behind *Capital* is now clear: the proletarian revolution merely prosecutes the inherent contradiction of the capitalist mode of production, its historical tendency to stagnation, through to its final consequence. Accordingly, Marx's concept of class is one that is based on exploitation and is *relational* and *antagonistic*, where classes embody the historical movement of social contradictions. He writes that the proletarian and the capitalist are merely "personifications" of the productive forces and relations of production (respectively) (Marx 1973: 303–4). The main idea is that the exploitation relation is the basis for the objective material interests of social classes. This is certainly not an income stratification or occupational status model. It is therefore quite unlike common sociological and popular conceptions of "class". It is also incomplete: Volume 3 of *Capital* broaches the question of definitions – and here the manuscript trails off into the ellipsis of Marx's death. In an incredible historical irony, Marx's influential theory of class struggle did not provide a full definition of social class.

Nonetheless, Marx did provide voluminous historical writings on class struggles (Draper 1977). Taking Marx's historical writings as a basis, a straightforward model of classes as formed through exploitation at the point of production has been successfully applied to ancient society and slave-based production (de Ste Croix 1981), and to feudal society in the late middle ages (Bois 1984). Nonetheless, Marx acknowledges in his historical writings that status gradations and control over the labour process play a significant role in the complexities of historically existing social classes.

Turning to capitalism, the working class, according to Marx, is the waged, collective worker who engages in the productive and unproductive labour that generates a social surplus product. Because of lack of ownership of the means of production, this surplus product is appropriated by the capitalists indirectly through the wage form. Marx considers not just manual production of surplus value, but also the unproductive waged work of domestic servants, commercial employees and administrative clerks (Marx 1973: 305–6). The capitalist class is the class that exploits waged labour through its ownership of the means of production. Marx argues that the entire class of exploiters redistributes the social surplus product through market mechanisms, so that industrial capitalists, financial capitalists and stock-holding "rentiers" are part of the same class (TSV2: 29). Capitalists generally delegate the control function implicit in property ownership to managers who may not be members of the ruling class. And third, there are the landed aristocracy, who live by exploiting ground rent from tenant farmers. Marx in general acknowledges that although there are "three great classes of modern society", there are many "intermediate and transitional strata [that] obliterate line of [class] demarcation" (C3: 794, 862). These are in addition to the family businesspeople ("petite bourgeoisie"), who are in Marx's terms small capitalists, because they labour collectively and share profits, while owning their own means of production. Finally, Marx describes as the "lumpenproletariat" those who are semi-permanently not in legal employment, including criminals and beggars.

In fact, many of the "classes" from the *Communist Manifesto* (and elsewhere) are actually status groups and not social classes. Marx and Engels acknowledge that the "manifold gradation of social rank" has an important role in pre-capitalist societies. The "intermediate strata" of capitalism suggest that the situation has remained complicated. Sometimes, Marx does indeed recognize that the proletariat "constitute[s] [a] constantly declining proportion (even though it increases absolutely) of the total population" (TSV3: 63). There is an extensive debate in Marxist theory on how to define the middle strata, so-called because, first, the middle class is not a fundamental class of production, but rather a series of gradations between bourgeoisie and proletariat, and, second, the term "middle class" is sometimes confused with the bourgeoisie, on grounds that the bourgeoisie were the class in between peasantry and aristocracy in the feudal mode of production. Erik Olin Wright helpfully defines classes primarily by the exploitation relation (e.g. wages), secondarily by a control relation in the means of production (e.g. management and employees) and thirdly by control over the labour process itself (e.g. professional occupations, salaried employees and waged workers; Wright 1979: 14–21). These definitions provide for a segmented scale with bourgeois and proletarian at either end, and a series of "contradictory class locations" that shade from fractions of the ruling class (e.g. senior corporate executives), through the vast middle strata, to fractions of the working class (e.g. office workers). Many salaried professionals with educational credentials would qualify on these definitions as members of the middle strata, because of their control of the labour process and direction of other employees, together with employment permanence and material privileges associated with social prestige.

Despite the ramifying complexity of class societies, Marx and Engels announce in *The Communist Manifesto* that "[capitalist] society as a whole is more and more splitting up into two great hostile camps" (MESW: 36). In *Capital*, Marx holds that an historical process of proletarianization of the working population is a necessary consequence of the general law of capital accumulation (C1: 763). This thesis on the simplification of class formation in advanced capitalism is stated with qualifications, but it performs important theoretical work, because it clearly links economic history with political strategy.

Women's liberation

Class formation – already complex – is further complicated by the gendered division of labour involving (mainly) unpaid domestic labour, performed mostly by women, and waged productive labour, undertaken most often by men. According to Lise Vogel, "Marx put forward positions that upheld the rights of women and protected, to the best of his understanding, the interests and future of all members of the working class" (Vogel 1983: 70). Marx was a consistent advocate of women's liberation, and Engels's work *The Origin of the Family, Private Property and the State* (1884) is a major Marxist statement on the oppression of women that is based on Marx's ethnographic notebooks of 1880–81. Marx and Engels identified the subordination of women as involving lack of political rights, denial of access to socially recognized and monetarily rewarded labour, and loss of control over their actions and bodies in the patriarchal household. They also denounced the system of enforced participation in an asymmetrical system of sexual morality – monogamy – that restricted women's sexuality while encouraging male promiscuity. Despite describing the position of the woman in the household of both bourgeois and proletarian families as "slavery", however, Marx does not regard the modern relation between men and women as a class relation.

The young Marx regards the relation between men and women as an elementary indicator of emancipation in general, for "the extent to which the other person, as a person, has become for him a need [is] the extent to which he in his individual existence is a social being" (MECW3: 296). In these passages (as elsewhere), Marx uses the German word *Mensch*, which means "human being", rather than *Männer*, which means "men", but English translations from the 1950s and 1960s give the misleading impression that Marx thinks that men exemplify humanity and that women are merely an additional specification. In fact, Marx was highly radical for his time, believing that the liberation of men and women would not only eliminate social inequalities, but also culminate in the abolition of the family and in a non-exclusive sexuality. By contrast, Engels, perhaps more conservatively, holds that human emancipation would make exclusive lifelong sexual bonds possible for the first time in history since the advent of class society (Draper 1972).

Both Marx and Engels documented the terrible social conditions of the European working classes. They described widespread child labour, the inability of pregnant women to stop working, and the leap in prostitution and alcoholism during the nineteenth century as bestialization and demoralization. They also described the "latent slavery in the family" that involved domestic labour and the agency of the male worker as a broker for the labour of his wife and children (Vogel 1983: 44–50). But in actuality, Marx and Engels maintained, patriarchal authoritarianism and property relations had been combined long before capitalism.

Engels's explanation for this situation, based on Marx's notebooks, was that the subordination of women originated with the advent of classes and that in fact the conditions of women's oppression improved with the progress of the productive forces. The institution of bourgeois marriage was basically a property transaction involving legalized prostitution, but the dissolution of traditional familial bonds at least fatally weakened the patriarchal authority of the male head of the household (MESW: 499, 507).

Tracing the evolution of the family and its relation to property, Engels argued that the division of labour with the advent of agrarian communities was the basis for class society, because it enabled the production of a social surplus. Engels proposed that the appropriation of the social surplus directly implied property relations, with the consequence that the accumulation of wealth becomes a social question for the minority able to command the surplus. This minority, Engels conjectured, consisted of men who had been charged in the natural division of labour with supplying the household with food and defending it from raids. The production of a surplus made possible the consolidation of power in men's hands, with the consequence that "mother right", the supremacy of the female head of the household, was defeated. "The overthrow of mother right was the world historic defeat of the female sex", Engels wrote: "the man seized the reins in the house; the woman was degraded, enthralled, the slave of the man's lust, a mere instrument for breeding children" (*ibid*.: 488).

In this context, Engels claimed that the monogamous family was "the first form of the family to be based not on natural but on economic conditions – on the victory of private property over primitive, natural, communal property" (*ibid*.: 494). He therefore maintains that "the first class antagonism which appears in history coincides with the development of the antagonism between man and woman in monogamous marriage, and the first class oppression is that of the female sex by the male" (*ibid*.: 495). The first classes, in other words, are men and women. For this reason, monogamous marriage appears at the end of the pre-historic era "as the subjection of one sex by the other, as the proclamation of a conflict between the sexes entirely unknown hitherto" (*ibid*.: 494).

The struggle to overcome the remainders from maternal right and matrilineal succession was historically protracted, Engels argues, and continued into antiquity. But sexual class antagonism quickly yielded to slave-based production as the social division of labour ramified and the productive forces increased. Marx and Engels accept the complication of the major theses of historical materialism that this implies. However, they argue that although the male member of an exploited class (slave, serf, worker) has the female member of that class perform domestic labour for him, that labour reproduces the labour power of the male, which is then exploited by the ruling class. Thus, Marx and Engels appear to reason, familial relations are oppressive (political and ideological), but not economically exploitative. Nonetheless, their hypothesis suggests that the family represents quasi-class oppression with potentially exploitative characteristics, something that sits uneasily with the demand for proletarian unity.

At any rate, the political programme of Marx and Engels is clear: the proletarian revolution must involve women's liberation. They demand the transformation of domestic labour into publically recognized and materially rewarded services, socialization of childcare and the education of children, abolition of the inheritance of property, and full political rights, labour market access and civic participation for women. With the nationalization of property, Engels predicts, "the single family ceases to be the economic unit of society [and] private housekeeping is transformed into a social industry" (MESW: 503). The economic basis for women's oppression is eliminated.

The state

Marx believes that economic flashpoints around the working day and the wages system spontaneously tend to become political conflicts, not least because of the need to struggle against unjust laws designed to support the capitalist interest. The restriction of unlimited exploitation through union organization, culminating in legislation on the eight hour day, for instance, was the result of "a protracted and more or less concealed civil war between the capitalist class and the working class" (C1: 412–13). From this perspective, Marx regards the modern nation state as an instrument of the capitalist class for the legal enforcement of the endogenous "laws of motion" of capital accumulation, and for the armed defence of the institution of private property in the means of production. The executive arm of the state, Marx and Engels write, is an expression of the collective exploitation of the working class by the capitalist class, a "committee for managing the common affairs of the whole bourgeoisie" (MESW: 37), whose centre of gravity is "armed bodies of men" expressly intended for the suppression of proletarian revolt against the capitalist class. The state is an instrument of class domination because "political power, properly so called, is merely the organised power of one class for oppressing another" (ibid.: 53), and, indeed, it is possession of a state apparatus that converts an economically dominant class into a ruling class properly speaking. According to Marx and Engels, then, politics is mainly a reflection of economics – specifically, politics is the result of the generalization of the economic interests of the exploiting class and the institutionalization of these interests in a special body of men and women whose detachment from particular interests enables them to represent the interests of that class as a whole (ibid.: 577).

Nonetheless, especially in his historical writings, Marx also acknowledges that the state apparatus, while based on economic interests, has relative autonomy of action not only from particular fractions of the ruling class, but indeed from that class as a whole. Marx waxes eloquent about this consequence of exploitation as an "enormous bureaucratic and military organisation, with its extensive and artificial state machinery [an] appalling parasitic body" (ibid.: 169), which has the capacity under exceptional circumstances to act as a neutral arbiter between contending classes. Even in 1852, the "state machinery" had at its disposal "an army of half a million officials" besides its military forces. This institutional apparatus makes possible the phenomenon of "Bonapartism", military dictatorship led by charismatic figures, where the state maintains the stability of the social order by preventing class conflict. Although this implies that the relatively autonomous state apparatus has the subordinate function of regulating the unity of the social formation, it has to be noted that, for Marx, the Bonapartist state, by preventing class conflict, effectively preserves private property. For this reason, Marx insists that the modern nation state, irrespective of its form of government, is a "dictatorship of the bourgeoisie", because the distinction between democracy and authoritarianism, although it makes a tactical political difference, does not alter the state's class foundation.

A lot of the subsequent debates in Marxism – beginning with Engels – about the "relative autonomy" of the state from capital and the ability of politics to "react back upon" its economic foundation are attempts to capture analytically these descriptive positions. Alongside an instrumental position that the state is a machine for maintaining class domination and economic exploitation (e.g. *ibid.*: 37, 169) there is what has been called, because of its logical primacy rather than frequency of occurrence in Marx's work, "Marx's general theory of the state" (Draper 1977: 584). The general claim is that although the state might sometimes be directly manipulated by the ruling class, fundamentally its class character is determined by the dominant property relations (e.g. MESW: 181–2). Parliamentary democracies sometimes enact reforms against the interests of the capitalist class, but these remain capitalist states by virtue of their legal defence of private property and their economic investment in national infrastructure, which are both beneficial to the capitalist class (e.g. C1: 229, 461).

For Marx, the bourgeois state apparatus is a "parasitic excrescence" (MESW: 288), not something that the proletarian party captures and deploys in the interests of the transformation of capitalism into socialism. Marx is adamant that "the first step in the revolution by the working class must be to raise the proletariat to the position of ruling class" (*ibid.*: 52), and that the second step is to dismantle the bourgeois state apparatus (*ibid.*: 288–90). The proletarian state is a "social republic" (*ibid.*: 287) based on participatory democracy by the armed population, which abolishes the "social slavery" of the working class through the nationalization of property (*ibid.*: 290–91). (Mass participatory bodies with direct election and open debate have arisen in most revolutions since 1871, and have subsequently been called "soviets", "workers' councils", "shoras" and so forth.) The replacement of the nation state and private property with a participatory democratic social republic based on socialized property provides the key to the meaning of Marx's notorious expression "the dictatorship of the proletariat" (*ibid.*: 259).

For Marx, *every* state is inherently a class dictatorship, because it is the political expression of the economic relations that form the anatomy of society, so that all states defend – with the coercive force that necessarily supports legal relations – the material interests of their ruling class. The term "dictatorship", then, is not used in opposition to "democracy" (for Marx, both parliamentary democracies and authoritarian regimes are dictatorships insofar as they express the interests of the dominant class) but in opposition to the "withering away of the state" (*ibid.*: 327–8). For Marx, the "social republic" organizes the elimination of capitalist property, the global federation of socialist republics abolishes remaining inequalities and the stateless communist world is a condition of abundance (*ibid.*: 319–20).

The "anarchist" element in Marx must not be forgotten. Marx remained all his life an advocate of democracy – initially of parliamentary democracy and then of participatory democracy – and a sometimes nostalgic enthusiasm for the democratic ancient Athenian polis. But Marx is not a *democrat*, if what that means is an advocate of democracy as the best regime for a good community and thus the final end of political strategy. To be exact, Marx is an instrumental democrat, an advocate of democracy as the best means for the self-emancipation of the oppressed and the only way to cooperatively organize the "rule of the associated producers" during the transition to communism. In terms of political strategy, of the ends or goal of social mobilization, Marx is actually anti-political, something that follows directly from the notion that the state is the expression of exploitation. For Marx, politics is the confrontation of class against class at the level of state power, and a society without exploitation would have no classes, and thus need no state.

Bourgeois ideology

According to Marx, the major limitation on the political action of the working class is not really the capitalist state, but bourgeois ideology, wherein "men and their relations appear upside down, as in a *camera obscura*" (MECW5: 36). The implication of this celebrated claim is that the working class has material interests in social revolution but is imbued with false consciousness regarding these material interests. For instance, Marx comments that "instead of the conservative motto 'a fair day's wages for a fair day's work', [the proletariat] ought to inscribe on its banner the revolutionary watchword 'abolition of the wages system'" (MESW: 226). As with the materialist inversion of Hegel, the reversal of perspective involved in going from bourgeois ideology to proletarian consciousness is said to entail a shift from ideological to scientific cognition.

In Marx's writings, the term "ideology" is used critically to mean a distorted representation of social relations centred on material production, which by concealing social contradictions serves the interests of the ruling class (Larrain 1979). Ideology refers only to that subset of ideas that have the social function of justifying class rule: it does not mean a class "worldview" (instead, it means specific elements *within* a worldview) and it definitely does not mean ideas in general. Marx's contention that "in every epoch, the ruling ideas are the ideas of the ruling class" is a claim about how the most prevalent social ideas are likely to be those that have beneficial consequences for the reigning set of material interests (a functionalist claim), rather than the notion that ideology is a conspiracy.

The most important way in which sets of ideas function to justify class rule is not through directly legitimating domination, but rather through rendering it invisible, by naturalizing exploitation and representing alternatives as impossible or unthinkable. This is a consequence of the indirect form of exploitation under capitalism, which presents relations of domination as relations of freedom, together with the tendency of the "ruling ideas" to represent society ahistorically. Marx lampoons the apologists for capitalism for their uncritical representation of capitalism as natural and inevitable, rather than social and historical, but he also recognizes that these ideological depictions accurately represent the way capitalist social relations superficially appear. The realm of market exchange really is characterized by formal "equality and freedom", Marx notes, but this merely conceals the way that "this apparent individual equality and liberty disappear" in the depths of production relations, where exploitation means they "prove to be inequality and unfreedom" (Marx 1973: 247–48).

Ideologies are not a deception but rather a structural limitation. Ideologies "do not [intellectually] go beyond the limits which [their class] do not go beyond in life", and these limits are fundamentally the relations of production (*ibid.*: 117). Marx maintains that the surface appearances of bourgeois economics (equal exchange) conceal the exploitative essence of the wage labour relation, and that classical political economy is ideological because it merely records these surface appearances (C3: 797). In an oft-cited passage, Marx proposes that the process of "real abstraction", the rule of equivalence based on abstract labour, means that the commodity is "a very queer thing indeed, abounding in metaphysical subtleties and theological niceties":

> A commodity is … a mysterious thing, simply because in it the social character of men's labour [the exchange value of abstract labour] appears to them as an objective character stamped upon the product of that labour; because the relation of the producers to the sum total of their own labour is presented to them as a social relation, existing not between themselves, but between the products of their labour … it is a definite social relation between men, that assumes, in their eyes, the fantastic form of a relation between things. (C1: 45)

Commodity production, Marx therefore maintains, generates an inverted world of representations that he describes as "commodity fetishism", where the commodity appears to take on the social properties of the agent and the worker seems merely a natural object ruled by the "general laws of motion" of the economy. This is an "enchanted, perverted, topsy-turvy world, in which Monsieur Le Capital and Madame La Terre do their ghost-walking as social characters and at the same time as mere things" (C3: 809).

Marx subtitled his major works "critiques", but he did not imagine that intellectual criticism alone would disperse ideological representations, for he held that because of their naturalization of limitations, ideologies represented a sort of necessary illusion vital to the perpetuation of production relations. The distinction between a class "in itself" (as a set of persons positioned in contradictory relations) and "for itself" (as a set of persons mobilized within a social antagonism under the banner of their material interests) expresses this difficulty. For the proletariat to overcome ideology, the organization of "the most advanced and resolute section of the working class" into a political party is necessary. For the mature Marx, emphatically, this is not a question of the intellectuals directing the proletariat, for "the emancipation of the working classes must be conquered by the working classes themselves" (Marx & Engels 1953: 395).

In the "1859 Preface", Marx claims that the relations of production in a social formation are the foundation not only for politics and the state, but also for ideological forms of social consciousness. A particular focus for criticism is "bourgeois morality", which is arraigned with being a non-scientific set of ideas that maintain a supposedly disinterested perspective, while in reality naturalizing the standpoint of the isolated individual. Political liberalism, with its negative conception of liberty as formal rights providing freedom from unwarranted interference by others, is likewise taxed with reflecting the same conception of formal equality that supports the wage contract (MESW: 97–8). For the mature Marx, the communist perspective is based on a scientific analysis of the material interests of the proletariat.

Communist freedom

The basic tension in Marx's thinking, between the normative critique of capitalist alienation and a scientific theory of material interests, becomes most evident in the question of post-capitalist society. I would like to broadly follow Habermas's analysis of this problem in what follows (Habermas 1972: 25–63, 1979a: 130–77). On the one hand, the "young Marx" has a normative theory of capitalist alienation, which proposes that capitalism involves moral wrong and that individualistic definitions of liberty violate higher ideals of political freedom. On the other hand, the "mature Marx" has a descriptive–explanatory theory of capitalist exploitation, which proposes that the laws of motion of capitalist economics are internally contradictory, so that humanity will soon confront a choice between social stagnation and revolutionary progress. Although the two are potentially compatible – the descriptive account might clarify the historical conditions of possibility for the realistic achievement of the goals of the normative account – in Marx's treatment, they tend to be in conflict.

For Marx, communist politics were distinctively anti-utopian because, instead of imposing "fantastic pictures of a future society" on the actual world, historical materialism meant a dialectical analysis of the potentials for a social alternative already latent in existing arrangements (MESW: 60). "We call communism the *real movement* which abolishes the present state of things", Marx and Engels wrote in *The German Ideology* (MECW5: 42). In the *Communist Manifesto*, they added that the "theoretical conclusions of the communists are in no way based on ideas or principles that have been invented, or discovered, by this or that would-be universal reformer [but] merely express, in general terms, actual relations springing from an existing class struggle" (MESW: 46). This position, held consistently throughout his lifetime, made Marx constitutionally allergic to theoretical speculations on post-capitalist social arrangements.

Nonetheless, in his *Critique of the Gotha Program*, Marx did outline some basic ideas on the transition from capitalism to socialism under the social republic, and then the transition from socialist states to communist society (*ibid.*: 319–21). Socialism, Marx proposed, involved:

> a communist society, not as it has *developed* on its own foundations, but, on the contrary, just as it *emerges* from capitalist society; which is thus in every respect, economically, morally and intellectually, still stamped with the birthmarks of the old society from whose womb it emerges. Accordingly, the individual producer receives back from society … exactly what he gives to it. … [E]*qual right* here is still in principle *bourgeois right*, although principle and practice are no longer at loggerheads.
> (*Ibid.*: 319)

Exploitation no longer happens, because payment is regulated by a contribution principle rather than the wage contract, but natural inequalities persist, together with social inequalities remaining from capitalism. Marx comments that justice in the form of rights "can never be higher than the economic structure of society and its cultural development conditioned thereby" (*ibid.*: 320).

The realm of communist freedom begins with the transcendence of naturally imposed necessity, through the generation of material abundance, whereupon the communist distributive maxim "from each according to his ability, to each according to his needs" replaces formal equality (*ibid.*: 321). Marx held that communism would abolish the enslavement of the individual to the division of labour and promote the all-round development of human beings (*ibid.*: 320). Despite comments by the young Marx that suggest the elimination of the division of labour entirely, the vision of the mature Marx appears to be one of individuals' socially unrestricted participation in material life, rather than the demand that each be capable of all, or that natural abilities would be irrelevant to individual fulfilment.

Although Marx advocates principles of distributive justice, it is not clear what their normative foundation actually consists in. According to Marx, "the communists do not preach morality at all" (MECW5: 72). Principles of distributive justice appear to be natural results of advances in the productive forces, not consequences of reasoning about the social conditions of moral autonomy and the forms of self-realization that constitute human flourishing. In *Capital*, Marx states unequivocally:

> The justice of the transactions between agents of production rests on the fact that these arise as natural consequences out of the production relationships. The juristic forms in which these economic transactions appear as wilful acts of the parties concerned, as expressions of their common will and as contracts that may be enforced by law against some individual party, cannot, being mere forms, determine this content. They merely express it. This content is just whenever it corresponds, is appropriate, to the mode of production. It is unjust whenever it contradicts that mode. (C3: 333)

The mature Marx therefore has a non-moral critique of capitalism as a fetter on development, which entails a historical relativization of morality. The base-and-superstructure model of the mature Marx's social theory claims that normative principles are themselves historically variable functions of economic developments. This is the idea that moral values and standards of justice are relative to the level of social evolution of a historical society, and that means, for Marx, relative to the mode of production. It follows that bourgeois morality and capitalist justice are valid for capitalist society, but not for future societies; conversely, however, there is no trans-historical perspective from which bourgeois justice will have been a form of social injustice. Such a relativization of normative principles leads Marx to frequently declare that communism has no place for morality and that freedom reduces to historical necessity.

Marx recognizes the importance of human freedom, in the form of political agency, in the socialist revolution, but he does not think that this involves a moral imperative. The practical activity of socialist revolution presupposes a relation between human freedom and historical necessity: "historical necessity" describes the material preconditions for a successful action; political strategy consists in the performance of successful actions once these preconditions are satisfied. There is, accordingly, no contradiction between Marx's insistence on economic developments as historically necessary, his claim that "freedom is the recognition of necessity" and the practical activism of Marx's politics. But there is also no connection to moral principles (Reiman 1991: 149–50).

It is not the case that there is a communist justice which represents a higher principle of justice beyond capitalism – for instance, substantive equality as opposed to formal equality. Marx does not appear to think that at all. Instead, he believed that justice involved conflicting claims under conditions of scarcity, from which it follows that communism is beyond justice. Norman Geras perhaps sums up the problem best: "Marx did think that capitalism was unjust, but he did not think he thought so" (Geras 1985: 70).

From the perspective of the addressees of the theory, however, it is crucial that an emancipatory social theory have rational normative foundations. Denunciations of "exploitation" and "oppression" appear to invoke the language of moral values and political ideals, and it is reasonable to ask what the moral wrongs and losses of freedom are that any individual proletarian is supposed to resist. Likewise, even when it is clear that no historical process is automatic, the projected "liberation" and "emancipation" must seem arbitrary if they arise merely from a descriptive account of social evolution, because it is not at all clear that consciously accelerating historical tendencies is the same as deliberate action towards desirable ends.

In principle, a normative clarification of the real stakes in the debate, despite what appears to be a set of evolutionary claims about normative validity, remains possible. Sometimes Marx *does* appear to be proposing that moral autonomy is a trans-historical principle and that historical societies constrain (or do not constrain, in the case of communism) its realization. Alternatively, from the perspective of a teleological conception of the goal of history in communist society, it might be possible to argue that stages of normative development also ascend in sequence. In that case, historical values are valid as approximations to an ideal of human flourishing that will only be realized in a final stage of history.

But the fact is that in Marx's conception, communism is a society without ideals. Communism is therefore beyond moral autonomy and any teleological ideal, despite the fact that it is said to provide the conditions for human flourishing. Why, then, did Marx deny that his was a normatively rich critique of capitalism? The answer must be that his theory of ideology led him to maintain that moral terminology represented bourgeois ideology with a merely "tactical" value. Marx appears to have thought that normative arguments were centred on the rational individual and therefore historically limited by the realities of capitalist society. The mature Marx therefore deprived himself of the clear normative perspective of the young Marx, whose critique of alienation brings together criticism of the social conditions that limit the exercise of moral autonomy with a teleological ideal of human flourishing in a truly social existence. From the young Marx's perspective, exploitation would be a clear moral wrong, because a fundamental principle of moral autonomy is the injunction to treat other human beings as free individuals with moral dignity, rather than instrumentally manipulating them for personal gain. But the mature Marx thought that exploitation was not an injustice, and therefore also not a moral wrong.

The problem is that a resolution of this confusion remained unlikely, insofar as Marx thought that there was no point in producing a blueprint for communism, especially not a moral one, or in discussing norms of justice when the state was going to wither away anyway. The result is a paradox, when not a tragedy: perhaps the most successful philosophy of politics in the history of Western thought lacked clear normative foundations for its social theory and a political philosophy for its strategic programme. Tensions within the thought of the mature Marx, between a theory of society with links to the natural sciences and an emancipatory philosophy in the heritage of the Enlightenment, exploded into open differences among the Marxists. This pulled at the synthesis of praxis, structure and history, teasing apart its elements as social conditions and historical experiences confronted mid-nineteenth century theory with mid-twentieth century problems. Marxism is the century of effort to confront this situation and resolve these problems.

Summary of key points

The "young Marx"

- Dialectical theory involves progress through contradiction and conflict. It emphasizes the unity of conceptual and social opposites, the way in which antagonism grows out of the limitations of a historical form of social life, and the tendency for inherent contradictions to transform a phenomenon into its opposite.
- Marx rejects Hegel's idealism for a materialist position based in a philosophical anthropology whose core is the idea of human labour as creative praxis, as the transformation of nature, and the self-transformation of humanity.
- Marx's critique of capitalism depends on the category of alienation – a condition of estrangement from nature, the products of labour, other persons and oneself, which is the consequence of the division of labour and private property.

The "mature Marx"

- Turns from a normative theory of alienation to a descriptive theory of exploitation, based on a critical appropriation of the labour theory of value, according to which commodities exchange for the socially necessary labour time embodied in them.
- Exploitation happens because of the difference between the value of the commodities a worker produces and the value of the worker's commodified labour power (the ability to work for a specified time in return for wages), which means that the hidden source of capitalist profit is unpaid labour time.
- The accumulation of capital and the exploitation of labour are the same thing, but Marx detects a long-term tendency to stagnation (the tendency of the falling rate of profit) in the very mechanism of capitalist dynamism, the way that capitalism promotes technological innovation.

- The bourgeoisie are the owners of the means of production, held to exploit the proletariat, the class of persons compelled by lack of ownership of the means of production to sell their labour power for a wage. These classes are fundamental to capitalism, but many other classes exist, including an extensive "middle strata" whose precise boundaries are disputed.
- Marx is an advocate of women's liberation, holding that although the oppression of women predates capitalism, both men and women of the working class have a common interest in the abolition of exploitation.
- Marx holds that the state exercises its monopoly of violence in the interests of a defence of the property relations that form its foundations, and that the main function of the state is to act as a committee of management for the capitalist class.
- Ideology is "false consciousness", which means a representation that is a motivated distortion of the material interests of a social group: "motivated" because in the interests of the ruling class; "distortion" because a representation of historical social relations as natural, just and inevitable.
- Communism is a hypothetical condition of a worldwide society, characterized by the achievement of material abundance, within which production would happen according to the abilities of each individual, and distribution would happen in line with the needs of every person.
- Socialism is a hypothetical condition of a post-capitalist society preliminary to communism, characterized by a world federation of socialist states, which would result from anti-capitalist revolutions led by proletarian, communist parties.

two

Classical Marxism

Karl Marx described his own social and political theory as "historical materialism", not as "Marxism". Indeed, upon learning of one early version of the consolidation of his ideas into a political doctrine, he famously announced that "I am not a Marxist!" (MESW: 679). The implication of Marx's statement is that there is a significant difference between the complex and provisional nature of a theoretical research programme, on the one hand, and the sort of practical simplification involved in a political doctrine capable of serving as the foundation for a party – and a state – on the other hand.

Marx was well aware that mass movements are not built around abstract research programmes, and he did not oppose turning the main conclusions of historical materialism into a political doctrine, formulating a party programme and putting the ideas into practice. Indeed, historical materialism calls for its own practical application as the definitive test of theory, for this lends the theory its historical falsifiability, differentiating it in an important way from traditional philosophy. Yet, as Marx's comments in his "Critique of the Gotha Program" (1875) indicate, doctrinal simplification can easily generate vulgarization and, ultimately, an oracular statement of "eternal truths" – an ideology.

Marx, then, did not espouse Marxism. Nonetheless, it was as Marxists, and not as "historical materialists", that the masses marched and the leaders acted during the convulsions of the twentieth century. In fact, the key figure in the emergence of one of the major political and intellectual forces of twentieth-century history is Engels. It was Engels who sorted "Marxism" out from a host of contradictory and open-ended research questions in the final work of the mature Marx, and then popularized and disseminated it as a political doctrine. The codification, systematization and simplification of Marx's positions that Engels performed in his major works centres on the reduction of dialectical philosophy to the method of the natural sciences.

Engels's transformation of historical materialism into Marxist politics under the title of "scientific socialism" inaugurates the period of "classical Marxism". Following Engels, the leaders of the socialist movement, such as Karl Kautsky (1854–1938), Georgi Plekhanov (1856–1918), Vladimir Ilych Lenin (1870–1924), Joseph Stalin (1878–1953), Leon Trotsky (1878–1940) and Mao Tse-Tung (1893–1976), modified specific predictions and strategies in light of historical developments and political successes. But from Engels onwards, during the century of historical Communism (1883–1989), the Marxism of the Second, Third and Fourth Internationals remained substantially the same. Marxism was a scientific politics that revolutionized history just as Darwin had radicalized nature. It formulated general laws of history that demonstrated a unilinear process of social evolution, which ascended through a historically necessary sequence of modes of production, culminating in communist society.

The result is a relation between practice, history and structure based on the adaptation of human society to the natural environment. Practice is accordingly defined through the level of technological development of the productive forces, which is held to be the motor of historical dynamics. Historical evolution is seen as passing through the emergence, maturation and then stagnation of a society's characteristic productive forces, as these are promoted and then retarded by its typical social relations of production. Because social structure depends upon the reflection of economic arrangements in politics, law and ideology (and the reaction back upon economics of these factors), mutations in the economic foundation of society catalyse wider changes.

The change in the meaning of the term "praxis" indicates the shift involved in this vision. Where for the young Marx praxis meant that creative human labour in which humanity transformed the natural environment while modifying itself, for classical Marxism, following Engels, "practice" referred to instrumental manipulation of the external world. Praxis, meanwhile, came to signify the unity of scientific theory with revolutionary practice. Social revolutions, in other words, were the laboratory experiments of the new science of history, the events where the hypotheses of Marxism were refined and demonstrated. Classical Marxism is therefore first and foremost *scientific* socialism, a science of history that explains past social evolution and links this to the material interests of present class agents involved in major structural transformations.

But classical Marxism is also, at the same time, an effort to protect this interpretation of historical materialism from revision, in the face of challenges emanating from within the socialist movement. Classical Marxism was, then, from the very beginning a "restoration" of the correct line against "revisionism", that is the recovery of an original doctrine from its subsequent distortion through neglect or revision.

The challenges around which orthodoxy and revisionism took shape in classical Marxism can be reduced to two basic sets of factors: intellectual and political. On the one hand, classical Marxism had to deal with a whole raft of historical developments and research discoveries that falsified specific predictions made by Marx. Although Marxism as a research programme in history provided an immense stimulus to the investigation of past societies, many of the findings disconfirmed fundamental elements of the classical position. And capitalism in the twentieth century proved far more complex than Marx and Engels had anticipated, catalysing major new theories and serious disputes within classical Marxism.

On the other hand, as might be expected from a perspective that regarded political success as the ultimate vindication of theoretical positions, revolutionary experience dominated the debate. For what changed between Engels's intervention and subsequent, bitter debates in the communist movement was the emergence of actual socialist revolutions. But these revolutions happened where Marx and Engels never imagined they would: in Russia and China – backwards, peasant-based economies, utterly different from the industrialized nations of today. From October 1917 in Russia onwards, the connection between historical experiences of revolution and the theoretical works of the leaders determined the arguments about the "authentic Marx". Yet these arguments, about parliamentary reform versus revolutionary insurrection and questions of socialist strategy, happened in a world unlike that predicted by the founders.

Engels's systematization of Marxism

Engels's codification of historical materialism as "scientific socialism" was greatly influenced by the prestige of the natural sciences, and especially by Engels's admiration for Charles Darwin. The result is a systematization of Marx's research into a theoretical doctrine that claims to rest upon the "general laws of motion of matter" undergoing "ceaseless flux" (Engels 1950a: 60, 65). Scientific materialism is supposed to provide a general social and historical theory of the economic infrastructure of society, together with the "ultimate explanation" of the whole superstructure (Engels 1950d: 124). The dialectical method, shorn of its normative dimension, systematically connects natural evolution and the historical process (Engels 1950c: 349), thus supplementing Darwin with Marx (MESW: 429). By virtue of this method, Marxism supposedly discovers "the general laws of motion ... in the history of human society" (Engels 1950c: 353). Although Engels's evolutionary vision of the Marxist worldview is characterized by revolutionary advances and social antagonisms – unlike the gradualism of the natural sciences – there is no doubt that he regards Marxism as the application of scientific method to human history.

Engels's presentation of Marxism as an evolutionary theory, supported by the dialectical method as a general science of everything, is centred on the monumental 542 pages of the Marxist primer *Anti-Dühring* (1878). Indeed, after Marx's death in 1883, Engels's output increased phenomenally. As Norman Levine summarizes:

> The height of Engels' career corresponded with the termination of Marx's life. It is, therefore, entirely consistent that five of Engels' major works were published in the years closely preceding Marx's death, or after the termination of Marx's life. *Anti-Dühring* appeared in 1878; *Socialism: Utopian and Scientific* in 1882; *The Origin of the Family, Private Property and the State* in 1884; and *Ludwig Feuerbach and the End of Classical German Philosophy* in 1888. *The Dialectic of Nature* was first published in 1927 by Riazanov, although the manuscript itself appears to have been completed by 1882. (Levine 1975: 233)

Although Marx certainly read the *Anti-Dühring* – from which *Socialism Utopian and Scientific* and *Ludwig Feuerbach* are taken, along with core ideas for *The Dialectic of Nature* – we should not conclude that his positions coincided with those of Engels. Getting the demarcation right, however, is a complex question. For Terrell Carver and Norman Levine, there is a clear opposition between the humanist Marx and the positivist Engels (Carver 1983: 156; Levine 1975: 174). Subsequent scholarship, in retrieving Engels from simplistic condemnation, has tended to stress the warrant in the mature Marx for Engels's interpretations (Hunley

1991). Nonetheless, defenders of Engels cannot press this to the point of total agreement, for Marx is on record rejecting supposed general laws of history (Marx & Engels 1953: 294), whereas Engels clearly proposes just such supra-historical laws (Engels 1950c: 353). But the underlying difference between Marx's historically specific materialism and Engels's highly general scientific socialism was probably masked by the intervention of Marx's death between their main publications (Carver 1983: 151–2; Levine 1975: 233–4).

Engels's appellation "scientific" was probably also intended to trail connotations of cultural certainty and political authority in the practical context of organizational struggles. Even before Marx's death, theoretical challenges began to arise within the socialist movement, in the form of a current demanding a philosophical rethink of socialist strategy. In this context, the subtitle of Engels's work against Professor Dühring's moderate views is meant ironically. *Herr Eugen Dühring's Revolution in Science* mocks the professor's overturning of Marxism's scientific findings with the abstract tools of philosophy. In place of the hopeless speculations of the red professor, Engels substitutes a total theory of human history framed in evolutionary terms and redolent of the natural sciences.

Inside the final decade of his life, Engels engaged in a monumental work of popularization, writing about a hundred publications between 1890 and 1895 (Carver 1983: 181; Levine 1975: 234). In Engels's treatment, Marxism's method of scientific analysis, although based on the dialectical theory of Hegel, has been "corrected" by splitting the revolutionary method from the conservative system by means of abstracting three core methodological principles from Hegel's work (Engels 1950c: 330). Basically, what this means is that the natural environment, together with the social and historical totality, is to be grasped as an antagonistic whole in a constant process of development through contradictions. This notion of antagonistic interconnections is *science*, Engels affirms, whereas *philosophy* is Hegel's conservative system, which boils down to his historical teleology. Thus the dynamic process grasped by Marxist science does not have an ideal goal outside of history that masquerades as "absolute truth" (*ibid.*: 329). Instead, it proposes laws of motion, formulated as historical tendencies (and counter-tendencies) that can be consciously catalysed, accelerated or retarded, with the assistance of scientific knowledge (*ibid.*: 354).

Furthermore, the dialectical method is said to generate a scientific politics totally unlike the utopian imposition of well-intentioned ideals onto society. Where natural science incorporates a process of theoretical correction through experimental testing, scientific socialism constantly corrects its social theory through analysing the results of revolutionary politics. In other words, the experimental laboratory of the new science of history is nothing less than social revolution and its applied technology is the transformation of society. The implication is that the relation between the theorist and the masses is the same as that between the chemist and her materials, because "the conflicts of innumerable individual wills and individual actions in the domain of history produce a state of affairs entirely analogous to that prevailing in the realm of unconscious nature" (*ibid.*: 354).

Scientific socialism

Although the idea that Marxism makes scientific claims cannot be wholeheartedly endorsed, it cannot be completely dismissed either. As we saw in the first chapter, the mature Marx suppressed the normative foundations of historical materialism. Sometimes he maintained that historical materialism was solely an explanatory theory of particular societies, grounded in a materialist reconstruction of classical political economy and supported by descriptive statements; at other times he provided textual authority for Engels to push historical materialism in the direction of a factually based set of explanatory generalizations capable of trans-historical application. The leaders of the Marxist parties followed Engels in arguing that, effectively, the evolution of humanity's productive forces should be regarded as that part of natural history which ultimately determines the economic foundation of society.

This has rightly been described as "productive force determinism" (Rigby 1998: 5–91), and before examining its specific claims, it is worth pausing to assess its scientific status. In principle, an argument that locates the dynamics of human history in a natural tendency of the human animal to innovate and relates this to social evolution is a scientifically testable theory. Furthermore, insofar as classical Marxism involves explanatory generalizations about historical causes, and locates these causes in the regularities of economic behaviour, it is a plausible candidate for being considered a properly scientific sociology.

Yet, despite its origins in a positivist conception of scientific method, the classical Marxist conception of scientific socialism has not satisfied positivist philosophers of science such as Karl Popper. For Popper, science does not advance through improved generalizations about the world. Instead, science progresses by knocking out false pretenders to scientific status. Scientists advocate bold conjectures about the natural world in a form that involves some specific (testable) predictions. Experimental testing involves efforts to falsify the claims of a theory, so that a real scientist will say of current orthodoxy that it has not yet been disproven, not that it is true. And Popper finds this combination of boldness and humility completely absent from Marxism.

Specifically, Popper accuses Marxism of being a pseudo-science on two grounds. First, he thinks that it does not contain any falsifiable propositions, because its hypotheses do not lead to a set of verifiable predictions. This is basically an attack on the dialectical method, which Popper regards as mere logical confusion: "the dialectician need never be afraid of refutation by forthcoming experiences" (Popper 1940: 424). More damagingly, Popper alleges that Marxism depends on confusion between trends and laws. Trends involve general conditional statements (if *condition* then *event*, where the event is something that holds, empirically, in a statistically significant way). By contrast, laws are logically universal and "assert the impossibility of something or other" (Popper 1964: 115). Marxism, he maintains, asserts that the accumulation of means of production, that is the relentless advance of the productive forces, is a universal historical law (*ibid*.: 129). But Marx himself admits the existence of counter-examples. Therefore the hypothesis is false.

Where does this leave us with respect to the scientific status of classical Marxism? Its defenders can either deny the validity of Popper's model of science or argue that Popper has misunderstood the Marxist argument.

On the one hand, Popper's own student, Imré Lakatos, soon corrected Popper's hard-line position by acknowledging that scientific theories are not in general directly falsifiable (Lakatos 1978: 25). Instead, scientific hypotheses are located in theoretical networks and operate through holistic frameworks, or research programmes, so that the distinction between scientific and non-scientific theories concerns the fallibility versus non-fallibility of entire bodies of knowledge. Non-scientific research programmes degenerate: faced with problems for specific theories, they try to "save the hypothesis" by adjusting the theory to fit with observations, rather than by advancing radical new explanations (*ibid*.: 25). Scientific research programmes risk failure – that is, they are fallible – because they promote radical new explanations when confronted with anomalies and falsifications, which often means abandonment of the original programme. From this perspective, classical Marxism without question began as a scientific research programme – indeed, as a radical new explanation within the programme of classical political economy that generated a new holistic framework in its wake (Kadvany 2011). The big question today would be whether classical Marxism is progressively continuing to produce radical hypotheses, or whether it has degenerated and become a non-scientific dogma.

On the other hand, defenders of classical Marxism could argue that Popper mistakenly interprets its hypotheses as general laws, when what is in fact claimed is the existence of general tendencies. Popper admits the validity of statements of tendency in the physical and social sciences, although he rightly points out that such claims are existential and conditional, not universal and determining (Popper 1964: 129). The problem with this line of defence is that it retrieves the scientific status of historical materialism by exploding the fundamental tenet of classical Marxism. A statement of tendency maintains that under specific conditions a certain result is (descriptively or exactly) likely to happen, thereby explaining the existence of a definite trend in the empirical data. The difficulty is that although this interpretation of historical materialism finds plentiful warrant in Marx's mature work, it is incompatible with the claims of productive force determinism. The classical dilemma is as follows. If Marxism provides statements of tendency, then it is grounded in an examination of the specific conditions of historical societies. In that case, it yields social scientific knowledge of social formations, but it must acknowledge that no general law connects their transformations. The consequence is that socialism is, like other revolutionary events in human history, a contingency, that is something that might or might not happen. Lacking a normative framework, such a set of claims cannot cross the threshold from "might occur" to "should happen". But if, by contrast, Marxism is a set of determining laws of trans-historical generality, then socialism becomes a question of causally determined social evolution, that is, a (non-moral) historical necessity. The political benefits of such an argument are obvious. In that case, however, classical Marxism is committed to producing a falsifiable set of predictions flowing from a deterministic interpretation of the role of the productive forces in social evolution. It is to the difficulties of this final strategy that we now turn.

Productive force determinism

According to S. H. Rigby, "the essence of productive force determinism is that the level of development of a society's productive forces explains the nature of its relations of production, so that as the productive forces develop, so society is obliged to change" (Rigby 1998: 28). Not only is it certain that the mature Marx advocated this position explicitly and repeatedly (*ibid.*: 27, 52), but there can also be no doubt that the classical Marxists subscribed to this view. Following Engels's lead, the leaders of the Second International, Plekhanov and Kautsky, "asserted [productive force determinism] as the basis of Marxist history and social theory" (*ibid.*: 60). The theoreticians of the Third International, Bukharin and Lenin, continued to advocate this reading of Marx despite major political differences with the Second International (*ibid.*: 66–8). Stalin and Trotsky, mutual political hostility notwithstanding, also both proposed productive force determinist interpretations of Marx (*ibid.*: 68–9). As Rigby summarizes:

> A productive force determinist reading of Marx was not only legitimate in terms of Marx's explicit statements. It was also well suited to the political practice of the Second International. … Yet although the political practice of the [Third International] implied a very different conception of Marxism from that of [the Second International], this change was *not* accompanied by any innovation in the realm of historical theory. … Plekhanov and Kautsky rejected the Bolshevik revolution led by Lenin; Bukharin, Stalin and Trotsky disagreed on the way forward for the revolution in an age of international isolation, yet *all* were united by a conception of historical materialism as a form of productive force determinism. (*Ibid.*: 61–2)

G. A. Cohen's *Karl Marx's Theory of History* (1978) represents the most cogent statement of the classical Marxist argument yet provided. He begins from a distinction between the social form of labour (the mode of production or economic foundation of society) and the material labour process (the development of the productive forces as the way in which human beings adapt to the natural environment). Cohen's aim is to locate the productive forces in natural history, in order to ground scientific socialism in a set of causally determined natural regularities. He expresses this commonplace of classical Marxism somewhat surprisingly by claiming that "the productive forces occur *below* the economic foundation" (*ibid.*: 30). For Cohen, the productive forces are "the foundation of the economy, but they do not belong to the economic foundation" (*ibid.*: 30).

The implication is that the advance of the productive forces *is part of natural history*. They are the "matter" that is "formed" by historical social formations (*ibid.*: 98). As Cohen puts it, "there are traces in

Marx of a Darwinian mechanism" in which adaptation to the natural environment by a labouring animal generates material and intellectual conditions that communal group dynamics must then respond to, by a filtering process based on social hierarchies (*ibid.*: 291). The aim is to use this argument to defend the perspective that "history is the history of *human industry*, which undergoes growth in *productive power*, the stimulus and vehicle of which is an *economic structure* which perishes when it has stimulated more growth than it can contain" (*ibid.*: 26).

This is the exciting, if contentious, claim that founds classical Marxism. It rests on the idea that it is human nature to develop and deploy technological means in the labour process. This is because it is human nature to exercise an instrumental form of rationality in calculations of efficiency, when it comes to the important question of satisfying desires by means of human effort. We are, in other words, rather lazy, but also rather desirous, creatures. This strong contradiction in our nature generates both progress and the utopian expectation of what progress is towards. For Cohen:

> (1) Men are, in a respect to be specified, somewhat rational. (2) The historical situation is one of scarcity. (3) Men possess intelligence of a kind and degree which enables them to improve their situation. [Thus] rational beings who know how to satisfy compelling wants that they have will be disposed to seize and employ the means of satisfaction of those wants.
>
> (*Ibid.*: 152)

The salient respect in which human beings are rational is that they innovate in the technological means by which they satisfy their wants, in order to decrease the effort and increase the yield involved in labour. Historical materialism is therefore an explanatory system that seeks to clarify how societies respond to the adaptive behaviour of human beings, in light of the "fact, which needs to be explained, that societies rarely replace a given set of productive forces by an inferior one" (*ibid.*: 153). On this basis, Cohen proposes two theses designed to justify the determinist perspective:

> (Development Thesis) The productive forces tend to develop throughout history. (Primacy Thesis) The nature of the production relations of a society is explained by the level of development of its productive forces. (*Ibid.*: 134)

The Development Thesis explains the state of the productive forces, and predicts their tendential advance on a natural-historical basis by virtue of "somewhat rational" human innovation. But notice how Cohen shifts from an argument for a determining law to the idea of conditional trends, while continuing to maintain the language of "determination". Logically speaking, Cohen should now state the condition under which the upwards trend in the productive forces happens, and it is clear that this condition is that the relations of production "fit" to the productive forces.

But the Primacy Thesis states that advances in the productive forces cause alterations in the relations of production, by virtue of a functional relationship between them (*ibid*.: 160). This is surely circular reasoning, because now the conditions under which a trend happens are described as effects of the trend that was to be explained.

Cohen appears to be unaware of this sort of objection, which is about the logical connection between two theses. But he is aware that objections to a proposed circular connection between two things (productive forces and relations of production) might arise. His rejoinder is that the relation between productive forces and productive relations, as well as between economics and the superstructures, is functional. Causation here involves *functional explanation*, which is quite different to mechanical cause-and-effect sorts of explanation.

Functional arguments involve consequence explanations, in which the occurrence of the event (a mutation in productive relations, for instance a change in property law) happens because its consequences are beneficial to the cause (the advance of the productive forces, for instance a technological innovation; *ibid*.: 263). For instance, classical Marxism maintains that the advent of capitalist relations happened because these relations were beneficial to the advance of the productive forces released by the modern scientific revolution. Generally speaking, for a functional explanation to be intellectually credible, a mechanism of selection has to be demonstrated, which clarifies how changes in Y that are beneficial for X are preferentially retained.

Let us assume that the relevant mechanism can be specified. Then functional explanations of the connection between productive forces and relations of production are perfectly acceptable. But this is not really a rejoinder to the objection of circular reasoning, which concerns the relation between the Development and the Primacy theses. Cohen never confronts this possibility, because he states the Development Thesis in the form of a determining law (i.e. unconditionally), but with the content of a statement of tendency (i.e. conditional).

Where that leaves us is with the asserted "fact ... that societies rarely replace a given set of productive forces by an inferior one". In other words, the most significant test case for the productive force determinism of classical Marxism is the existence of an ascending sequence of modes of production.

Modes of production

In line with the Development Thesis, classical Marxists expect that human history should show evidence of a tendential ascent of the productive forces, from scarcity towards abundance. These should be accompanied by a series of distinct forms of productive relations, corresponding to each stage of advance of the productive forces. Further, these stages in economic history should lead to a defined sequence of forms of the state together with characteristic official ideologies, especially religions. History, in other words, should exhibit a stepwise progression within what is, overall, a unilinear evolutionary curve upwards, as shown in Figure 2.

Marx's quip that "the hand mill gives you society with the feudal lord; the steam mill society with the industrial capitalist" (MESW: 200) does indeed provide some guide to the classical position on modes

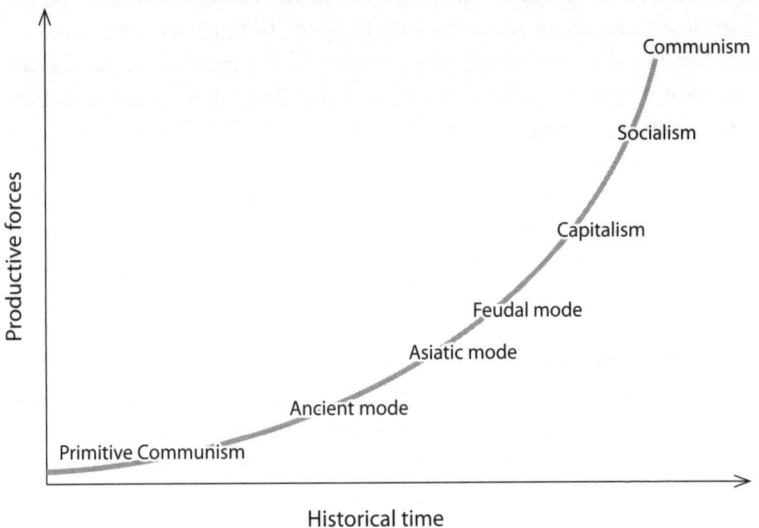

Figure 2 The classical sequence of modes of production.

of production. But, despite appearances, it must not be imagined that classical Marxists are technological determinists, because the concept of a mode of production relates technology to social forms rather than reducing social forms to technological inventions. Specifically, a mode of production designates the connection between a characteristic set of productive forces and the social relations of production that provide beneficial consequences for them. Although the productive forces include instruments of production and raw materials, the most important productive force is labour power, that is the class of direct producers. Likewise, although the social relations of production are comprized by property relations, the crucial thing is how effective possession of the means of production leads to control of the distribution arrangements regarding the product of labour. Therefore (and following Balibar's postclassical clarification of the logical relations involved in these concepts; Althusser & Balibar 1970: 212–16):

- "Work relations" designates the connection between labour power and the means of production, which reduces to the question of the extent to which the direct producers are separate, that is whether or not the direct producers are regarded as *part* of the instruments or means of production. Under so-called primitive modes, there is minimal separation between the collective, shared implements and the common land. In slavery, ancient law regarded the producer as an instrument, a "talking tool". In rent-based modes (feudalism and the so-called Asiatic mode of production), the serf (i.e. unfree peasant farmer) is tied to the land, that is to the means of production. Under capitalism, and in a hypothetical socialist society, the producers are free, that is regarded as separate from the instruments and means of production. In exploitative modes of production, classical Marxists often speak of the distinction in work relations between "economic compulsion" (wages) and "extra-economic coercion" (slavery, rent).
- "Property relations" refers to effective possession of the means of production by the property-owning class, which is generally a class of non-producers but sometimes the direct producers themselves. Ultimately, what is meant by effective possession is the ability to appropriate the social surplus product. This is the sum total of social production left over once those necessities required for the maintenance of the labour power of the direct producers have been deducted. In so-called primitive societies, the direct producers are the property owners and the (minimal)

social surplus product is distributed in an egalitarian way, or in ways that reflect forms of political and cultural authority. Under slavery, the slave-owners appropriate the entire product and make deductions, often at less than subsistence levels, to feed, clothe and house the slaves. In rent-based societies, the serfs provide for their own subsistence but are compelled to perform several days a week of surplus labour for the landlord, which is appropriated by this propertied class. Under capitalism, Marx's labour theory of value holds that the social surplus product is appropriated through the difference between wages and profits. Finally, in a hypothetical future society, the propertied class and the direct producers coincide, so that the social surplus product is distributed equally (socialism) or as needed by each (communism).

Modes of production, then, are in the final analysis all about exploitation, that is the way that the combination of work relations and property relations determines the form through which the social surplus product is appropriated. For reasons of space, I will just discuss two of these forms, slavery and rent, as we examined Marx's theory of the wage-based society in the last chapter. How well do these general descriptions of historical societies perform when confronted by the historical evidence? Do the transitions between them correspond to the predictions made by productive force determinism?

Ancient slavery

For classical Marxism, the ancient civilizations of the Mediterranean, especially Greece and Rome, are paradigmatic examples of the slave-based mode of production. Slaves are people who have become items of property, and who therefore cannot direct and control their own labour power, but are instead able to be bought and sold. In the ancient world, the slave was – as Marx reminds us – *instrumentum vocale*, a "talking tool", whose enslavement was the result of accumulated debts, military conquest, sale of children or an inherited condition. The form of appropriation of surplus labour in slavery was through the most brutal forms of extra-economic coercion, ranging from the murderous regime of the galleys, mines and plantations, through to the application of severe corporal punishments in the cases of manufacturing, domestic and body slaves. Slaves receive, at their masters' discretion, a portion of the product of labour sufficient to reproduce their labour power, and the constant threat of coercion is applied to maintain productivity.

The hypothesis that ancient Greece and Rome were slave societies has been tested by classical Marxist research, but the results are somewhat inconclusive. G. E. M. de Ste Croix's monumental *The Class Struggle in the Ancient World* sets forth from classical premises, but then concedes that the majority of the population in Greece and Rome were in fact free peasants and independent artisans (de Ste Croix 1981: 52–4). Additionally, although slave revolts were common in the ancient world, in celebrated instances managing to liberate whole provinces and entire cities, the political struggles of the ancient world mainly happened between the wealthy patricians and the impoverished plebeians. Perhaps in an effort to salvage the hypothesis, de Ste Croix then claims that although the bulk of the social surplus product was not in general derived from slavery, the ancient ruling class specifically "derived their surpluses … from unfree labour" (*ibid.*: 53). Indeed, he points out that the surplus product generated on the vast plantations and in state-held mines, together with the constant influx of cheap slaves following military conquests, was the most important civil weapon at the disposal of the patrician class. De Ste Croix analytically conflates the unfree peasantry (serfs) with agricultural slaves, under the title of "unfree labour", while accepting that "it is serfdom which provides the propertied class with much of its surplus" (*ibid.*: 173). Nonetheless, this is a reasonable way to modify the classical position in light of empirical evidence. In effect, it claims that the societies of the ancient world were based on a combination of production modes, where slavery and serfdom are not legally differentiated.

Much more troublesome for the classical account is the transition from antiquity to feudalism in Europe. Marx and Engels were well aware that the collapse of the Roman Empire after 450 CE led to economic regression. Now in general, the classical expectation is that the productive forces display an inherent tendency to increase, which leads the productive relations to become fetters on development. Once this occurs, the increase of the productive forces is temporarily blocked, generating stagnation, crisis and then either collapse or revolution. But that is not what historical research indicates happened. "This was not a case", writes Ellen Wood, "where dynamic forces taxed the limits of restrictive relations. … But rather … the prevailing relations … encouraged the extension of extra-economic surplus extraction instead of the improvement of labour productivity" (Wood 1995: 130). The economic problems of Rome depended on the conflict between efforts to broaden the base of exploitation (not to increase its depth) by enserfing the free peasantry (the *colonii*) and the staggering expenditures of the expanding state (Anderson 1974b: 18–28).

Engels constructed an argument to circumvent this problem: the enserfment of the *colonii* represented the nucleus of an increase in labour productivity through technological innovation. Late Roman development was on its way to feudalism when contingent events (lasting fully 500 years!) interrupted the historically necessary sequence with a sort of barbarian intermission. Subsequent classical Marxist historians have followed suit, arguing that feudalism represented a significant productivity advance on antiquity and that the Roman peasantry were proto-feudal. In other words, feudalism represents the resumption of a unilinear historical sequence determined by economic productive forces. This argumentative strategy preserves the series of modes of production, but it sacrifices the explanatory account of the transitions between them.

Rent-based modes

Medieval eastern and western Europe is regarded by classical Marxists as the paradigmatic instance of feudal society, but Mughal India and Han Dynasty China are also examples (Rigby 1998: 222). Alongside feudalism, classical Marxism also debated the existence of another rent-based mode of production, the "Asiatic", which I will discuss in a moment. The rent-based modes are characterized by agricultural production under conditions where money rent is highly restricted in favour of rent-in-kind, and markets for agricultural goods are limited. Two common characteristics define these rent-based modes: the supreme landlord is the monarch, who theoretically possesses the entire country on behalf of the ethnic collectivity; the labourers are legally bonded to the soil and this legal restraint facilitates extra-economic coercion of surplus labour through royal taxes and customary obligations.

Under European feudalism, a serf (sometimes called a peasant) is an agricultural labourer who is legally tied to a particular landholding as *glebae adscripti*, bondsman or bondswoman, which juridically prevents their movement. Work relations were therefore characterized by lack of control over materials (plus lack of access to major instruments, such as mills, irrigation and oxen teams), creating a relation of dependence on the landlord for the serf's means of subsistence. The appropriation of the surplus social product through property relations happens by means of a division of the serf's week into days spent on their private plot (reproduction of labour power) and days served on the lord's fields (production of surplus). As Perry Anderson writes:

agrarian property was privately controlled by a class of feudal lords, who extracted a surplus from the peasants by politico-legal relations of compulsion. This extra-economic coercion, taking the form of labour services, rents in kind or customary dues owed to the individual lord by the peasant, was exercized both on the manorial demesne attached directly to the person of the lord and on the strip tenancies or virgates cultivated by the peasant. (Anderson 1974b: 147)

Meanwhile, although landownership is technically invested in the monarch, in practice the sovereign parcelled out estates through a descending hierarchy of feudal nobles, in a chain of dependent tenures that contracted military services for the opportunity to exploit a landholding and its serfs. The partitioning of sovereignty into manors, baronies, earldoms and so forth prevented the unification of the feudal state, with two historically significant consequences. First, the church played an extraordinarily important role in the suppression of dissent, supplementing the political weakness of the aristocratic centre with ideological control of the popular periphery. And second, feudal ruling classes could not establish control over the free towns, which eventually provided the seat for the rise of the bourgeoisie.

The controversy in classical Marxism regarding the so-called Asiatic mode of production concerns whether the entire historical world of Asia can reasonably be regarded under a single description. Additionally, Marx's own description of this mode in terms of state-based irrigation works, prolonged by Karl Wittfogel into a massive survey of "oriental despotism" that embraced everything from the Incas to Imperial China, is highly misleading (Wittfogel 1957). Although some Marxists dismiss the entire category, there is a distinction to be made between the generic form of a rent-based mode characterized by sovereign ownership of land and its deviant form in European feudalism, characterized by the parcellization of sovereignty. In ancient Egypt and the Mesopotamian civilizations, for instance, land tenure was organized through the state and rent collected as tax (in money, goods and services), and this would in fact appear to be typical of pre-modern agrarian economies (Rigby 1998: 222–4). But these rent-based societies were notoriously conservative in terms of technological innovation and economic development. In the case of Europe, by contrast, the rent-based mode represents a significant productive improvement on the ancient mode:

[Although] there was no simple, terminal halt to technique in the classical world … no major cluster of inventions ever occurred to propel the ancient economy forward to qualitatively new forces of production. Nothing is more striking, in any comparative retrospect, than the overall technological stagnation of antiquity. It is enough to contrast the record of its eight centuries of existence, from the rise of Athens to the fall of Rome, with the equivalent span of the feudal mode of production which succeeded it, to perceive the difference between a relatively static and a relatively dynamic economy.

(Anderson 1974b: 26)

Indeed the entire narrative of the maturation and stagnation of feudalism, with the long crisis of feudalism in the fourteenth century as a placemarker for its incipient collapse, seems better evidenced than the equivalent account of the transition from antiquity to feudalism. Capitalism, on the classical account, matures in the womb of feudalism until it is reflected throughout late feudal society in the development of absolutism in the seventeenth and eighteenth centuries. Absolutism is already bourgeois in content, although feudal in form, and it nurtures the productivity advances that the free towns and the scientific revolution make possible. Once the late eighteenth century has generated bourgeois revolutions, the productive forces of capitalism are liberated from feudal restraints, producing the Industrial Revolution as a spectacular proof of the superior dynamism of capitalism compared with feudalism.

In other words, as was perhaps expected, the classical Marxist account of historical transitions fits well with the western European case of the shift from feudalism to capitalism. Elsewhere, in terms of the test of historical evidence in the ancient world, and the comparison between European and non-European rent-based societies, classical Marxism fares badly. This suggests what we might already have suspected, that the theory represents a premature generalization from a special case.

Challenges in the twentieth century

The theoretical limitations of classical Marxism, however, did not prevent productive force determinism from having a significant political effect. Indeed in the demonstration of the value of classical Marxism, revolutionary success tended to be substituted for research findings, and this is hardly surprising. The Marxist parties were mass formations, not intellectual seminars, and they recruited members on the basis of taking political action around the legitimate grievances of the oppressed. Under these circumstances, Marxists' political effectiveness in revolutionary situations appeared to corroborate the basic correctness of the central idea of productive force determinism, which was that the march of history pointed necessarily towards socialism.

The thesis of the advance of productive forces implied that by the end of the nineteenth century, mature capitalism would begin to decay into stagnant forms. This would generate a series of economic crises that would be reflected in political authoritarianism and ideological reaction. Classical Marxists from Kautsky and Plekhanov through to Stalin and Trotsky argued that the breakdown of capitalism was on the horizon after the First World War (1914–18), and with it the disintegration of liberal ideology and the abandonment of parliamentary democracy. The economic turbulence and political convulsions of the interwar decades (1920–40), such as the Great Depression of the 1930s and the rise of German and Italian fascism, together with successful socialist revolutions in Russia (1917) and then China (1949), certainly appeared to confirm the basic theses of classical Marxism.

Yet throughout this period, because of a paradoxical combination of political successes and failed predictions, classical Marxism was itself in crisis. In 1918, the Second International, founded around the authority of Marx and Engels in the 1880s, split, with its radical wing, the pro-Leninist Third (or Communist) International, breaking from the social democratic majority. Then, in 1938, the radical, Trotskyist minority of the Communist International, already long since expelled from the pro-Stalin national parties that composed the movement, formed the Fourth International.

Two basic sets of questions were at work in these splits. The first concerned how complex new social phenomena were to be interpreted by classical Marxism in ways consistent with productive force determinism. These phenomena included developments such as the massive expansion of the middle strata, the strikingly uneven development of the former colonies, the unprecedented economic boom of the post-war era, the spread of social rights and civil liberties in the industrialized world, and the failure of the socialist countries to economically compete with the capitalist world. Although the stagnation of the productive forces that should, theoretically, have been produced by the fetter of capitalist social relations did appear to be confirmed before the Second World War, post-war capitalism seemed to have returned to a progressive dynamic, with economic boom, political progress and a historical advantage relative to the socialist bloc. The basic discursive strategy of classical Marxism was to interpret these phenomena as misleading appearances concealing the global and historical essence of a mode of production in decline. One way to do this is to argue a theory of imperialism, proposing that material prosperity and expanding rights in the industrialized centres, or "metropolitan countries", is the direct consequence of impoverishment and authoritarianism in the industrializing periphery, or "semi-colonial countries". There is plenty of evidence of unequal exchange, dependent development and political distortion that supports this sort of contention, but it is not really a defence of the *classical* hypothesis unless it is also shown that this results in overall stagnation in the global level of productive forces. Perhaps because this is rather difficult to demonstrate, the other strategy is to remove the requirement that the productive forces be involved in a zero-sum game. This involves building up a contemporary classical picture of the determining role of the economy in relation to politics and ideology on a world scale. The most impressive classical Marxist synthesis of this sort is Ernst Mandel's *Late Capitalism*, which, together with his interpretation of twentieth-century history (Mandel 1978b, 1986), provides a productive forces determinist reading of multinational capitalism (Mandel 1978a). Probably the most striking element of this account is Mandel's shift from a theory of the emergence, maturation and stagnation of capitalist productive forces to a theory of long waves of capitalist development (Mandel 1995). According to Mandel's classical determinism, the up-and-down historical rhythm of expansion and contraction is built into capitalism, rather than signifying the breakdown of the mode of production.

The second set of questions concerned the opposition between political voluntarism and evolutionary gradualism. These were ultimately arguments about the relation between the economic base and the ideologico-political superstructure. Engels had insisted in the 1890s that the Marxist understanding of history and society did not imply the passive reflection, in politics, of economic trends. In a famous letter to Joseph Bloch, Engels maintains that:

> According to the materialist conception of history, the ultimately determining element in history is the production and reproduction of real life. More than this neither Marx nor I have ever asserted. Hence if somebody twists this into saying that the economic element is the *only* determining one, he transforms that proposition into a meaningless, abstract,

senseless phrase. The economic situation is the basis, but the various elements of the superstructure – ... political, juristic, philosophical ... religious ... – also exercise their influence upon the course of the historical struggles and in many cases preponderate in determining their form. There is an interaction of all these elements in which, amid all the endless host of accidents, ... the economic movement finally asserts itself as necessary.   (Engels 1950b: 443)

The notion of "economic determination in the final instance" is here related to the *class content* of political history. Meanwhile, an example of the superstructural determination of the *political form* of a social struggle arising on the basis of economic interests is provided by Engels's analysis of the relation between emergent capitalism and the Protestant Reformation. For both Marx and Engels, the doctrines of Luther and Calvin were ideological representations of the class interests of the fledgling bourgeoisie, "the true religious disguise of the interests of the bourgeoisie" (Engels 1950c: 362).

In terms of social structure, the classical position is that economic determination is ultimately decisive, but politics and ideology nonetheless "react back" on the economic foundation to limit or enable development (Engels 1950b: 444). In the dynamic terms of historical events, Engels speaks of a "parallelogram of forces", whose "resultant" is the direction of historical change. This implies that although politics and ideology might point away from class forces, their total effect is best analysed in class terms, because historical agents are ultimately economically constituted *class* agents. The whole question of the action of the superstructural institutions on the class infrastructure, and the historical effectiveness of the ideology and politics of popular movements in transforming economics, becomes particularly pointed when it comes to revolutionary states. The Leninist Third International ultimately split from the social democratic Second International on just this issue. Could a Marxist party, based in a tiny industrial proletariat, successfully set up a socialist state in a country whose economic foundations were mainly pre-capitalist?

Lenin's politics and the Leninist party

For the leading theoreticians of the Second International, such as Kautsky and Plekhanov, Marxism predicts the need for a prolonged period of capitalist development before socialist revolution becomes a possibility. By contrast, in his celebrated *Imperialism, the Highest Stage of Capitalism* (1916), Lenin argues that capitalism has completed its historical mission in the creation of a world economy regulated by nation states, and has now entered into its epoch of decay (Lenin 1977c: 728). The big corporations and the most powerful states try to stave off economic stagnation by exploiting cheap labour and raw materials in the colonies, but this only leads to world wars between the imperialist powers. The implication is that there would be no "prolonged period of capitalist development" in Russia, because capitalism as a global system has ceased to secure well-rounded, as opposed to uneven, development. The stark alternatives are socialist revolution or chronic under-development.

Lenin's explanation for imperialism is based on economic factors (*ibid*.: 700–08). The emergence of monopolistic firms that have integrated with banking concerns generates what Lenin calls "finance capital", the merger of industry and banking in international corporations. These firms generate "monopoly super-profits" because their international scope means that they can "export capital" through foreign investment, taking advantage of cheap labour, abundant raw materials, high rates of profit and pliant colonial governments. The implication is that the nature of capitalism has changed: where once the capitalists had sought to liberate humanity from feudalism, they now seek global domination; where once capitalism had aspired to cosmopolitan peace and international unification, it now represents a force for nationalist aggression and imperialist rivalries. To prevent rebellion in the colonies and revolution at home, the imperialist powers enlist sections of the working class as a "labour aristocracy" in support of their policies, through special conditions, and try to manage crises through the integration of the state with capital in a semi-planned economy. The super-exploitation of the colonial peoples and the devastation of the natural resources of the developing world are not accompanied by well-rounded industrial development or the improvement of living standards. Instead, Lenin argues, the imperialist powers use their military superiority to impoverish and dominate their colonial empires. But since colonialism in the nineteenth century has already partitioned the globe, the only solution for rising imperialist powers such as Japan and Germany is to militarily force a re-division of the world (*ibid*.: 708–26).

Hastily returning to Russia upon the outbreak of democratic revolution in February 1917, Lenin drew the final conclusion from this analysis. Amidst the chaos of imperialist wars, economic crises and revolutionary uprisings, an extremely centralized party can seize the opportunity and lead a socialist insurrection. This is despite the developmental backwardness of these "weak links" and the fact that the proletariat is a tiny minority of the population in the semi-colonies. If the central committee is prepared to exercise military discipline among its small number of highly trained militants, the party can expand rapidly among the radicalizing population and win support by combining democratic and socialist slogans with land reforms aimed at the vast peasantry.

And it so happened that such a party was on hand in April 1917, because Lenin had been arguing for just such a formation since *What Is To Be Done?* (1902) had split the Russian Social Democratic Party. In *State and Revolution* (1917), written in the heat of the action, Lenin insists that the authentic Marxist doctrine on the state maintains that every state has a fundamental class character. The class character of the state is decided by the property relations enshrined in its legal system, while the unity of the state resides at the level of executive power. A weapon for the oppression of one class by another class, the state is an instrument of violence that basically consists of "armed bodies of men" (Lenin 1977b: 243). The bourgeois state is a national state dedicated to private property, especially in the means of production, Lenin concludes, something that has become reactionary in an era of the world economy and the possibility of socialism. Against the bourgeois state, Lenin proposes a workers' council republic modelled on the Paris Commune, pointing out that although Marx foresaw the necessity of a socialist state, the ultimate aim is to smash the state altogether (*ibid.*: 269–74). Accordingly, Lenin distinguishes between a workers' state (a revolutionary republic within a recently nationalized capitalist economy in transition to socialism), a world federation of socialist states (a global arrangement of states defending collective property within economic arrangements based on worldwide planning) and communism (a world arrangement of planned production without states or property; *ibid.*: 303–13).

In opposition, then, to capital and the nation state, Lenin places the working class and its participatory-democratic workers' councils. Yet Lenin also argues that the link between class and councils is the revolutionary party, arguing that the task of the party is organization of the armed insurrection followed by political representation within the workers' council republic. From the very beginning, Lenin's framing of the class/party relationship attracted the criticism that it was "substitutionist", that is that Lenin was preparing to substitute a minority party for the working class as a whole. Lenin's conception of the role and organization of the party did nothing to reassure the critics within the

Russian, French and German social democratic parties on this score, for Lenin insists on a party of the militant minority controlled by the central committee through "democratic centralism" (Lenin 1977c: 186–7).

Lenin claimed that although the party represents the historical interests of the whole class, the party cannot be a broad formation or reflect anything other than the majority view in the party itself, because it must consist only of the "highest consciousness". He therefore gladly took the name "Bolshevik" ("majority") when the Russian Social Democratic Party split on these questions. It must be said that the party's consciousness-raising activities certainly included a militant defence of human rights, for Lenin insists that "working-class consciousness cannot be genuine political consciousness unless the workers are trained to respond to all cases of tyranny, oppression, violence and abuse, no matter what class is affected" (*ibid.*: 145). Nonetheless, although Lenin insists that the highly disciplined and well-educated party members – or "cadres" – act as a transmission belt in both directions between class and central committee, in practice the central committee determined policy from exile, using the party newspaper as a propaganda organ.

That many socialists were suspicious of Lenin's conception of political organization was the result of one of his most controversial positions, on the relation between workers' experience and class consciousness. In a notorious passage, Lenin writes that:

> there could not have been Social-Democratic consciousness among the workers. It would have to be brought to them from without. The history of all countries shows that the working class, exclusively and by its own efforts, is able to develop only trade union consciousness. … The theory of socialism, however, grew out of the philosophical, historical and economic theories elaborated by educated representatives of the propertied classes, by intellectuals. (*Ibid.*: 114)

The entailment of this position is that working class spontaneity is to be distrusted as merely "reformist", by contrast with the correct, revolutionary line of the party militants. It also means that when workers learn about politics from experience, their conclusions are always wrong, as opposed to the right interpretation of historical events by the central committee. In fairness to Lenin, these were *never* conclusions that he explicitly drew. But the implications are disturbing, especially when this is placed next to Lenin's views on the dictatorship of the proletariat. Although Lenin maintains that this expression means popular participatory democracy, he also insisted that the proletarian dictatorship was above the law and beyond "bourgeois" morality.

By October 1917, Lenin's Bolshevik Party had won a majority in the urban centres on the demands of "land, bread and peace", and Lenin felt ready to start the insurrection. The Russian Revolution completely transformed world politics and led to the breakaway of the Third (Communist) International (or "Comintern") from the Second (Socialist) International. Lenin, probably the most unorthodox of the orthodox Marxists in the period 1902–17, overnight redefined what orthodoxy meant. Meanwhile Kautsky, yesterday's "pope" of orthodox Marxism, suddenly became not just a "revisionist", but a veritable "renegade" (Lenin 1977a: 17–97).

Actually existing socialism

The Russian Revolution provided the template for insurrectionary politics and socialist construction in the twentieth century. These states have been described as "historical Communism" or "actually existing socialism", designations that are imprecise but widely used. The questions surrounding the destinies of the revolutions made by the communist parties that grew from the Third International are complex. Nonetheless, there are some historical facts that frame the entire experience, which must be taken into consideration in any account of the implementation of classical Marxism. As Howard Chodos summarizes:

> First, the fact that the vision that inspired the creation of historical communism did not survive the twentieth century intact. The main states that were built in the name of Marxism either collapsed, as in the case of the former Soviet Union and its allied People's Democracies, or have been so thoroughly transformed as to result in a series of economic reforms, as in the case of China, as to be completely unrecognisable. ... Second, the fact that serious violations of human rights, not to say outright criminal behaviour, have repeatedly occurred in states purporting to implement the [classical] Marxist vision, under a sufficiently wide array of circumstances to constitute a prima facie case that there was something amiss at the heart of the twentieth-century socialist project. And finally, the fact that historical communist regimes were never able to live up to the standard that they themselves established as the criterion by

which they should ultimately be judged, that is they never did surpass capitalist liberal democracies either in terms of their ability to sustain economic growth, or in terms of meeting the material needs of their citizens.   (Chodos 2007: 177)

For most people today, the future society envisaged by Marxism as a whole, and not just its classical variant, is fatally compromised by the experiences of Russia and China. The designation "actually existing socialism", which originates from its defenders, is apologetic, because it implicitly contrasts what was imagined before any of this happened with what became possible under historical circumstances. Indeed even the most resolute advocates of the political arrangements modelled on the Soviet Union acknowledged that the results were hardly ideal (Stalin 1943: 656–7). Following internal political struggles against the left opposition of Bukharin and Trotsky, Stalin's control of the central committee of the Bolshevik Party made it possible to instigate a particular version of the classical programme. Under conditions of imperialist encirclement, invasion by a militarily superior fascist power and then Cold War stand-off against the technologically advanced West, the Soviet Union engaged in a form of the national construction of socialism that had four elements. These were forced agricultural collectivization and modernization, the socialization of industry and rapid industrialization, centralized economic planning using a five-year timeframe, and political centralization of a dictatorial, one-party state with an extensive secret police.

Where Stalin pioneered a particular vision of socialist construction that was extensively implemented following revolutions in the developing world, it was really Mao who worked out how to apply classical Marxism to political strategy in peasant societies, that is to actually make revolutions happen. Following Stalin's interpretation of Lenin's theory of imperialism and its application in Russia, Mao foresaw a two-stage process. In the first stage, the Communist Party leads (on behalf of the absent proletariat) an alliance of peasants and the national bourgeoisie against the alliance of imperialist forces, local fascists and the pro-imperialist bourgeoisie. The resulting People's Democracy then manages a peaceful transition to socialism in one country, as the Communist Party within the provisional government of national unity rapidly consolidates power.

Confronted with the problem of socialist strategy in a peasant society, Mao concluded that the Communist Party must create revolutionary zones within the countryside and only arrive at the end of the revolution at the gates of the cities. In essence, the revolution sets up a proto-state in one part of the country and then extends this outwards by infiltration into the popular masses and guerrilla actions against the army and police (Tse-Tung 1967–69: 113–94 Vol II, 147–54 Vol IV). Furthermore, given the arms imbalance between pro-imperialist forces and the communist movement, the revolution must reckon with a "prolonged popular war" involving serious casualties, where revolutionary policy, democratic centralism and military discipline collapse into the same thing. Once the Communist Party holds a majority in the organs of state and the national assembly, it moves to alter the constitution to reflect a socialist state by collectivizing property, revolutionizing agriculture, forcing industrialization and expropriating foreign corporations. After the socialist revolution, the proletariat becomes a majority of the population, although, happily, it is not a proletariat by this stage but just "the people" of a classless republic.

Because classical Marxism regarded practice as the test of theory, Marx's vision of socialism has been held to stand or fall with the success or failure of historical Communism. Most evaluations of actually existing socialism have sought to balance the difficult historical circumstances of its birth against the social achievements of these regimes. Their strategy for socialist construction centred on the breakneck advance of technological productive forces at the expense of the political rights and economic control of the labour force. These were traded against an expectation of material prosperity in the future. Nonetheless, defenders of the regimes can point to some real achievements. Successful revolutions demonstrated that capitalism could be overthrown, while the initial phases of agricultural reform and industrialization generated significantly higher growth rates than Western alternatives. Socialist construction – however flawed – resulted in better material conditions for the population compared to the pre-revolutionary regimes, where vast wealth gaps were replaced by relatively egalitarian distribution arrangements and massively improved access to social services. The socialist bloc supported national liberation from colonial domination and imperialist military interventions worldwide, and the existence of an alternative to capitalism influenced the setting up of the welfare state in the West (Chodos 2007: 185).

Critics of these regimes have powerful arguments at their disposal, however, beginning with the way that the terminus of these regimes in atrocity or stagnation has almost completely discredited social alternatives to capitalism. Despite some social and economic advances, popular support for actual socialism has proven absent in the moment of political truth, possibly because of persistent material shortages, bureaucratic manipulation of distribution arrangements, the suppression of dissent and debate, and failure to actually surpass the West technologically. To protect a system of political clientalism, the governing bureaucracy engaged in ferocious repression of any popular movements, including massive criminal acts, on the scale of the atrocities that fascism perpetrated (*ibid.*: 185).

The official declarations of the leaders of these states ring in chilling counterpoint to the factual record of their regimes. "All of the exploiting classes have been eliminated", Stalin wrote triumphantly in 1936; "the exploitation of man by man has been abolished, eliminated, while … in the sphere of the national economy of the USSR, we now have a new, Socialist economy [advancing] along the road to Communism" (Stalin 1943: 566). It is reliably estimated that the construction of this "new, classless, Socialist society" (*ibid.*: 567) cost at least 10 million lives between 1929 and 1953 (Davies 1995: 72–3). Mao's efforts to implement the Stalinist blueprint from the 1930s under Chinese circumstances of the 1950s also had catastrophic consequences for the popular masses. The policies of agricultural collectivization and forced industrialization were continued in the Great Leap Forward (1958–62), which resulted in famine and 38 million deaths (Chang & Halliday 2005: 456–7). In the Great Proletarian Cultural Revolution, party cadres consisting of layers of workers and students were mobilized against intellectuals and bureaucrats, not in order to create a participatory democracy, but in order to cleanse the state of "cultivation", by removing these layers from power and sending intellectuals to forced "re-education" camps (Shu-Tse 1980: 380–415). Nonetheless, Mao's strategy of guerrilla warfare and socialist construction led by the Communist Party was successfully prosecuted by Ho Chi Minh in Vietnam (a relatively benevolent regime) and by Pol Pot in Cambodia (an extremely malevolent regime).

Explanations of actually existing socialism and accounts of these societies have ranged from right-wing arguments that they demonstrate that Marxism as a whole is inherently totalitarian, through to apologies for their political and economic defects as the result of imperialist encirclement, rather than some problem with the classical vision (Chodos 2007: 182). These societies have been described as immature forms of socialism, workers' states that have degenerated into bureaucratic despotisms, forms of state capitalism and even new types of bureaucratic class society. Adjudication of these claims would require a separate volume, but in relation to classical Marxism, two things can be said. The first is that the combination of a vision of historically necessary social evolution with a conception of socialism as a morally neutral scientific politics most certainly played a part in the disaster of historical Communism. The second is that this by no means incriminates classical Marxism as a whole, because it was certainly possible to be a classical Marxist and yet directly oppose the regimes of actually existing socialism.

The classical critique of Stalin's Russia

Trotsky's is far from the only classical critique of Stalinism. Nonetheless, because of his historical significance, this analysis of the Soviet Union cannot be overlooked in any evaluation of productive force determinism and its political consequences. Although the Fourth International failed to lead a mass mobilization (Frank 1979: 3–4), it provides evidence that the politics of Stalin are not the whole story about scientific socialism. Trotsky's claim that the Soviet Union was a "degenerate workers' state" that had resulted from a political counter-revolution by the Stalinist bureaucracy, and his alternative to national liberation in "permanent revolution", remain controversial and contentious. The point here, however, is not to reach a final judgment on the object of Trotsky's analyses, but to illustrate the classical approach by looking at an historical figure's response to Stalin's national model of socialist construction.

According to Trotsky's mature theory, although capitalism as a world system of combined and uneven development is *as a whole* a fetter on the productive forces – making socialist revolution in the developing world possible – it is absurd to suggest that a backward economy could *on its own* advance to socialism (Trotsky 1970). In *The Revolution Betrayed* (1936), Trotsky argues that, from the classical perspective, the Stalin regime can only be regarded as a counter-revolutionary force within what Trotsky calls a "degenerate workers' state".

This is fundamentally an argument from the historical condition of the global sum of productive forces to the negative consequences of isolated national development, exacerbated by imperialist blockade. Additionally, Trotsky denounces the suppression of participatory democracy in the workers' soviets and ridicules Stalin's declaration of the achievement of socialism as a farce, given the industrial backwardness of the Russian economy. "By the lowest stage of communism [i.e. socialism]", Trotsky writes, "Marx meant, at any rate, a society which from the very beginning stands higher in its economic development than the most advanced capitalism." He continues:

[T]he present Soviet Union does not stand above the level of world economy, but is only trying to catch up to the capitalist countries. Marx called that society, formed upon the basis of a socialization of the productive forces of the most advanced capitalism of its epoch, the lowest stage of communism. This designation obviously does not apply to the Soviet Union. ... [T]he present Soviet regime, in all its contradictoriness, [is] not a socialist regime, but a preparatory regime transitional from capitalism to socialism. (Trotsky 1972: 47)

In his analysis of the class character of the Soviet state, Trotsky begins from the economic base and then argues that the contradictions of the political superstructure are determined in the last instance by an economic antagonism. This is between socialist property relations in production and capitalist monetary relations in distribution. Because it is compelled by material scarcity to use monetary wages to distribute the social product, Trotsky proposes:

The state assumes directly and from the very beginning a dual character: socialistic, insofar as it defends social property in the means of production; bourgeois, insofar as the distribution of life's goods is carried out with a capitalistic measure of value and all the consequences ensuing therefrom. (*Ibid.*: 54)

In other words, the institutional structure of the state reflects the fundamental laws of motion of the economy, so that political struggles must respond – according to the specific factors at work in the political arena – to economic antagonisms of a class character. Accordingly, the administration is being run by a class layer that is distinctly non-proletarian, at the same time that the government in the soviets has excluded proletarian participation. The Stalin regime, Trotsky concludes, represents a political counter-revolution. Although Trotsky does consider the possibility that the Soviet Union is a form of state capitalism, he remains unconvinced, because he believes that that would have to involve the reversal of socialist property relations:

The means of production belong to the state. But the state, so to speak, "belongs" to the bureaucracy. If these as yet wholly new relations should solidify, become the norm and be legalized, whether with or without resistance from the workers, they would, in the long run, lead to a complete liquidation of the social conquests of the proletarian revolution. But to speak of that now is at least premature. The proletariat has not yet said its last word. The bureaucracy has not yet created social supports for its dominion in the form of special types of property. It is compelled to defend state property as the source of its power and its income.   (*Ibid.*: 249)

The class characterization of the Soviet state remained an important question in the post-war era. Some Trotskyists adapted a "state capitalist" position, while others described the post-Stalin regime as a "degenerate workers' state". But they agreed on the practical tasks involved in Russia. These included launching new soviets against the post-Stalinist bureaucracy, the democratization of the economy and the complete dismantling of what Trotsky had called "a totalitarian-bureaucratic state" (*ibid.*: 108).

In the event, that did not happen. Instead, historical Communism collapsed through economic stagnation and lack of political legitimacy. Many Marxists had long recognized that these states were not viable and had rejected the official orthodoxies that went with them. From the 1970s onwards, many classical Marxists, drawn by both Trotskyist and Maoist critiques of the Soviet Union, began to move away from productive force determinism. A new focus on the relations of production was accompanied by recognition of multiple paths of historical evolution and the importance of political contingency in social development. This might well be called post-classical by thinkers such as Perry Anderson and Ellen Wood, for instance, although they affirm a base-and-superstructure perspective, emphasizing the centrality of the political superstructure in class dynamics (Wood 1986, 1995) and the multiplicity of possible trajectories confronting historical societies (Anderson 1974a, b). Others affirm the centrality of the concept of imperialism but locate this in a world-system perspective that concentrates on economic and political relations (Wallerstein 1990, 2002). Either way, the unfolding of historical necessity through a sequence of modes of production, and the politics of national infrastructural development that accompanied it, no longer represent the mainstream of Marxist thinking.

Summary of key points

The codification of historical materialism

- In the context of debates in the socialist movement, Engels formalized "Marxism" as the science of human history that complemented Darwin's science of natural evolution.
- From this perspective, social revolutions are the laboratory experiments of Marxist science, whose major hypothesis is that social evolution follows development of the productive forces.

Lenin's politics

- Lenin's rediscovery of Hegel was a return to historical teleology, in the form of the thesis that imperialism is the "epoch of capitalist decay", an era of wars and revolutions which implies that the communist party must have a quasi-military discipline.
- Imperialism is caused by five economic factors (monopoly corporations, finance capital, the export of capital, world economy and colonial re-division of the globe), but the resulting uneven development creates revolutionary opportunities in the "weak links" in the "imperialist chain".
- Lenin argues that the capitalist state is a machine for the defence of private property and must be smashed in a proletarian insurrection, replaced by a workers' council republic led by the victorious communist party.
- Lenin proposes that the vanguard role of the party springs not only from the imperialism it opposes, but also from the inability of the proletariat to spontaneously transcend trade union consciousness.

Trotsky and Stalin on socialism

- Stalin declared it possible to achieve socialism in an isolated and backward country by virtue of state property, industrialization campaigns, collectivized agriculture and the suppression of dissent, announcing in 1936 that the Soviet Union, despite its state apparatus, had arrived at communism.
- On Trotsky's analysis, the Soviet Union was a degenerated workers' state characterized by contradictions between socialized production and bourgeois distribution, and by a totalitarian political regime whose interests are contrary to the interests of the proletariat.

three

Hegelian Marxism

The Hegelian Marxism of the Hungarian philosopher György Lukács and Italian Communist Party (PCI) leader Antonio Gramsci heralded the renaissance in Marxism that followed the Russian Revolution. Alongside many other Marxist thinkers at the time, Lukács and Gramsci returned to the Hegelian roots of Marx's theory in order to rethink its conclusions. Dissatisfaction with orthodox Marxism's combination of evolutionary gradualism and scientific socialism was widespread. Speaking for many, Gramsci described the Bolshevik insurrection as a "revolution against [Marx's] *Capital*" (rather than capital!). This formulation meant, for Gramsci, the rejection of politically fatalistic determinism and vulgar economic reductionism. A theoretical renaissance involves taking the fundamental principles of a research programme and systematically varying one of them. In the case of Hegelian Marxism, that meant retaining praxis and history while varying structure. For both Lukács and Gramsci, Marxist theory was meaningless outside political activism in the class struggle, so instead of a scientific theory of social structure, Marxism was a philosophy of praxis.

Arising from a materialist radicalization of Hegelian dialectics, Marxism as a philosophy of praxis locates the source of the impasses of philosophy in the contradictions of social life. The consequence is that the transcendence of philosophical limitations can take place only through the practical resolution of these real contradictions. In proposing this, Lukács and Gramsci certainly considered themselves to be Leninists, although they insisted that the problems confronting the western European revolutionary movement could not be solved by the mechanical application of Lenin's positions. Indeed, most of the other Hegelian Marxists, such as Karl Korsch (*Marxism and Philosophy*, 1923) and Jose-Carlos Mariategui (*Seven Interpretive Essays on Peruvian Reality*, 1928), also regarded themselves as Leninists. But the truth was that Hegelian Marxism had broken with Lenin's militant version of the base-and-superstructure model. The result is two extraordinarily influential new Marxist conceptions of the structure of capitalist society, in terms of "reification" (Lukács) and "hegemony" (Gramsci). In the context of the failure of the western European revolutions in the 1920s and the rise of fascism in the 1930s, these ideas provided powerful new explanations of the "lag in consciousness" that had undone the Italian and German workers, despite objectively revolutionary conditions. With Hegelian Marxism, the Marxists in the West began a long "cultural turn", seeking to understand how supposedly "superstructural" factors had decisively influenced history.

History and class consciousness

György Lukács (1885–1971) was already a significant cultural intellectual when the crisis of the First World War and Russian Revolution burst upon Hungary in 1919. His philosophically inclined literary criticism, *The Soul and Forms* (1910) and *Theory of the Novel* ([1916] 1971b), had made a considerable impression on western European intellectual circles, with their post-Hegelian existential treatment of cultural fragmentation. In both works, Lukács diagnosed a yearning for psychological wholeness and communal unity. Describing this as a longing for totality that was everywhere denied by bourgeois conditions, Lukács regarded it as primarily a cultural problem until he radicalized at the end of the war. During the short-lived socialist uprising, Lukács served as a revolutionary commissar, as well as being a member of the Communist Party (Arato & Breines 1979: 91).

From exile in Vienna in the 1920s, Lukács wrote his enormously influential *History and Class Consciousness* ([1923] 1971a), which, although it electrified the radical intellectual milieu in western Europe, was greeted by the Leninist leadership of the Communist International as a dangerous deviation. Its central claim is that the orthodox Marxism of the Second International represents a complete falsification of the dialectical philosophy that animated Marx's theory. Once the historical dialectic is returned to the forefront of materialist social theory, Lukács proposes, two major breakthroughs become possible. The first is

recognition that Marxism advocates the idea of totality as both a theoretical lens for revealing the systematic interconnection of all aspects of
social life and a normative ideal upon which to reconstruct a truly social
existence. The second is that from the totalizing perspective of Marxist
theory, capitalist dehumanization and cultural fragmentation turn out
to be deeply related processes and, indeed, represent the main barriers
to revolutionary class consciousness. Clearly influenced by sustained
reading of Hegel and the dialectics of alienation, as well as detailed
knowledge of Marx's published works, *History and Class Consciousness*
anticipated the release of Marx's *Economic and Philosophical Manuscripts
of 1844* at the end of the 1920s (Feenberg 1981).

The significance of *History and Class Consciousness* is twofold. As
already mentioned, it is emblematic of the "cultural turn" of the Western
Marxists, a process that orthodox Marxists have represented as a turn
away from class struggle to the forms of cultural critique beloved of
intellectuals (Anderson 1979). Certainly that book's disregard for the
structural analysis of capitalist society and the concept of laws of motion
of the economic foundation meant that it was instantly distrusted by
the Comintern's leadership. And there is no doubt that with the recession of the tide of proletarian political mobilization in the 1920s, the
Marxist intellectuals to some extent lost contact with mass movements.
But the central problem for newly converted Leninists in the Western
revolutions of 1918–23 was that the majority of the working class continued to follow the moderate social democrats. Most workers displayed
highly conservative cultural attitudes that prevented their entry into the
ferment of radicalization happening among a minority of the population. The cultural turn was a turn *to* central problems of revolutionary
strategy, not a turn *away* from Marxist theory.

At the same time, *History and Class Consciousness* was a *philosophical* treatment of problems of revolutionary strategy that highlighted
the normative dimension of Marxism. Lukács's work advocated moral
universality and human flourishing in ways that had been suppressed
by the reception of historical materialism as social science. Its central
essay, "Reification and the Consciousness of the Proletariat", centres on
the section critiquing "The Antinomies of Bourgeois Thought", where
Lukács confronts Kantian philosophy. Lukács criticizes Kant for his
notorious divisions between value and fact, freedom and determinism, practice and theory, and subject and object, maintaining that these
reflect the conditions of existence of the bourgeois individual (Lukács
1971a). Adapting Hegel's critique of Kant in the *Phenomenology of Spirit*
(Hegel 1977: 355–74), Lukács proposes that the social conditions of

bourgeois society generate an individualistic understanding of freedom and a contemplative attitude towards the world. These prevent bourgeois consciousness from acknowledging that the realization of freedom, the revolutionization of the social world and the transformation of the natural environment in labour practice are all the same thing.

The concept of reification

Marx linked his analysis of political economy with his critique of ideology through the concept of commodity fetishism, the ideological illusion that structured the interactions of individuals in a market society. "A commodity is therefore a mysterious thing", Marx wrote:

> simply because in it the social character of men's labour appears to them as an objective character stamped upon the product of that labour ... It is only a definite social relation between men that assumes, in their eyes, the fantastic form of a relation between things. (C1: 72)

What Marx describes here Lukács calls the "reification" (*Verdinglichung* – petrifaction) of social relations under capitalism, where reification colloquially refers to treating persons as things. More technically, it names the fallacy of misplaced concreteness, the mistake of treating an abstraction as a material thing, and attributing causal powers to it. This is Lukács' point of departure for his analysis of the commodity as the "universal category of society as a whole", a "central structural problem" whose "consequences are able to influence the *total* ... life of society" (Lukács 1971a: 86, 84). The commodity form becomes a universal structuring principle of both society and the psyche, because the principle of equivalence – the exchange of commodities in proportion to abstract labour – is both a psychological requirement, as a necessary illusion, and sociological compulsion, as a "real abstraction". The real abstractions of capitalist society create a world that is highly rationalized, yet utterly irrational. Although the "principle of rationalisation is based on what can be calculated", these calculations represent society as governed by anonymous economic laws that have the appearance of laws of nature. The anarchy of the market means that the operation of social processes happens behind the backs of agents, to whom the world appears as a "second nature" ruled by a capricious fate. Everyday life, meanwhile, becomes dominated by quantitative calculations of efficient means, not qualitative considerations of human ends, so that "time is everything; man is nothing" (*ibid*.: 88–9).

In light of the phenomenon of reification, Lukács radicalizes the sociology of Max Weber on social and cultural rationalization. For Weber, the modern world of capitalism and bureaucracy are formed through a new type of "formal rationality", the application of the principle of calculation to reason itself. Mainly, individuals exercise "purposive rationality", calculations of the most efficient means to (potentially irrational) goals; reflection on the goals of action happens in "value rationality", submission of reason's ends to procedures which reduce to tests of logical consistency. What is lost from everyday life under formal rationality is not only traditional, religious worldviews, but also other aspects of "substantive rationality", considerations of human flourishing and the good life. As Lukács notes, "quality no longer matters", for "quantity alone decides everything", so the modern person becomes a "human being without qualities" (*ibid*.: 89–90). The individual under capitalism is a socially atomized, anonymous functionary who suppresses their unique individuality and regards the sum of their personality in terms of their quantitative performance, considering themselves a calculable object located in an anonymous chain of causes and effects (*ibid*.: 89–90).

The development of vast bureaucracies in state and corporate administration is one consequence of the "dehumanising function of the commodity relation" (*ibid*.: 92). Another is the submission of every element of human life (law, culture, ethics, politics) to the procedures of the natural sciences, in the interests of a "disinterested" effective manipulation of social routines. Lukács maintains that the objectification and rationalization of social relations means that the major aspects of social life break apart into reified "things", departments of activity such as law, politics, culture and economics, which appear to relate to one another externally, through mechanical cause-and-effect relations.

Reification "leads to the destruction of every image of the whole", that is to a condition of cultural fragmentation (*ibid*.: 103). The formalism of modern bourgeois philosophy reflects this reality, especially in its characteristic antinomies. An "antinomy" is a set of mutually exclusive and logically contradictory conclusions arrived at from identical premises, such as Kant's simultaneous claims that the empirical individual is entirely determined, yet the "transcendental ego" is completely free. Bourgeois philosophy cannot resolve its own antinomies, Lukács argues, because its characteristic standpoint is that of the isolated individual contemplating nature from the perspective of judging between competing scientific theories. This perspective leads Kant to propose that the substratum of the natural and social worlds is unknowable in principle. For all its rationalism and elevation of the mathematical as the paradigm of thinking, bourgeois philosophy is fundamentally irrational. Thus, Lukács concludes:

> the attempt to universalise rationalism necessarily issues in the demand for a system but, at the same time, as soon as one reflects upon the conditions in which a universal system is possible, i.e. as soon as the question of the system is consciously posed, it is seen that such a demand is incapable of fulfilment.
> (*Ibid.*: 117)

To solve the problem of the antinomies of bourgeois thought, Lukács shifts from the epistemological focus on "theoretical reason" of Kantian philosophy. He rejects the standpoint of the contemplative subject investigating an object domain in society using formal procedures reminiscent of the natural sciences. Instead, he advocates the activist focus of Fichte's idealism of "practical reason", with its free subject transforming the object domain through rationally willed action. Lukács states that:

> What is relevant to our problem here is the statement that the subject of knowledge, the ego-principle, is known as to its content and, hence, can be taken as a starting-point and as a guide to method. In the most general terms, we see here the origin of the philosophical tendency to press forward to a conception of the subject which can be thought of as the creator of the totality of content.
> (*Ibid.*: 122)

It was Fichte who radicalized Kant's formalistic ideas about practical reason into a philosophy that placed "the practical, action and activity in the centre of his unifying philosophical system" (*ibid.*: 123). But it was Hegel who fully understood the revolutionary implications of the subject as creator of totality, an insight that Hegel expresses as the idea of the active subject who consciously creates the world and at the same time transforms themselves (*ibid.*: 128).

The category of totality

Lukács' materialist interpretation of Hegel as a sort of bourgeois Marx was later to extend to a demonstration that Hegel's economic research had substantially anticipated Marx. In *History and Class Consciousness*, Lukács restricts himself to the claim that "economic determination in the last instance" is actually *not* the centrepiece of Marxism:

> It is not the primacy of economic motives in historical explanation that constitutes the decisive difference between Marxism and bourgeois thought, but the point of view of totality. The category of totality, the all-pervasive supremacy of the whole over the parts, is the essence of the method which Marx took over from Hegel and brilliantly transformed into the foundations of a wholly new science ... Proletarian science is revolutionary not just by virtue of its revolutionary ideas which it opposes to bourgeois society, but above all because of its method. *The primacy of the category of the totality is the bearer of the principle of revolution in science.* (*Ibid.*: 27)

Instead of a bourgeois "purely formal" ethics "lacking in content", Lukács proposes that "the essence of praxis consists in annulling that indifference of form towards content" of bourgeois philosophy. This happens by recognizing that the material object (nature and society) is something generated by the active subject (human labour; *ibid.*: 126–8). In other words, from the perspective of praxis, the antinomies of bourgeois philosophy and the cultural fragmentation of the bourgeois world are resolved by means of a methodological totality that anticipates and guides the totalizing praxis of socialist revolution.

Now, this reasoning requires some questionable premises to carry the argument. As Lukács acknowledged in his 1967 self-critique, the main one is the claim that "nature is a social category" (*ibid.*: 130). This certainly makes possible the idea that theory and practice, and subject and object, are a unity. But it is a regression to idealism, potentially at its most absurd. Technically, in order to make subject and object *and* theory and practice a complete unity, the ontological difference between subject and object has to be annulled, along with any distinction between scientific knowledge of the natural environment and normative agreement within the social world. The problem with this position, as he later conceded, is that performs an idealist conflation of the material properties of the natural environment with the theoretical discoveries that scientifically model these. Then it reduces the question of scientific validity, idealistically conceived, to a political question of the correct line.

Moreover, if "nature is a social category", then society is basically an artwork. It is an intelligible and transformable totality, which can be entirely known because it is exhaustively the product of human action. Since the material substrate of human labour and the social totality has been rendered transparent, there are no opaque social relations that need to be grasped through scientific procedures, because the connection between material scarcity and productive forces has vanished. Not surprisingly, Lukács maintains that bourgeois aesthetics is a perfect exemplification of the category of totality in operation:

> [Art's] principle is the creation of a concrete totality that springs from a conception of form orientated towards the concrete content of its material substratum. In this view, form is therefore able to demolish the "contingent" relation of the parts to the whole and to resolve the merely apparent opposition between chance and necessity. (*Ibid*.: 137)

Bourgeois aesthetics grasps "the principle whereby man having been socially destroyed, fragmented and divided between different partial systems is to be made whole again", but it does this only in ideas, not through actions (*ibid*.: 139). Instead, art's aesthetic redemption of the world remains a compensation for the loss of substantive meaningfulness and the reality of the mutilation of human flourishing, one restricted to a specialized compartment of social life characterized by its uselessness. With the dialectical method, Lukács argues, Hegel applies the aesthetic principle to thinking in response to an "impulse to overcome the reified disintegration of the subject and the – likewise reified – rigidity and impenetrability of its objects" (*ibid*.: 141).

Reality can be understood as the product of human action, so that the rationality of the material substratum and the concrete individuality of the contents of thought are the same problem. Its solution, Lukács flourishes, is the identification of a "subject of the genesis" of the totality of forms, a "methodologically indispensible subject-object" (*ibid*.: 146). Hegel identified this subject with humanity as a whole, idealistically reified into the "world spirit". But Lukács argues that Marx's discovery of the proletariat demonstrates that Hegel's subject is a premature designation:

> Only when a historical situation has arisen in which a class must understand society if it is to assert itself; only when the fact that a class understands itself means that it understands society as a whole and when, in consequence, the class becomes both the subject and object of knowledge; in short, only when

these conditions are all satisfied will the unity of theory and practice, the precondition of the revolutionary function of theory, become possible. Such a situation has in fact arisen with the entry of the proletariat into history. (*Ibid.*: 2–3)

The proletariat, Lukács unequivocally states, is the "identical subject-object of history" (*ibid.*: 206).

The proletarian revolution

Lukács eventually conceded that "the proletariat seen as the identical subject-object of the real history of mankind is no materialist consummation that overcomes the constructions of idealism [but] rather an attempt to out-Hegel Hegel" (Lukács 1971a: xxiii). That was not, however, until 1967, almost half a century afterwards. In the meantime, Lukács' defense of *History and Class Consciousness* found him announcing that, in effect, Marx was a continuation of Hegel. "Like the classical German philosophers, particularly Hegel," Lukács writes, "Marx perceived world history as a homogeneous process, as an uninterrupted, revolutionary process of liberation" (Lukács 1972: 24–5).

The accent in Lukács's version of Hegelian Marxism falls solidly on praxis as the key to both structure and history. This is not only because the proletarian subject "expresses" itself in the socio-historical totality. It is also because the theory itself reduces to an expression of political practice:

Historical materialism is the theory of the proletarian revolution. It is so because it is in essence an intellectual synthesis of the social existence which produces and fundamentally determines the proletariat; and because the proletariat struggling for liberation finds its clear self-consciousness in it.
(Lukács 1970b: 9)

Along the way, scientific experimentation and the objectivity of knowledge are denounced as "contemplation at its purest" (Lukács 1971a: 132). This sort of critique of orthodox Marxism was badly received in the increasingly Stalinist Comintern, as Stalin drove Marxism back in the direction of "proletarian science". Lukács was forced to recant publicly and he only just escaped being purged.

During the period between about 1927 and 1967, Lukács's participation in cultural debates and philosophical interventions was intensively regulated by the government. In Lukács's aesthetics of the realist novel, however, the category of totality and the notion of an identical subject-object made a lot more sense. This is because the world of the novel, being, after all, entirely composed of linguistically mediated idealizations, has none of the stubborn resistance of the material world that renders such notions so dubious in relation to social structure and world history.

According to Lukács, the realist novel is politically progressive irrespective of authorial intentions, because literary realism depends upon the construction of psychologically plausible and socially typical individuals, acting and being acted upon within a created ("diegetic") world that must strike the reader as believable. The requirements of literary diegesis mean that the author must construct a social world composed of realistic social relations, within which the characters interact in ways consistent with their worldly position and psychological characterization. What this means, in effect, is that the realist work reconstructs the reified totality of surface appearances of a historical society as in actuality the effects generated by the sum total of human actions undertaken by socialized agents. The realist work *totalizes*, both historically and socially, revealing society to be the work of socially and historically determined human agency.

By contrast with the literary realism of authors such as Walter Scott, Charles Dickens, Honoré de Balzac and Thomas Mann, Lukács argued, stood two degenerate tendencies that reflected reification. On the side of the object was "naturalism", the realistic depiction of the objective world, including the accurate representation of empirical individuals, but lacking the synthetic connection between historical background, social context and typical character of literary realism. Naturalism "describes" but does not "narrate", because it represents the reified totality but does not reconstruct it as a social process, and it is populated by individuals but not characters, because it reproduces idiosyncrasies but cannot achieve typification. On the side of the subject was modernism, a sort of psychological naturalism that accurately reported the subjective experience of reification, in terms of cultural fragmentation and personal disintegration. Modernism, for Lukács, was utterly hostile to progressive culture, because its protest against reification was conducted in terms that rendered the real causes of the problem in historical social relations completely invisible, substituting instead a politically reactionary naturalization of subjective distortion (Lukács 2007: 34–9).

The totalizing perspective of the realist work overcomes the reified fragmentation of the reader's immediate experiences, because it represents the antagonism between the particular and the general as a social process. But this totalizing perspective awakens a dormant dimension of those experiences and this may lead to a moment of acknowledgment (recognition) of the truth of the artwork and a desire for liberation. "The [realist] work", Lukács says, "by its very nature, offers a truer, more complete, more vivid and more dynamic reflection of reality than the recipient otherwise possesses" (Lukács 1970a: 36). Art therefore preserves and expresses the yearning for the realization of human creative potential and the desire for human agency of everyday individuals. The collision between the rounded development of literary characters and their social agency, and the reified perspective of everyday life, results in a cathartic shock with the potential to catalyse ethical regeneration in the audience (Lukács 1963: 767, 786).

Indeed, with fascism on the rise, Lukács detected a strong current of philosophical modernism in the works of bourgeois philosophy since Hegel, with a turn to subjectivity amounting, Lukács argued, to an embrace of irrationality. In somewhat shrill tones, Lukács documented the hypothesis that in the age of imperialism, bourgeois thought passively reflected the fettering of the productive forces, in the form of a gradual renunciation of reason. The deepest valleys in this dark landscape were labelled Kierkegaard, Bergson, Nietzsche and Heidegger – philosophers who might indeed be accused of irrationalism – but Lukács's monochrome treatment of major thinkers meant that neo-Kantianism and Husserl's phenomenology were also included in the generalized retreat from reason. That everyone else had abandoned the heights achieved by Marx and Hegel perhaps provided psychological compensation, however, for Lukács's own failure to complete his major late projects, on social ontology and philosophical aesthetics, satisfactorily.

The philosophy of praxis

The second concept to be explored in this chapter is the category of "hegemony", or leadership based on a combination of domination and direction, developed by the Italian Marxist Antonio Gramsci (1891–1937). With the category of hegemony, Gramsci arrived at a conceptualization of social structure, based on the typically Hegelian–Marxist emphasis on praxis and history, which profoundly modified the base-and-superstructure topography of orthodox Marxism. Orthodoxy's static, external relation between economic foundation and ideologico-political superstructure regards the state as an instrument of domination only. But Gramsci proposes that "the supremacy of a social group manifests itself in *two* ways, as 'domination' *and* as 'intellectual and moral leadership'" (Gramsci 1971: 57). Hegemony, which Gramsci defines in terms of a mobile equilibrium of consent and coercion operating in both state and civil society (*ibid*.: 245), introduces a dynamic, dialectical relation, in which politics and ideology play an interventionist role in economics.

A small and highly intellectual man, who suffered from a spinal deformation that left him with a permanently hunched back as a result of a childhood accident, Gramsci is one of Marxism's heroic figures, alongside Luxemburg, Trotsky and Che Guevara. For despite constant ill health, Gramsci became a founding member of the powerful Italian Communist Party (PCI) and a leader of the anti-fascist resistance against Mussolini in the 1920s and 1930s, right up until his death in a fascist gaol just before the beginning of the Second World War. His visionary imagination and role as one of western Europe's most important socialist humanists meant that Gramsci incorporated successive historical developments – the workers' councils of 1918–23, the Bolshevik Revolution and formation of the Third International, the emergence of mass popular movements against fascism – into his theoretical writings in ways that reach beyond the dark days of the 1930s.

Hegemony is a category that Gramsci uses in several – possibly conflicting – senses. It therefore hovers uncertainly between a theoretical concept and a descriptive metaphor. This is not Gramsci's fault. It was imposed on him by the conditions under which he wrote, in a series of 33 notebooks that he wrote in prison in the late 1920s and the 1930s (Boggs 1976: 11–20; Gramsci 1971: xvii–xcvi). The 2,848 pages of the *Prison Notebooks* use numerous euphemisms designed to evade the censorship of Mussolini's political police – Marxism is "the philosophy of praxis", the PCI is "the Modern Prince", socialism is an "integral civilization" – but they also systematically aim at double-meanings. This unsystematic system of metaphors and disguises has aptly been described as a "labyrinth" for the interpreter (Anderson 1976: 72). Alongside Perry Anderson's superb analysis of "The Antinomies of Antonio Gramsci" (Anderson 1976) and Carl Boggs's scholarly and objective reconstruction of *Gramsci's Marxism* (Boggs 1976), I have also drawn on Martin Jay's analysis of Gramsci's concept of totality (Jay 1984: 150–73). Probably the best way to grasp what is meant by hegemony is to explore its conceptual genesis in Gramsci's developing ideas, before locating it in the broader problems of political strategy that it was supposed to resolve.

Gramsci's theory reflects the impact of pragmatist philosophies of language (*ibid*.: 160–63). A semantic approach to language is an approach that seeks to understand how correctly constructed sentences refer to the world, that is to a material reality that is assumed to be external to the words and ideas contained in utterances. By contrast, pragmatism overturns the traditional, correspondence theory of truth (a true sentence is one that accurately describes the external world) and replaces it with the idea of truth as warranted assertion (a true sentence is one that we all agree will allow us to get things done). Cooperative action in the world (because it is mediated by language) is the same thing as understanding the world.

"Philosophy", Gramsci maintains:

> is not to be conceived as the individual elaboration of system-atically coherent concepts, but as a cultural battle to transform the popular mentality and diffuse ... philosophical innova-tions, which will demonstrate themselves to be 'historically true' to the extent that they become concretely – i.e. historically and socially – universal.   (Gramsci 1971: 348)

Gramsci's "philosophy of praxis" is therefore a reading of Marx in pragmatist terms, and specifically an interpretation of the concept of praxis – the "dialectic of theory and practice" – as the idea that action and culture are a unity. "The fundamental concept [of the] philosophy of praxis [is that it] is 'sufficient unto itself'", Gramsci writes:

> It contains in itself all the fundamental elements needed to construct a total and integral conception of the world, a total philosophy and theory of natural science, and not only that, but everything that is needed to give life to an integral practical organization of society, that is to become a total integral civili-zation. ... [T]he philosophy of praxis is a completely autono-mous and independent structure of thought in antagonism to all traditional philosophies and religions ... that is begin-ning to exercise its own hegemony over traditional culture.
> (*Ibid.*: 462)

Beyond language pragmatics, Gramsci's views are shaped by the neo-Hegelianism of Italian philosopher Benedetto Croce. Gramsci explic-itly concedes that his critique of the base-and-superstructure model is inspired by Croce (*ibid.*: 458–61). He also adopts the Crocean term for Hegelianism, "absolute historicism", and uses it to describe Marxism:

> It has been forgotten that in the case of [historical material-ism] one should put the accent on the first term – "historical"

– and not on the second, which is of metaphysical origin. The philosophy of praxis [i.e. Gramsci's Marxism – GB] is absolute "historicism", the absolute secularisation and earthliness of thought, an absolute humanism of history.   (*Ibid.*: 465)

The "philosophy of praxis", then, is a pragmatist version of Marxism, one that turns away from orthodox Marxism to the Hegelian roots of historical materialism in order to understand the wider implications of its own pragmatic theory of action. History is the succession of struggles for universality, in which the nature of universality is extended and deepened until, finally, with socialism, a form of universality arrives that derives from the majority and not from the minority of the population. "Absolute historicism", then, means not just that universality is historical, but that it is relative – every contending social group has its own universal, or definition of universality. The connection, then, between praxis and history is, according to Gramsci, not a question – as it is for Lukács – of the teleological unfolding through the historical process of the goal of a de-reified society. Instead, it is a radically open-ended process of social struggle in which political mobilization and party organization must bring together the fragmented germs of that new culture already present in workers' consciousness, systematize and extend this, and expand this integral vision to the entire society.

Historical bloc and national unification

Against this conceptual background, the problem that Gramsci's theory of hegemony is intended to solve has two aspects. First, it copes with the incomplete nature of the bourgeois revolution in Italy and the way in which, because of this, tasks of socialist construction overlap with the completion of democratic development. And second, it deals with the way that, despite this uneven development in Italian capitalism, the revolutionary upsurge of the 1920s failed because of a lack of cultural and political preparation among the oppressed classes of Italian society. Both of these problems involve "hegemony", but in different ways. The first complex of problems brings Gramsci into proximity with classical theories of uneven development. The second set of problems complicates the first in ways that go beyond classical Marxism, because it raises the question of the existing integration of workers, peasants, intellectuals and the middle classes into capitalism. In Italy between 1918 and 1922, historical conditions meant that the moment that the radical wing of the socialist party began to form workers' councils, a broad popular alliance formed in support of Mussolini's fascist "march on Rome" and its effort to save the monarchy.

Gramsci understood that this had historical roots going all the way back to the incomplete Italian democratic revolution of 1848 and the Mazzini (and Garibaldi) movement of the 1860s. Not only did the revolutionary movement of the 1840s fail to dislodge the northern monarchy, but the Mazzini–Garibaldi movement of the 1860s had failed to enlist the peasantry against the feudal southern landlords. Instead, the northern liberals were quickly satisfied with a constitutional monarchy that encouraged market relations, while the southern landlords basically traded their renunciation of a claim on political power for military support from the north to suppress Garibaldi's radical movement (Gramsci 1971: 74–5, 95–6). While the north industrialized rapidly, the south stagnated, thanks to a lack of agricultural reforms, which blocked market relations and subordinated the south to the north (*ibid.*: 98–9). Rather than releasing peasants from the land in an agricultural revolution that could fuel an industrial revolution with wage labourers, capitalist development in the south inched forward through corruption, inefficiency and indiscipline. By the beginning of the twentieth century, northern and southern Italy were like two historical eras – capitalist and feudal – soldered together by a political compromise of historical proportions (*ibid.*: 101–3). Under the dominance of the moderate northern liberals, and without disrupting the interests of southern landlords, Italy in the nineteenth century underwent a "passive revolution", in which national unification and bourgeois consolidation crept forwards without seriously destabilizing this system of political compromises (*ibid.*: 106–14).

Gramsci conceptualized this situation as a "historical bloc" of north and south, liberal capitalists and reactionary landlords, that had managed to recruit important elements of the white-collar workers and middle-class professionals in the north, and small traders and prosperous peasants in the south, to this major social alliance (*ibid.*: 102–6). The social alliance functioned by satisfying the historical interests – that is to say, the fundamental material interests, such as ownership of the means of production and the legal relations that accompany this – of the major parties. At the same time, the major players in the social alliance provided significant material concessions – financial rewards, political power, cultural prestige – for the minor alliance partners. Thus the liberal parties of the north were run by middle-class professionals with a conservative outlook on behalf of the liberal capitalists, with a union movement whose leadership was staffed by similarly conservative white-collar employees. Meanwhile, the parties of the south drew their strength from small businesspersons and wealthy farmers, whose ability to command a popular following was used to block land reform on behalf of the feudal landlords (*ibid.*: 92–6). Although this historic bloc maintained its power through coercive force – for instance the military suppression of Garibaldi – its real stability was due to the pervasive consent to this arrangement throughout Italian society. In the absence of real alternatives, "subaltern groups", such as workers and peasants, radical intellectuals, and junior employees, regarded their best chances for advancement as springing from cutting a deal with the power brokers. And besides, nowhere did a clear conception of an alternative to this system of liberal conservatism and historical compromise exist. All of the major ideas about reform, such as those presented by Croce's liberalism, had already capitulated to the status quo by declaring that fundamentals were off limits when it came to social change (*ibid.*: 114–18).

Especially against the background of the disaster of failed proletarian insurrection in the north, followed by mass popular backlash and fascist takeover, Gramsci understood that the key to socialist strategy in Italy was the building of a social counter-alliance. Encompassing all of the oppressed, such an alliance would need to address their most fundamental interests in order to cement these groups together in a historically binding way. The key to this was an analysis of the connection between the interests of the southern peasantry and the tasks of capitalist modernization. The creation of a unified national economy, the provision of national infrastructure, a single legal code enforced by a professional (i.e. non-familial) state, a national system of political representation based on democratic principles – all of these things could benefit the poor peasantry, but only on one proviso. This was that land reform must dispossess the landlords and redistribute the land, thereby replacing feudal relations with an agricultural market. In essence, that meant the transformation of peasants into farmers, that is into small agrarian businesspeople, a dream that Gramsci believed (on good evidence) was close to the heart of every struggling peasant. On Gramsci's analysis, this was not in contradiction to the initial tasks of socialist construction, which must rest upon raising the level of the productive forces in Italy and expanding the ranks of the proletariat, mainly through the completion of the bourgeois revolution. And such a liberal socialism would be able to offer significant concessions to middle-class professionals and white-collar employees, because it would involve a dramatic expansion in state industry and administration, together with new opportunities for political representation and cultural recognition (*ibid.*: 272–6).

The category of hegemony

Although Gramsci's category of hegemony represents a profound modification of the base-and-superstructure model, this is not always expressed with clarity in the *Prison Notebooks*. "Structures and super-structures form a 'historical bloc,'" Gramsci maintains: "that is to say, the complex, contradictory and discordant ensemble of the superstructures is the reflection of the ensemble of the relations of production" (Gramsci 1971: 366). That sounds like the base-and-superstructure model; but, in actuality, it explicates a different idea: "though hegemony is ethical-political, it must also be economic, must necessarily be based on the decisive function exercised by the leading group in the decisive nucleus of economic activity" (*ibid*.: 166). Gramsci's position is *inconsistent* with the idea that class subjects are formed in production and must then use the state solely as an instrument for domination, while concealing their interests through ideological falsifications. Instead classes – such as the Italian bourgeoisie – form in the economic foundation, but they only become historical subjects in social alliances, through "intellectual and moral leadership" or "ethical-political hegemony", as in the historical bloc of northern capitalists with southern landlords just discussed.

In the theory of hegemony, then, the collective subject is the historical bloc, not the economic class, and hegemony is how the subject maintains its position of social dominance in opposition to contending subjects. Hegemony, then, means leadership by a historically cemented social alliance through its control of the state and its ability to secure consent in civil society. Gramsci describes this in terms of a mobile equilibrium of coercion and consent, because it reflects a dynamic condition, where a threatened ideological consensus can always be protected using force. Although Gramsci is not entirely consistent in how he thinks about the relationship between the terms "consent and coercion" and "political state and civil society", probably the most plausible position that the *Prison Notebooks* formulate, in line with Anderson's discussion, is as follows (Anderson 1976). The state holds a monopoly over coercion in bourgeois society, through its executive and juridical components. But it is also an agent promoting consent, through its legislative arm and its educational apparatus. Bourgeois civil society – that is, economic institutions together with civil organizations such as unions, parties, churches and associations – does not normally directly involve coercion, because it rests upon individual liberty (rather than forced labour). Instead, civil society is the major locus of the formation of consent, through public debate, protest movements, the spread of ideas and the transmission of the cultural forms of everyday life. That is not to say that there is no state coercion regularly applied to civil society organizations – such as union-busting legislation backed by police powers, or police lines to defend strike breakers. But the point is that this is legally sanctioned state force. Coercion, then, happens through the state, while consent is generated by the state and within civil society. It is not correct, therefore, to speak of "political force and cultural hegemony". Hegemony describes that combination of political force and political and cultural consent that makes *authority* different to *domination*.

The hegemonic position of the dominant historical bloc over all subaltern groups, then, is not just the result of a lack of "lawyers, guns and money", but also the consequence of the subaltern groups consenting to the dominant position of the groups composing the historical bloc. Subaltern groups see their interests in terms of the interests of the dominant alliance partners, because the dominant particular interests are framed as universal ideals, that is as human rights and national interests. Thus, for instance, Italian workers framed their wage claims in terms of the national interest and in terms of claims for rights. Subaltern groups also regard the world through the values of the dominant alliance, sharing ideals of patriotic nationalism and individual liberty with the groups who in fact benefit most from these ideas. Gramsci's recognition of this situation is the key to his explanation of the failure of the western European revolutions, by contrast with the success of the eastern European revolutions:

> In Russia, the State was everything, civil society was primordial and gelatinous; in the West there was a proper relation between State and civil society, and when the State trembled, a sturdy structure of civil society was at once revealed. The State was only an outer ditch, behind which there stood a powerful system of fortresses and earthworks. (Gramsci 1971: 238)

This contrast, between western capitalist hegemony and eastern absolutist domination, leads to Gramsci's celebrated opposition between western trench warfare, or the "war of position", and eastern breakthroughs, or the "war of manoeuvre". Where the Bolsheviks could achieve a sudden breakthrough by virtue of the Eastern reduction of hegemony to domination, the Italians must engage in a protracted process of building up counter-hegemony in civil society before the seizure of state power. With the conquest of state power, proletarian and peasant hegemony would be directed through the instrument of a new sort of mass, participatory state apparatus, but would nonetheless continue to involve a mobile equilibrium of consent and coercion (*ibid.*: 228–76).

Gramsci's interest in Machiavelli is best understood in this context. For Gramsci, Machiavelli is a Renaissance thinker trying to work out for the nascent capitalist class what Gramsci is theorizing for the rising proletarian class, namely a theory of hegemony. Machiavelli's notion of the state as a centaur – half beast (i.e. coercion) and half human (i.e. consent) – together with his insistence that the state is an educator that creates a new type of civilization (*ibid.*: 246–52) are indices of this. Machiavelli's notorious separation of politics from ethics, then, expresses only the distinction between coercion and consent, and his awareness that the state must engage in both. Equally, Gramsci's notions of "ethical-political hegemony", and an "ethical state", must be framed by the "Machiavellian" idea that although the state promotes an intellectual and moral culture among the population, it also reserves to itself the right to deploy force when persuasion fails (*ibid.*: 263). But, probably most importantly for Gramsci, Machiavelli provides a reflection on intellectuals and the moral and cultural elements of hegemony that is particularly fertile for the communist thinker. Gramsci was, after all, trying to work out how party intellectuals, such as himself, could prepare a counter-hegemony that would, by means of a process of political education and cultural reform, disintegrate bourgeois hegemony and replace it with a national-popular alliance. In this process, Gramsci jettisons the negative and critical implications of the term ideology (i.e. a distorted representation of material interests) for the positive version of ideology as a worldview.

The modern prince

Although hegemony cannot be reduced to culture, cultural questions are clearly central to the category. Cultural forms provide the medium for the formation of consent and therefore the ideological cement for social cohesion, together with the universal ideals within which individuals and classes formulate their material interests. For Gramsci, the intellectuals are therefore crucial to the formation of hegemony (and counter-hegemony), because it is the intellectuals who elaborate cultural forms. But Gramsci insists that the articulation of hegemony is a popular process, because "all men are intellectuals", although he concedes that "not all men have in society the function of intellectuals" (Gramsci 1971: 9).

To understand what Gramsci means here it is important to situate his position in relation to two central Marxist questions – the nature of class consciousness and the implications of the division between mental and manual labour. While he refuses the conception of ideology as false consciousness, Gramsci does not quite think that the proletariat spontaneously develops a representation of its historical interests. On the one hand, the material interests of subaltern groups such as the proletariat are typically represented within the hegemonic ideology. On the other hand, where representations of interests do break with the hegemonic ideology, they remain fragmentary until systematized into a new culture and new morality. The task of intellectuals is therefore the systematization of popular ideas rather than the fabrication of an entirely alien doctrine that is to be imposed on the masses by the party (*ibid.*: 330–36). Exactly who these intellectuals are, in light of Gramsci's assertion that all persons are intellectuals, is a question of historical contingency. The intellectuals are those who the division of labour have allocated to that function; but, under socialism, this distinction will wither away. Moreover, the party is a "collective intellectual" (the conceptual direction perhaps of the proletariat as a "collective worker") which adverts to its educational function in not just raising class consciousness, but also providing a forum for the development of individuals' own intellectual capacities (*ibid.*: 16). According to Gramsci, "the philosophy of praxis does not tend to leave the 'simple' in their primitive philosophy of common sense, but rather to lead them to a higher conception of life" (*ibid.*: 332). Intellectuals should combine their theoretical knowledge with the practical wisdom of the masses, forming an "intellectual/moral bloc" with the "cultural movement as a whole" (*ibid.*: 333–4).

This analysis is complicated by Gramsci's claim that the intellectuals within the division of labour fall into two main groups: traditional intellectuals (those who belong to the professions as a consequence of mental labour) and organic intellectuals (those who, although they perform manual labour, are the thinkers of their groups). The traditional intellectuals, historically speaking, were once organic intellectuals of the bourgeois class, at an earlier stage of the division of labour. Gramsci hoped that the proletariat would generate its own organic intellectuals from among all strata of the labouring population and that these would assemble beneath the banner of the communist movement. But he did acknowledge that renegade traditional intellectuals – such as Marx and Engels – had played a crucial role in the formation of the socialist movement, and so were not to be rejected from Italian communism.

The communist party, then, as a "collective intellectual", is the modern equivalent of Machiavelli's Renaissance prince: the political agency without which the organic intellectuals of the rising class could not hope to articulate a new hegemony (*ibid.*: 249). Although Gramsci's conception of socialist strategy certainly involves what has been described as a "long march through the institutions" of civil society, that is a protracted struggle by progressive intellectuals to transform popular and high culture in line with a new morality and new vision of society, it is not restricted to this. At some stage, and despite an extended preparatory phase of political education and cultural struggle, politics means conflict for and through the state, which in turn means the necessity for an organization capable of seizing power and directing society through the state apparatus. The "modern prince", the communist party, like Machiavelli's Renaissance prince, must be capable of applying coercive force, including armed insurrection and the repression of the formerly hegemonic group.

Gramsci's aim is to connect mass enthusiasm for progressive change with Machiavellian republicanism, connecting the Leninist conception of politics with the national-popular unification of Italy (Boggs 1976: 114). At this juncture, as Jay has noted, there is a tension in Gramsci between ethical humanism and an instrumental vision of politics (Jay 1984: 169). Unfortunately, Gramsci's theory of hegemony does not provide definitive clues to resolving this ambivalence in one direction or the other, because its central feature is the idea that normative universality arises through instrumentally successful action, and functions as a means to represent material interests. Gramsci clearly believes that the proletariat is a universal class with universal interests, whose liberation is also emancipatory for the entire society. The problem is that his theory does not and cannot justify this belief, because, in fact, it leads to the opposite conclusion, namely that antagonistic interests result in different worldviews. Gramsci's "historicism", that is moral and epistemological relativism, threatens to revenge itself upon the claims of universality that the theory needs in order to ground its understanding of political struggle in something other than the arbitrary assertion of group interests. In the end, politics for Gramsci was less about moral universality than about the formation of collective subjects through the struggle to educate and discipline the masses for republican self-government, reflecting his embrace of political, rather than ethical, values. The idea that hegemony is a process of the formation of a new collective will, a national-popular identity that consolidates a social alliance into an historic bloc through cultural and political, as well as economic, struggles, has been immensely influential in subsequent Marxist political thought.

Summary of key points

The primacy of practice

- For Lukács, Marxism is the dialectical method, the revolutionary outlook of the insurgent proletariat and the political strategy of socialist revolution all at once, because it is an activist unity of theory and practice, a conceptual totality that creates a new world.
- For Gramsci, Marxism is a "philosophy of praxis", a worldview based on creative labour that is capable of generating a new, integral civilization, and which must struggle to assert its universal vision.

The structure of capitalism and ideology

- Lukács's concept of reification combines Marx's alienation with Weber's rationalization: commodity fetishism structures society and rationality, resulting in the reduction of quality to quantity, and the appearance that society is governed by pseudo-natural laws of economic development.
- Bourgeois philosophy is characterized by antinomies, because it reflects the limitations of capitalism as a form of life that is affected by reification, especially the opposition between a free subject and society as governed by the laws of motion of capital.
- The category of the totality represents the revolutionary principle in thought, because it reconstructs the social structure as a whole with a historical genesis through human action, which exposes how capitalism is not natural, but historical.
- For Gramsci, society is structured through historical blocs, social alliances based on fundamental classes, which fuse economic foundation and ideologico-political superstructure into a unity.
- Historical blocs exercise ideological and political power through hegemony, a mobile equilibrium of consent and coercion fundamentally based on the representation of the particular interests of the social alliance as the general interest.

Historical change and class politics

- For Lukács, the proletariat is the author of social reality, the identical subject-object of history, who, led by the proletariat, will expressively generate a new totality following the socialist revolution.

- For Gramsci, the proletarian party is key, because it must construct a progressive class alliance capable of bringing a counter-hegemonic force to power and creating a new historical bloc of the oppressed.

four

The Frankfurt School

Although strongly influenced by Lukács's critique of commodity reification and advocacy of the principle of totality, and highly sympathetic to the rediscovery of the radical humanism of the young Marx,
the historical materialism of the "Frankfurt School" developed along
entirely different lines to Hegelian Marxism. The research programme
led by figures such as Max Horkheimer (1895–1973), Theodor Adorno
(1903–69), Herbert Marcuse (1898–1979) and Erich Fromm (1900–80)
is called the Frankfurt School because it originated at the Institute for
Social Research at Frankfurt University in the 1920s and 1930s. The
first Marxist research institute to be attached to a university department
outside the Soviet Union, the Institute for Social Research was eventually relocated to New York in 1934 because of the Nazi dictatorship.
Its leading members understood Lukács's breakthrough to mandate an
interdisciplinary research programme that employed a materialist version of the dialectical method. Their aim was to integrate specialized
inquiry into political economy, culture and ideology, psychology, and
philosophy into an open-ended and ongoing intellectual totalization,
in order to update historical materialism. Sharply critical, however,
of Lukács's proletarian "identical subject-object of history" and his
reduction of materialist knowledge to an action programme for revolutionary politics, the major thinkers of the Frankfurt School sought
to pose fundamental questions about revolutionary experiences and
contemporary capitalism without making historical materialism into
a left-wing Hegelianism. At the same time, they were deeply critical
of the orthodox Marxism of the Stalinist parties, regarding historical

materialism as a means to re-open ancient questions about the good life and meaningful existence, rather than as a positivist social science. Members of the Frankfurt School prudently described their research programme as "Critical Theory" partly as a euphemism for historical materialism that they hoped would deflect hostile attention, and partly to signify their distance from orthodox forms of Marxism.

The key element in the Frankfurt School's Marxism is their critique of the labour model of praxis, combined with a return to conceptions of structure and history close to those of the young Marx. Max Horkheimer's initial outline of Critical Theory in the 1930s, as an interdisciplinary, materialist research programme, set the scene for the development of a fairly systematic theory of monopoly capitalism, the bureaucratic state, the modern individual and consumer society. At the same time, scepticism towards Hegelian Marxism's activist reduction of historical materialism – its conflation of proletarian experience with radical theory – combined with the integration of psychoanalytic positions into Marxist theory, led to a questioning of the relationship between the labour process and an objectifying attitude. In the 1940s, leading members of the Frankfurt School significantly radicalized the critique of commodity reification in the context of an anthropological inquiry into the roots of social domination. They concluded that "instrumental reason", the formal rationality of reified calculations, arose long before capitalism, from the effort to master nature through technological progress.

After the Second World War, the paths of the key members of the group began to diverge, with what has become the major statement of the first generation of Critical Theory, Adorno and Horkheimer's *Dialectic of Enlightenment* ([1947] 2002), in fact representing only one intellectual possibility. Adorno's subsequent work on negative dialectics and dissonant modernism in the post-war era was mainly an effort to clarify and extend the theses of this breakthrough work. A significant alternative, however, was Marcuse's synthesis of psychoanalysis and Marxism, in works that directly inspired the student movements of the 1960s and 1970s. Marcuse and Adorno, in different ways, opened up questions around individuality and the family, bureaucracy and authority, consumption and culture, and dialectical methodology, which conventional approaches in historical materialism have rarely broached, before or after the Frankfurt School. This chapter, then, explores the development and diversification of Frankfurt School Marxism among its key, first-generation members, up until the 1950s. The second generation of the Frankfurt School, many of whom were students radicalized in the 1960s around the positions of their professors, are examined later, in the chapter on Critical Theory.

The Institute for Social Research and the "cultural turn"

The Frankfurt School's critique of labour and its interest in art have been widely misunderstood. Leninists in particular have strongly criticized the Frankfurt School for its insistence on the importance of culture and its members' political quietism (Marcuse excepted). For György Lukács, the Frankfurt School had installed itself at the "Grand Hotel Abyss", a contemplative and pessimistic intellectual space from which to justify their lack of political engagement with speculations on difficult art and high theory (Lukács 1971b: xv). For Perry Anderson, the Frankfurt School's "cultural turn" is a reflection of political defeat in the 1920s and 1930s that, together with the consequent isolation of radical intellectuals from mass movements, results in a theory that has lost contact with revolutionary practice (Anderson 1979: 32). Phil Slater proposes that, because the Frankfurt School is not an "agitational weapon", it fails to "achieve the relation to praxis which is central to the Marxist project" (Slater 1977: xiv). Zoltan Tar maintains that, lacking a scientific socialism, the critique of labour practice makes Critical Theory "in the last analysis [just] another existentialist philosophy" (Tar 1977: 205). The notion of "praxis" as the unity of Marxist theory, articulated by the Leninist party, with revolutionary practice by the proletarian movement, in which theory exists to guide strategy, and according to which truth is determined by political success, looms large in these criticisms.

The problem here is that some sorts of Marxism have reduced Marx's thought to a dour blue-collar workerism, for which "praxis" has no more meaning than experimental verification of scientific hypotheses in the "laboratory" of class politics. For the Frankfurt School, Leninist objections instrumentalized theory and made the central committee into the arbiter of philosophical truth, something whose negative intellectual consequences were reflected in Lukács' own fate (Adorno 2007c: 151–76). More damagingly, such objections also strategically "forgot" that for Marx, praxis meant human flourishing through creative labour (MECW5: 47), rather than theoretically guided political success. Generally speaking, the Frankfurt School's combination, of radical humanism under conditions of proletarian demobilization with social theory arising from a critique of the labour model of praxis, is understood by critics as leading to hopeless despair. There is a gap between ideals and reality that refuses to close, because – unlike for Marx in 1847 – no revolutionary upsurge seems to loom on the horizon.

But perhaps it would be simpler to express surprise that, given a grim assessment of revolutionary chances in the 1920s to 1940s, what the members of the Frankfurt School did was not to adapt to political conditions by moderating their stances, but to radicalize further. The specific form that this radicalization took was a deepening of the philosophical implications of Marxism by means of its fertilization with Weberian sociology, in the context of an encounter with Freudian psychoanalysis. Possibly the best way to think about the Frankfurt School is as a unique research programme that unites the Marxist question – what are the roots of the modern loss of freedom? – with the Weberian question – what is the ground of the modern loss of meaningfulness? – in a critical theory with an emancipatory practical intention (Bernstein 1995: 12). It was the intertwining of the problem of domination with the problem of nihilism, together with the integration of Freudian psychoanalysis into historical materialism, which defined the Marxism of the Frankfurt School.

Although the members of the Frankfurt School initially accepted Marx's idea that creative labour represented the model of practice, this eventually came under critical scrutiny. Freud had linked labour discipline to what he called "the renunciation of instinctual satisfactions" through delayed gratification, and had pointed to the increasing tendency under capitalism for this delay to become permanent (Freud 2001c: 57–146). But if the mastery of external nature through labour practice actually involved a problematic domination of internal nature, and if this problematic domination of internal nature threatened to lead to social irrationality and the mistreatment of others, then labour practice no longer looked like the key to liberation. Revision of the idea of labour practice as central to the utopian hopes of the socialist movement resulted in the distinctive and controversial character of Frankfurt School Marxism, because this triggered a search for alternative sorts of action on which to base emancipatory possibilities.

Additionally, members of the Frankfurt School radicalized in a context of a disastrous Leninist voluntarism, whose fatal neglect of cultural factors led to the failed Western revolutions of 1918–23. Further, the apparently irresistible rise of European fascism was the result not only of the political paralysis of radical forces, but also of the fascists' ability to appeal to the mentality of major sectors of the population. Like Gramsci, members of the Frankfurt School understood that during this period, although the capitalist state was completely vulnerable, what had been revealed was that the mentality of the working class lagged far behind political developments. An exhaustive empirical survey of psychological attitudes among German workers, conducted by the Institute in the 1920s, revealed that most had personality structures that were highly conservative and resistant to socio-cultural changes (Jay 1973: 124–35). These personality structures, Institute members discovered, were the result of childhood socialization, forming the templates by which individuals responded to economic and cultural transformations, so that there was a generational lag in the adaptation of individuals to society. Moreover, German fascism exhibited violent irrationality in a form widely described on the German Left as "mass hysteria". Turning to psychoanalysis to understand the unconscious roots of political unreason made sound sense. The "cultural turn" was entirely connected to the urgent political questions of the inter-war years.

Critical Theory versus Traditional Theory

Frankfurt School Marxism only took on its distinctive form once Max Horkheimer became the Director of the Institute in 1930. Nonetheless, under the direction of Carl Grünberg in the 1920s the Institute had published Karl Korsch's *Marxism and Philosophy* (1923) and discussed Lukács's *History and Class Consciousness* ([1923] 1971a). Against this intellectual and historical background, Horkheimer presented the differences between the ideas of Frankfurt School Marxism and rival socialist and bourgeois approaches in a series of articles for the Institute's journal that culminated in "Traditional and Critical Theory" in 1937 (Horkheimer 1982: 188–243). Influenced by Lukács, Horkheimer argued that the difference between social philosophy and traditional sociology consisted in the historical and materialist dialectical methodology that the former used to integrate the fragmented knowledge provided by the latter into an ongoing totalization. From this perspective, Marxism is a materialist prolongation of Hegel's use of "determinate negation". This refers to the process of specifying the social connections between isolated abstractions, so as to locate them in their contextual determinants. The method constructs a "concrete totality" of "many determinations and relations" that represents the dialectical "unity of the diverse" (Marx 1973: 100–101). Long before the publication of Marx's *Grundrisse*, Horkheimer had reconstructed the dialectical method from his knowledge of Hegel, but he had also realized that, although this resulted in a concrete totality, a truly *historical* materialism precluded finished systems (Horkheimer 1982: 226–8, 242–3).

The dialectical methodology of Critical Theory aims at an interdisciplinary materialism as the Frankfurt School's interpretation of Lukács's "category of the totality as the [intellectual] bearer of the principle of revolution". Implicitly drawing upon the critique of reification, Horkheimer argued that capitalist society appears to bourgeois consciousness as a "sum total of facts" submitted to "the classificatory thinking of each individual" in the interests of effective adaptation to social reality (*ibid*.: 199). The resulting disciplinary silos of traditional sociology and bourgeois philosophy therefore compartmentalize social reality in line with the prevalent cultural fragmentation caused by reification, even as they eliminate substantive questions through a formalistic method whose paradigm is the closed system of mathematical demonstrations (*ibid*.: 199–205).

Unlike the isolated silos of the bourgeois academic disciplines, dialectical theory relates the latest research findings in distinct areas to one another by grasping the material interconnections between economic science, sociology, political science, cultural criticism, psychology and philosophy. At the same time, Critical Theory inquires into the historical genesis of the object of inquiry, insisting that the economy, society, the state, culture, the psyche and thinking all change because of their mutual interrelation. Thus in order to construct an interdisciplinary materialism, members of the Frankfurt School had to reconstruct bourgeois disciplines within the historical genesis of their social context, while rejecting ideological limitations such as reified "laws of motion" and an unhistorical "human nature". A classic instance of this is the Frankfurt School's appropriative critique of Freudian psychoanalysis, in which it is argued that Freud had ideologically assumed that the nuclear family was an unchanging reality and so transformed his valuable dissection of the bourgeois individual into an unchanging model of the psyche (Adorno 1967).

Frankfurt School Marxism represents self-reflexive sociology, that is a sociology that reflects on its own social location in the division of labour and on its own historical conditions of possibility (Horkheimer 1982: 213). Because of his stress on the historical genesis of the object of analysis and the social connections between domains of human knowledge, Horkheimer regards the theorist as a participant in the socio-historical processes under diagnosis. Consequently, the synthesis of knowledge of society gained through integrating different disciplines using materialist dialectics is not a final truth, but the provisional result of an ongoing effort to grasp the totality in thought. There is a Hegelian distinction here that it is crucial to grasp. For Hegel, Kantian formalism was merely the classificatory "Understanding" operating on a fragmented and unhistorical "factual" world. By contrast, self-reflexive dialectical "Reason", grasping the totality as generated by antagonisms, knows that the totality can only be conceptualized by thinking in contradictions. Horkheimer's Marxist version of this idea is to propose that reality be grasped as a historically developing, concrete totality of social contradictions.

By contrast with Lukács, the members of the Frankfurt School sought to reopen a set of ancient questions about the good life *as questions*, turning to the doctrine of hedonism in particular for the roots of a materialist understanding of human existence. They also engaged extensively with what they described as the "dark writers of the bourgeoisie", reactionary philosophers such as Schopenhauer and Nietzsche, in a bid to fully comprehend the limits of the bourgeois Enlightenment. Like Lukács, they were attracted to a synthesis of Marx and Weber, and strongly influenced by Hegel's critique of Kant, but they also investigated Freud, existentialism (Heidegger and Kierkegaard), Bergson and Husserl (Held 1980: 29–39, 175–99; Jay 1973: 41–85).

As Horkheimer notes, if the social theorist commited to human freedom is a participant in antagonistic contradictions, then this implies an emancipatory sociology with the practical intent to change the world (Horkheimer 1982: 208–11). But the members of the Frankfurt School rejected Lukács' idea that the proletariat is the privileged historical subject whose revolutionary praxis entails absolute knowledge and which is capable of expressively generating the social totality from its conscious transformation of the natural environment (Jay 1984: 207). Not only does this reduce philosophical truth to the instrumental success of a political strategy, it also denies the resistance of matter to human consciousness, and it proclaims the idealist unity of subject and object in a way that can only lead to a closed system of finished truths. Instead, the addressee of the Frankfurt School's Marxism increasingly becomes humanity as a whole, understood as historical individuals rather than a collective subject (Held 1980: 24–6).

Administered society

The research of the Institute involved an informal division of labour (Held 1980: 14). Members were to investigate society (Henryk Grossmann,

Friedrich Pollock and Arkadij Gurland – political economy; Franz Neumann and Otto Kirchheimer – law and the state), culture (Leo Löwenthal, Theodor Adorno and Walter Benjamin – art; Herbert Marcuse and Max Horkheimer – philosophy) and personality (Erich Fromm – depth psychology, including Freudian psychoanalysis). The independent results were to be integrated into a social theory by means of the dialectical methods of historical materialism, mainly by Horkheimer, but in such a way as to place back on the agenda ancient philosophical questions about human happiness and the good life. Before long, Adorno was playing a role alongside Horkheimer in summarizing the research findings and synthesizing them into a global theory, based on the idea that the equivalence principle of commodity exchange dominated society. The equivalence principle refers to Marx's notion of "real abstraction", where unlike use values, embodying qualitatively different concrete labour, exchange for like exchange values, embodying the same amount of abstract labour. The equivalence principle became Horkheimer and Adorno's version of commodity reification.

Although the positions of the Frankfurt School were never formulated as a new orthodoxy, there was general agreement in the 1930s and 1940s that the historical materialist analysis of capitalism must begin from the economic structure of society (Kellner 1989: 51–82; Held 1980: 41–2). It was clear to the political economists, Neumann, Kirscheimer, Pollock, Gurland and Grossmann, that nineteenth-century liberal capitalism, with its reliance on market mechanisms and the minimal state, was finished. The new phenomena to be explained included fascist dictatorships, economic depression and the emergence of consumer society, the economic developments of monopoly capitalism, and the bureaucratic state. The capitalism described by Marx had been replaced by a new fusion of monopoly corporations, international banking and the interventionist state, which sought to manage crisis tendencies through rational planning. This was disturbing, because a central demand of the socialist movement from Engels onward was for the rational planning of the economy as a replacement for the anarchy of the market. For the members of the Frankfurt School, experiencing firsthand the stabilization of the Great Depression through authoritarian politics, this was being realized before their eyes – in the form of National Socialism. Moreover, the Russian experiment, which the Frankfurt School initially enthusiastically endorsed and then critically supported, had begun to suspiciously resemble Nazi Germany.

Although the members of the Frankfurt School agreed that liberal capitalism was finished, disagreements arose around the characterization of the form of capitalism that had replaced it. Despite some differences, Neumann, Gurland and Kirscheimer held that post-liberal capitalism was a crisis-prone form of authoritarian society that they described as "totalitarian monopoly capitalism" (Kellner 1989: 61–76; Held 1980: 53–8). On their analysis, the formation of monopoly corporations and their fusion with the banking sector distorts the operation of the law of value but cannot suppress it. The consequence is that the rate of profit must necessarily fall. Monopoly capitalism, in other words, has an inherent tendency towards stagnation – even breakdown – offset by political intervention by state authorities seeking to prevent collapse. "Rational planning" in this context means a reactive posture of constant crisis management, linked to an authoritarian approach to labour and a belligerent stance towards competing nations. Such a fundamental social arrangement, typified by German capitalism under the Nazi regime, must be accompanied by a totalitarian political system, because the state cannot afford to satisfy the material demands of the population or to risk the delays of democratic processes. Accordingly, Neumann argues in his classic work *Behemoth* (1942) that "in a monopolistic system, profits cannot be made and retained without totalitarian political power" (Neumann 1942: 354). The implication is that totalitarian government is to monopoly capitalism as parliamentary democracy is to liberal capitalism: the natural regime for that social formation.

By contrast, the approach taken by Pollock (and supported by Horkheimer, Adorno and Marcuse) was to describe post-liberal capitalism as a rationally managed form of "state capitalism", with democratic and totalitarian variants (Kellner 1989: 52–60, 74–6; Held 1980: 58–63). Despite the potentially misleading terminology, Pollock certainly did not mean by "state capitalism" the amalgamation of all capitals with the state in a single giant enterprise-cum-bureaucracy. Instead, his analysis indicates that the monopoly corporations and the major banks rely on state intervention to provide the conditions for the formation and realization of value. They do this through state support for strategic industries, control over labour regulations and distortion of market laws in the interests of preventing economic crises. Constant state intervention in the economy and regulation of labour markets, together with aggressive programmes of imperialist expansion and the creation of vast military industries, means that the crisis potentials of capitalism have been suppressed, although not totally eliminated (Adorno 1987: 33–56).

The analysis of state capitalism begins from a critique of the Soviet Union that rejects its socialist claims entirely (Jay 1973: 152). Pollock's argument that rational planning has successfully dampened down crisis potentials means that he can acknowledge the existence of state capitalism in the United States and Great Britain, for instance, without having to propose that these democracies would inevitably turn fascist. Instead, Pollock adopts a critical attitude towards the democratic variant of state capitalism by examining the ways in which the advertising industry and consumer goods belong to the rational management of the new capitalism. At the same time, however, Pollock's analysis tends to overstate the ability of state capitalism to control mass mobilizations and to prevent economic crises, leading to an analysis that risks concluding that there is no significant difference between parliamentary democracy and fascist totalitarianism (Picone 1978: ix–xxi).

The Pollock–Adorno–Horkheimer line, which leads key members of the Frankfurt School to describe both parliamentary democracy and authoritarian statism as the "administered society" (Habermas 1989: 296), has many advantages and some disadvantages. It clarifies members' opposition to both Stalinism and Hitlerism without forcing the Frankfurt School into the characteristic position of Cold War liberalism, which was to proclaim the relative superiority of the Western democracies (Held 1980: 70–76). It locates the basis for political apathy in the 1950s and 1960s not in some defect of the masses, but in the disempowering implications of consumerism and bureaucracy. And it leads other members of the Frankfurt School, such as Wolfgang Haug, to penetrating analyses of the advertising industry and post-war consumerism, which regard "commodity aesthetics" in terms of pseudo-sexual substitute gratifications with strong links to aggressive competitiveness (Haug 1986). This is a powerful analysis of how and why "sex sells", of status-driven consumption, and of the ways in which advertising generates consumer desire. On the negative side, however, the notion of an "administered society" tends to generate a model of society as monolithic, where the stress falls on the tendential elimination of crisis potentials.

Marx and Freud

The mainstream of Marxism has generally criticized Freud's theory as a pessimistic anthropology that is really an ideological naturalization of capitalist individualism. By contrast, for the Frankfurt School, from the beginning of Horkheimer's directorship of the Institute in 1930 onwards, psychoanalysis was regarded as a crucial part of any analysis of society. Individual psychology provided a conceptual corridor between ideological formations and social structure (Held 1980: 110–47; Jay 1973: 86–112). Extensive contact with progressive psychoanalytic thinkers through the Frankfurt Psychoanalytic Institute, led by Otto Fenichel and directly attached to the Institute for Social Research, convinced Institute members of the radicalism of Freud's theory (Jacoby 1986). They were persuaded that Freud's focus on socialization through the family and his materialist analysis of the personality represented a critique of the basic unhappiness of existing society, not an endorsement of current arrangements. Nonetheless, under the leadership of Fromm initially, and later at the hands of Adorno and Marcuse, the Frankfurt School attempted something other than merely adding psychoanalysis as a finished doctrine to the Marxist theory of society. Unlike orthodox Freudians, the members of the Frankfurt School insisted on a historicization of psychoanalysis through a philosophical critique of instinct theory and a sociological reconstruction of the relationship between changing forms of the family and historically variable structures of personality.

Based on the anthropological position in Marx's *Economic and Philosophical Manuscripts of 1844*, it was clear to Fromm that Marx did not in fact believe that the human being, as a natural animal, was an infinitely plastic expression of social relations. Marx held that the human animal had some basic natural drives (hunger, sexuality, etc.) whose expression was shaped (or distorted) by a historically specific array of (socially generated) human needs. Accordingly, Marx criticized the suffering caused by capitalist alienation as the result of an unnatural condition (Fromm 1966). For Fromm, then, what Freud could supply to Marxism was a theoretical description of the interaction between natural instincts, socialized needs and personality structures, one capable of explaining the psychological bases of hope as well as the mechanisms behind destructiveness and conformity. In *The Development of the Dogma of Christ* (1931), for instance, Fromm connects important shifts in religious doctrine to social shifts, on the one side, and changes in personality structure, on the other side, in a significant early integration of Marx and Freud (Burston 1991: 98–133). For Fromm, Freud's theory implies the formation of socially typical class "character", because common conditions of socialization, and therefore characteristic renunciations demanded of individuals, obtain across classes at any historical moment. The application of psychoanalysis to sociology is accompanied by the historicization of the categories of Freudian theory, especially the illegitimate universalization of the Oedipus Complex, which Fromm regards as specific to the liberal capitalist era. The destructiveness implied by the notion of a death drive, Fromm proposes, naturalized the aggression of possessive individualism and the market society. A better explanation, Fromm argues, is that from the Reformation onwards, European culture has displayed a strong preference for "anal" (i.e. ascetic and acquisitive) personality structures, something that the development of capitalism actively fosters. For such persons, conscious revulsion from sexuality as "unclean" has as its flipside an unconscious sexual excitement at the punishment of "deviants", which Fromm does not hesitate to describe as a sado-masochistic psychological identification with authoritarian figures. Eventually, however, Fromm rejected Freud's libido theory and eliminated the erotic dimensions of his explanations of fascism and capitalism (respectively) altogether.

Other members of the Frankfurt School regarded Fromm's rejection of the concept of libido as evidence for his adaptation to the post-war de-radicalization happening around the "neo-Freudian revisionism" of American ego psychology (Burston 1991: 207–29; Rickert 1986: 351–400). For Adorno and Marcuse, Freud's conception of the instincts is the ballast that prevents psychoanalysis from thinking that the ego might successfully adapt to social reality (Adorno 1967: 86–8; Marcuse 1966: 238–74). According to Freud's libido theory, the human animal adapts to its natural and social environment through the formation of a psychic structure – the ego – that reflects a "precipitate of aban-doned object-cathexes" (Freud 2001b: 29). Freud proposes that for each individual, an instinctually derived psychic energy, or libido, resident in the unconscious and operating according to the pleasure principle, is attached, or cathected, onto representations of objects, once these objects have provided pleasurable satisfaction to that human animal. The theory states that the reality principle disciplines the expression of the pleasure principle by forcing it, by means of the apparatus of the ego, to accept delayed gratification in accordance with the dictates of external reality. In effect that means that the socialization of the infant involves the renunciation of satisfying objects, especially sexual objects, and the "precipitation" of these sacrifices in the structure of the personality.

Freud proposes that a portion of libido is permanently invested in the ego as "desexualized narcissistic libido" around each conquest of repression, and he eventually described this precipitated structure as the superego, the psychic representation of social ideals. Only gradually does the infantile ego learn to partially replace early object-images with adult substitute satisfactions, and Freud in this connection speaks of the "vicissitudes" of the sexual inclinations as they mature through oral, anal and then genital forms of expression. These stages of development,

Freud holds, are deposited in the ego as personality structures that reflect fundamental attitudes of the ego toward the libidinal strivings of the rest of the psyche (Freud 2001a: 141–58, b: 1–66).

Adorno, Horkheimer and Marcuse connect these ideas with the late Freud of the anthropological theory of *Civilization and its Discontents* ([1930] 2001c). As already mentioned, in that extraordinary work, Freud proposes that the advance of civilization is necessarily accompanied by the increasing "renunciation of instinctual satisfactions", that is historically developing social reality demands the delay of gratification on an ever-expanding scale (Freud 2001c: 57–146). This condition, which Freud with dark irony calls "secular progress in repression", means that industrial capitalism has become a sickness-inducing society filled with potentially neurotic individuals, whose resentment of the demands of constant increases in productivity is likely to erupt in outbreaks of volcanic irrationality.

Culture industry

For Adorno and Horkheimer, the potentials of Freudian psychoanalysis go further than just a clarification of the appeal of fascism and Stalinism to the "authoritarian personality" (Adorno *et al.* 1964). The advent of an administered society, they argue, is accompanied by state intervention in family structures, with the consequence that the familial conflict dynamics that form the autonomous ego are institutionally circumvented, replaced by submission to social authority. Adorno in particular is concerned that the autonomous individual of liberal capitalism is becoming historically superseded by a morally heteronomous, or externally directed, "organizational individual", one with distinctly narcissistic traits (Kellner 1989: 83–120; Held 1980: 130–34; Jay 1973: 104–5). Accordingly, changes in the historical form of individuality are expressed in a significant superstructural modification that some members of the Frankfurt School describe as the "culture industry", the cultural complement to the administered society. In focused studies of the corporatization of culture happening in the entertainment industries, in radio, film, television and sport, Adorno, Horkheimer, Lowenthal and Marcuse reveal a significant shift in the nature of ideology. Bourgeois ideology had spoken of negative liberty and liberal justice, and its artworks expressed these aspirations in their highly individuated forms and idealistic contents. What this meant was that radical criticism could pointedly contrast the idealistic representations with social reality in ways that made potent contact with mass aspirations. By contrast, American democracy, Soviet totalitarianism and fascist propaganda all provide evidence of direct manipulation of individuals' consciousness by means of techniques that entirely bypassed potentially incriminating reference to ideals. Adaptation to existing society is presented as a desirable goal for the exhausted individual, for whom light entertainment provides some relief from that life of boredom and fatigue which the culture industries represent as entirely natural.

It is sometimes imagined that the Frankfurt School's idea of the culture industries pits commodified mass culture against non-commercial high art. But a Marxist sociology of culture that proposed that art had only recently become commodified would be at right-angles to reality, and this is emphatically not the Frankfurt School's position (Adorno & Horkheimer 2002: 107–9). Rather, their position is the dialectical one that, as Marcuse states in his key essay "Affirmative Culture", bourgeois art was emancipated from liturgical functions precisely because of a shift from religious tutelage to art markets (Marcuse 1968: 95–115). In the revolutionary era of the bourgeoisie, its autonomous art performed a radical role in undermining late feudal society and the absolute state, not because of any particular political content, but because its artistic form expressed an explosive desire for individuation.

Bourgeois art, Marcuse holds, has two special properties that make it historically unique: its "purposeful purposivelessness", a Kantian mouthful expressing the idea of deliberate uselessness, and its conception of aesthetic beauty as the harmonious proportionality of an organic whole. Deliberate uselessness means that art is an end in itself. Just like the free particular that is the human being enjoying individual liberty, the artwork "self-legislates" through its form and realizes ends inherent to itself, rather than those imposed from without. This results in a harmonious balance between parts and the whole, such that the whole is greater than the sum of its parts without at any moment arbitrarily subjugating any part to the total conception. This relationship is called "beauty" and it releases a pleasure unrelated to instrumental satisfaction of instinctual needs. Marcuse argued that this meant that bourgeois art contained a "promise of happiness" in its implicit vision of the well-rounded individual achieving non-instrumental well-being under conditions of individual liberty (*ibid.*: 115):

> By affirmative culture is meant that culture of the bourgeois epoch, which led in the course of its own development to the segregation from civilization of the mental and spiritual world

as an independent realm of value that is also considered superior to civilization. Its decisive characteristic is the assertion of a universal, obligatory, eternally better and more valuable world, that must be unconditionally affirmed: a world essentially different from the factual world of the daily struggle for existence, yet realizable in every individual "from within", without any transformation of the state of fact.   (*Ibid.*: 95)

Although this was revolutionary in relation to the *ancient régime*, with the shift of the bourgeoisie to the side of reaction after 1848, bourgeois art ceases to play an unequivocally progressive historical role. Its promise of happiness begins to promote not a radical challenge to the existing arrangements, but the ideological illusion that the social conditions for individual self-fulfilment have already arrived. In losing its critical negativity in relation to society, the mainstream of bourgeois art becomes merely "affirmative culture", degenerating in the next hundred years into a set of generic repetitions of established conventions.

Accordingly, the Frankfurt School's most radical theses, explored in Adorno and Horkheimer's *Dialectic of Enlightenment*, propose that this brings about the entry of the logic of the commodity into the structure of the artwork (Adorno & Horkheimer 2002: 114–15). The theses on the culture industry, therefore, are not primarily about the commercialization of art, but about the *standardization* of its forms and the consequent *trivialization* of its contents (Kellner 1989: 120–45). Art as light entertainment, produced only as a commodity for the purpose of diversion from the dissatisfactions of everyday life and the grind of work, is art characterized by generic clichés, stereotypical contents and repetitious forms, designed to elicit routine responses (Adorno & Horkheimer 2002: 107–12). The uniqueness of the bourgeois artwork, its unfolding according to a law of form that it evolves from the heart of its own concerns, is replaced by pseudo-individuation, the marginal distinctiveness of brand differentiation through the star system, in a marketplace that tolerates no real diversity (*ibid.*: 102–18). The promise of deep happiness is replaced by superficial instant gratification, based on infantile regression through representations of successful aggression and quasi-sexual pleasure through adaptation to power (*ibid.*: 120–25). The products of the culture industry avoid the really new like the plague, for this would challenge conventional tastes with fresh perceptions, new feelings and alternative values, implying a demanding experience that includes the risk of artistic failure as the flipside to real experimentation (*ibid.*: 125–8). "As the demand for the marketability of art becomes total, a shift in the inner economic composition of cultural commodities is becoming apparent", they conclude. "In adapting itself entirely to need, the [standardized] work of art defrauds human beings in advance of liberation from the principle of utility" (*ibid.*: 128).

Whereas artworks are generated through what Freud called "sublimation", a non-repressive detour of instinctual energies into cultural goals, the products of the culture industries represent a repressive channelling of sexual drives into conformist ideals. In Adorno's memorable phrase, "works of art are ascetic and shameless; the culture industry is pornographic and prudish" (*ibid.*: 111). Adorno's highly influential *Philosophy of Modern Music* ([1947] 2007b) represents a defence of autonomous art as a potentially liberating social practice in a reified society. This is conducted along the lines of his later assertion that "this is not a time for political art, but politics has migrated into autonomous art, and nowhere more so than where art appears to be politically dead" (Adorno 2007a: 194). The radical musical forms of Schönberg and Stravinsky break with the organic totality of the classical bourgeois artwork precisely in order to assert their independence from kitsch radio hits and the museum classics of the national symphony orchestra. Nonetheless, the dialectics of instrumental reason penetrate even the most hermetic and dissonant of modernist artworks, filling them with unresolved contradictions. Where Schönberg rationalizes and systematizes music, he liberates it from classical tonality only to make atonality into a formal prison (Adorno 2007b: 87); Stravinsky, meanwhile, uses avant-garde forms with folkloric contents to present a regressive modernism with affinities to fascism (*ibid.*: 115). Only Adorno's beloved "free atonality" preserves the liberating dynamics of dissonant modernism – but that is so rare that he has difficulty in specifying examples (Adorno 1998: 269–322, esp. 272, 293).

By contrast with Adorno and Horkheimer's view of the culture industry, unorthodox member of the Frankfurt School Walter Benjamin (1892–1940) holds that the production techniques of popular culture, especially cinema, have demystified art. By stripping the work's "aura", or quasi-magical mystique, popular cinema completes the secularization of bourgeois art and makes possible an engaged and participatory viewing experience. "Mechanical reproduction of art changes the reaction of the masses toward art", he writes:

> The reactionary attitude toward a Picasso painting changes into the progressive reaction toward a Chaplin movie. The progressive reaction is characterized by the direct, intimate

fusion of visual and emotional enjoyment with the orientation of the expert. Such fusion is of great social significance. The greater the decrease in the social significance of an art form, the sharper the distinction between criticism and enjoyment by the public. The conventional is uncritically enjoyed, and the truly new is criticized with aversion. With regard to the screen, the critical and the receptive attitudes of the public coincide. The decisive reason for this is that individual reactions are pre-determined by the mass audience response they are about to produce and this is nowhere more pronounced than in the film.

(Benjamin 1973: 236)

Whether Benjamin would have been able to sustain this optimistic position in the post-war era is a matter of speculation, for he suicided in 1940 when, fleeing from the Nazis, fascist Spain refused him entry from France.

Instrumental reason

The idea that Marxism involves liberation from utility, an emancipation from what Adorno and Horkheimer describe as the "functional context of self-preservation" (Adorno & Horkheimer 2002: 22), is a strikingly unconventional way of expressing Marx's notion that the society of abundance is a release from material scarcity. But *Dialectic of Enlightenment* is an enigmatic book, written between Stalingrad and Normandy, "to explain why humanity, instead of entering a truly human state, is sinking into a new kind of barbarism" (*ibid.*: xiv). As rival sci-entifically enlightened state capitalisms slugged it out by means of high-tech war machines and rationally administered death camps, Adorno and Horkheimer expressed a deep dismay at the results of the universal rule of the equivalence principle of bourgeois society. "Enlightenment", they write, "aimed at liberating human beings from fear and installing them as masters [of nature]. Yet the wholly enlightened earth is radiant with triumphant calamity" (*ibid.*: 1). Adorno was to write soon after-wards that the prospects of socialism are extremely bleak: the best that can be done is to keep alive hope for the good society by reflecting on the "damaged life" of the administered world (Adorno 2005: 39).

Adorno and Horkheimer's critique of instrumental reason extends the concept of commodity reification in several directions, most nota-bly by combining reification and rationalization with repression. By repression is meant both social domination and psychic repression of instinctual satisfactions. Thus the basic idea of instrumental reason is that of a calculating manipulation of human beings and the natural environment that reduces persons and things to raw materials for the production of use values, in order to assist socialized individuals in their goal of self-preservation. At the same time, growing technological control of the world by instrumental reason involves increasing instinctual renunciations on the part of socialized individuals, who as a result become potentially irrational in direct proportion to the accomplished rationalization of their world. The combination of rationalization and repression results in the transformation of society into a reified object, a total system that can be calculated mathematically, which becomes a second nature for the modern individual, ruling over them like a capricious fate. Under the signs of ideas of "progress" and "community", the administered society turns its vision of complete control and its nostalgia for lost solidarity into a potent ideology that functions as the modern myth, under various designations ("the socialist motherland", "the German Fatherland", "the American Dream"). But via Freud, Adorno and Horkheimer also reconstruct the anthropological genesis of instrumental reason, pushing the origins of this process back to before capitalism, in human pre-history. Hence their book has a title that alludes to the social process of rationalization, the tragedy of enlightenment, rather than a critique of capitalism alone.

Unfortunately, in line with the idea that this is a message in a bottle rather than a manifesto for action, Adorno and Horkheimer express this through a series of cryptic aphorisms about the mutual entanglement of myth and enlightenment, rational control and instinctual renunciation (Adorno & Horkheimer 2002: 8, 14). Although they do not explicitly clarify it, the underlying idea is that enlightenment is a historical process before it is a distinct historical moment (*the* Enlightenment). Finally, they are rather unclear about their alternatives to instrumental reason, which turn out to be a combination of dialectical thinking in the mode of negative dialectics and mimetic expression in line with avant-garde art – a combination that would be praxis and not labour, they insist.

It is therefore helpful to break the idea down into the relation to Lukács and the relation to Freud and treat them sequentially. It is also helpful to interpret *Dialectic of Enlightenment* by means of Horkheimer's more accessible co-text *Eclipse of Reason* ([1947] 1974).

As with Lukács, Adorno and Horkheimer synthesize Weber with Marx, suggesting that quantitative calculation and formal rationality are linked together in systems of thinking that have as their model mathematical formalizations, and which have a real material basis in social domination. The classificatory intellect dominates its object because it subordinates substantive particularity to universal forms and general regularities. When the social world is regarded as consisting of uniform regularities that can be described using the mathematical calculations of scientific sociology and economic laws, this is evidence that human beings have been socially reduced to mere objects. Unlike Lukács, however, rather than regarding capitalist culture as hopelessly fragmented into particulars and lacking the concrete universality of the category of totality, they link instrumental reason to the process of "determining judgement". This is the general intellectual process of subsuming a particular instance under a universal rule, which Adorno and Horkheimer propose is grounded in the equivalence principle. Accordingly, instrumental reason involves the domination of the particular by the universal along the lines of a process of intellectual classification that reflects economic calculations and bureaucratic procedures. Intellectual resistance to instrumental reason must accordingly take the form of a dialectical history in "philosophical fragments", rather than conceptual totality.

Instrumental reason involves a substitution of calculated means for rational ends, leading to the loss of substantive ideals of human flourishing, so that finally capitalism liquidates its own universal liberal ideals as "scientifically unverifiable" (Horkheimer 1974: 22–3). The concept of negative liberty central to liberal political philosophy was based on the assumption that self-preservation represented the ultimate goal of human existence. This is the philosophical meaning of the social contract, whereby self-preserving individuals unite around a state that defends universal principles, in order to protect themselves from lethal instrumentalization by aggressive others. This prolongs and socializes self-preservation, rather than transforming it into a higher principle, enshrining instrumental reason as the basic social mechanism of a technological society based on the equivalence principle. The instrumentalization of others and the self implicit in instrumental reason involves the generalization of utilitarianism, the idea that an ethic can be derived from calculations of utility applied to social relations. In liberal utilitarian Jeremy Bentham's notorious "felicific calculus", for instance, the individual is supposed to perform actions only when these maximize "the greatest happiness for the greatest number", a position that fairly obviously licenses the sacrifice of individuals and the imposition of totalitarian restraints on minorities. According to Adorno and Horkheimer, all that the Marquis de Sade's sadistic perversions do is to render explicit the underlying human irrationality of this system, which is why they claim that "enlightenment is totalitarian" (Adorno & Horkheimer 2002: 4). Liberalism contains within it the seeds of its totalitarian opposite. "In Sade", Adorno and Horkheimer conclude in disgust, "private vices are the anticipatory historiography of public virtues in the totalitarian era" (*ibid.*: 92).

Dialectic of enlightenment

Accordingly, Adorno and Horkheimer introduce Freud into the analysis of reification, linking formal rationality's suppression of qualitative distinctions and substantive goals to the repression of inner nature. The fundamental point that they are making is that in order to discipline themselves to a world organized on the lines of a mathematical formula, individuals must subject their internal nature to fierce controls. "Humanity had to inflict terrible injuries on itself", they write, "before the self, the identical, purpose-directed, masculine character of human beings, was created, and something of this process is repeated in every childhood" (Adorno & Horkheimer 2002: 26). Drawing on psychoanalysis, they propose that the corollary to this is a tendency to regard the unknown as the uncontrolled, and to respond with pre-emptive aggression to the potential threat. The "return of the repressed", then, involves the mechanism of projection, where unmastered aggression from the self is projected outwards as aggression from the other, and the self reacts with pre-emptive violence, together with irrational justifications about the "threat" posed by unassimilated aliens. Not for nothing does *Dialectic of Enlightenment* conclude with a long analysis of anti-Semitism.

Adorno and Horkheimer argue that instrumental reason develops through four stages, implicitly corresponding to Marx's sequence of modes of production. But they trace its anthropological origins to instinctual self-preservation in the natural environment. The basic aim of "enlightenment", in line with its underlying instinctual thrust, is the mastery of a threateningly unknown and potentially deadly nature. It achieves this through increasing detachment from nature, that is demystification and domination of the natural environment, including the mastery of human nature. This implies a thesis of staggering generality: technological advance in the productive forces, the historical movement of relations of social domination, scientific progress in the disenchantment of nature, the rationalization of cultural forms and religious worldviews, secular progress in the renunciation of instinctual satisfactions, the historical genesis of personality structures centred on an increasingly narcissistic ego, and the growth of calculating forms of rational conduct are all the same process.

What that means is that instrumental reason gradually generates formalist "enlightenment" and the personality structures belonging to it, beginning with the Greek Enlightenment of ancient Athens and culminating in the European Enlightenment of the eighteenth century. This process of "enlightenment" does not emerge at a stroke, but instead develops dialectically from within pre-scientific modes of thought, in that combination of objectification and repression that we have already explored. Accordingly, Adorno and Horkheimer announce that:

> mimetic, mythical and metaphysical forms of behaviour were successively regarded as stages of world history which had been left behind, and the idea of reverting to them held the terror that the self would be changed back into the mere nature from which it had extricated itself with unspeakable exertions, and which for that reason filled it with unspeakable dread.
> (*Ibid.*: 24)

Not only does the social self progressively detach itself from (external and internal) nature, it also increasingly treats others as things to be manipulated, so that social domination keeps pace with objectification, in what is recognizably a Freudian recasting of Marx's theses on alienation.

Although the whole book sometimes looks like a tragedy of "enlightenment" along the pessimistic lines of Weber's "iron cage of rationality", where the inexorable advance of formal rationality leads inescapably to the incremental reduction of freedom, in fact it follows a divergent variant on the standard dialectical schema. For Marx and Hegel, the master narrative of historical progress follows a convergent dialectic, where the minuet between domination and liberation flows in the direction of increasing freedom: the potential for emancipation and the actualization of freedom eventually converge on the goal of history. Throwing Freud into the mix makes the potential for emancipation and the actualization of freedom diverge, because the actualization of (apparent) freedom involves growing (psychic) repression, resulting in an ego that is increasingly cold and calculating, together with growing potential for irrational resentment against society's demands. The autonomous individual is therefore decoded as the lonely neurotic, the manipulative personality springing from a set of ego defences that tend to project unmastered internal aggression onto imagined external threats.

Liberalism is unmasked as the doctrine that self-preservation is the only value, a situation whose truth is the atomization of social solidarity into market relations, the construction of a state whose paramount task is to preserve life, and the elimination of moral restraints on human conduct. Thus liberalism morphs into totalitarianism, and democracy meekly submits to dictatorship. Instrumental reason advances in stages characterized by increasing potential for emancipation and human welfare combined with decreasing actualization of freedom and meaningfulness. Speaking *very* carefully in the context of post-war anticommunist hysteria, they write:

> The enslavement to nature of people today cannot be separated from social progress. The increase in economic productivity which creates the conditions for a more just world also affords the technical apparatus and the social groups controlling it a disproportionate advantage over the rest of the population. The individual is entirely nullified in the face of the economic powers. These powers are taking society's domination over nature to unimagined heights. While individuals as such are vanishing before the apparatus they serve, they are provided for by that apparatus better than ever before. In the unjust state of society, the pliability and powerlessness of the masses increase with [this] materially considerable but socially paltry rise in the living standard of the [working] classes.   (*Ibid.*: xvii)

Because Adorno and Horkheimer are interested in a dialectical reading of the "dark writers of the bourgeoisie", the reactionary critics of the European Enlightenment (e.g. Nietzsche), their thesis is sometimes brutally misinterpreted as just a neo-Romantic (i.e. irrationalist) rejection of enlightenment. That is false. What Adorno and Horkheimer are up to in *Dialectic of Enlightenment* is an anthropological variant of Lukács's essay "Reification and the Consciousness of the Proletariat" (Lukács 1971a: 83–222), that is a dialectical critique of formal rationality. But their dialectic is not just divergent: domination has a master narrative; liberation exists in fragments. Instrumental reason, the mastery of nature springing from self-preservation, is exemplified by the labour process. In opposition to domination is the utopian hope for a post-capitalist reconciliation between human beings and the natural environment, best expressed through creative praxis. Dialectical thinking corresponds to the only form of social praxis that refuses calculation and utility, the useless labour of modernist artworks, which contains the last glimpse of the potential for a utopian reconciliation in the administered world (*ibid.*: 23). Nonetheless, "in light of the catastrophes that have happened, and in view of the catastrophes to come", Adorno writes, "no universal history leads from savagery to humanitarianism, but there is one leading from the slingshot to the megaton bomb" (Adorno 1973: 320). Adorno's *Negative Dialectics* represents a sustained effort to develop this divergent dialectic as the method of a critique of the capitalist totality presented through a series of fragments, each of which reflects a potential for emancipation in the midst of the universal history of social domination.

Creative praxis and erotic liberation

The downbeat note struck by Adorno and Horkheimer in the post-war era is entirely alien to Marcuse's explicitly utopian connection between Freud and Marx in his major work, *Eros and Civilization* ([1955] 1966). Despite major engagement with psychoanalysis, dialectics of labour remain central to Marcuse, even though he distrusts the version of Marxism that proceeds from the cumulative advance of the productive forces. Although he had been a soldiers' deputy in the Berlin workers' councils of 1919, he too eventually became convinced that the proletariat in the industrialized world had become integrated into capitalist society to the extent that its revolutionary potential was questionable. Although the work of Adorno and Horkheimer radicalized some students, it was "Marcuse alone among the [founding members of the Frankfurt School] who identified with and defended the radical movements" of the 1960s (Kellner 1989: 210).

In keeping with the broad approach of Frankfurt School Marxism, Marcuse's introduction to *Eros and Civilization* strikes a familiar note, declaring that "intensified progress seems to be bound up with intensified unfreedom" (Marcuse 1966: 4). In this context, "utopian" means both apparently impossible and actually desirable, and it is the combination of a critique of alienation profoundly influenced by the young Marx with a politics of desire that sides decisively with the pleasure principle against social reality which characterizes Marcuse. In his classic exposition of the Hegelian roots of Marxian social theory, *Reason and Revolution* (1941), Marcuse represents Marxism as a whole as a prolongation of the dialectical philosophy by historical materialist means (Marcuse 1999: 273–322). Drawing on his work in the 1930s

on Hegel's ontology and Heidegger's philosophy, however, he empha-
sized the reconciliation of humanity and nature in his reconstruction
of socialist politics. Until the 1940s, Marcuse held that the proletariat
is the transformative class of capitalist society and that the anti-fascist
struggle is a prelude to socialist revolution. Emphasizing the young
Marx's claims of normative universality on behalf of the working class,
Marcuse maintains that "the proletariat is distinguished by the fact that,
as a class, it signifies the negation of all classes" (*ibid.*: 291). At the
same time, Marcuse's interest in a balanced relation between humanity
and nature led him to be highly suspicious towards capitalist technology (Feenberg 2005) and in *One-Dimensional Man* (1964), Marcuse
describes instrumental reason as "technological rationality" (Marcuse
1964: 115). The significance of this is that in the post-war era, Marcuse
increasingly believed that the proletariat had become materially integrated into capitalist society by means of the technological manufacture of pseudo-needs, linked to the substitute gratifications provided by
the culture industries. In the second edition of *Reason and Revolution*
([1958] 1999), Marcuse added that:

> Technological progress multiplied the needs and satisfactions
> [in consumer society], while its utilization made the needs as
> well as their satisfactions repressive: they themselves sustain
> submission and domination.   (Marcuse 1999: 437)

Marcuse believes that human needs that potentially transcend the capitalist system have been mainly replaced by false needs generated by
the culture industries. The next question is, of course, how to liberate
radical, system-transcending human needs from the gilded cage of the
consumer paradise. Despite a certain estrangement from other members in the post-war era, Marcuse remains consistent with the rest of
the Frankfurt School in rejecting labour as the source of this liberation.
Like Adorno, he turns instead to art, grasped dialectically as at once a
potentially liberating anticipation of creative praxis *and* a component of
the social division of labour with the potential to generate escapist com-
pensations for actual unfreedom. Artworks are the key to re-awakening
the longing for the release of creative human potentials that instant
gratification dulls, for the humanist perspective of authentic art provides a contrast with everyday life. Moreover, art, as a form of creative
play, operates under the pleasure principle, where the repressed desire
for a realization of individuals' full humanity can be openly expressed
(Marcuse 1966: 140). Accordingly "the revolution involves a radical

transformation of the needs and aspirations themselves, cultural as well as material" (Marcuse 1972: 33). To do this requires the overthrow of the connection between social domination and the reality principle in late capitalism, which Marcuse describes as the "performance principle". Consequently, a key task of socialist construction is the replacement of the performance principle, the reality principle adapted to capitalist discipline, with a "non-repressive reality principle" (Marcuse 1966: 129).

The connection between creative praxis and sexual liberation outlined in *Eros and Civilization* was fundamental to the positive reception of Marcuse's work among 1960s radicals, for it spoke of an erotic revolt against instrumental reason. Marcuse acknowledges that material scarcity imposes restraints on individuals' ability to gratify their instincts and that disciplined labour is the necessary foundation for social prosperity (Marcuse 1966: 21–77). But the "dialectics of civilization" have now made possible the elimination of those restraints that have to do with maintaining an unequal distribution of material wealth (*ibid.*: 78–126). With the society of abundance on the horizon, the instinctual renunciations necessary to drag humanity into the modern world can be progressively relaxed. In a key section, misleadingly entitled "Beyond the Reality Principle", Marcuse argues that repression is unnecessary under socialism and that his proposed non-repressive reality principle would involve the release into society of the pleasures hitherto dammed up within authentic artworks (*ibid.*: 172–96). In terms that echo how Adorno's understands art, but with a distinct preference for realism over modernism, Marcuse suggests that the sublimations reflected in humanist artworks can now be de-sublimated, through their application to reality. The revolution is both a political and a psychological liberation, whose major effect on the individual will be the freeing of erotic impulses from the narrow scope of sexual expression alone. Arduous work will become pleasurable play.

Subsequent developments and arguments led Marcuse to clarify and correct the hypotheses presented in *Eros and Civilization*. In *An Essay on Liberation* (1969) and *Counter-revolution and Revolt* (1972), Marcuse accepts that *some* repression is necessary to *any* form of civilization whatsoever (i.e. the repression of impulses to incest and murder) and that the real problem is what he calls "surplus repression", the repression needed to sustain the performance principle (Marcuse 1969: 33). Furthermore, a danger has emerged of the cooptation of radical culture by the capitalist system through "repressive de-sublimation", the explicit sexualization of cultural forms combined with the aggressive destruction of classical bourgeois art (Marcuse 1972: 103). Although the youth movement's radical cultural politics retain a progressive potential, the strategic aim of socialist revolution must not be derailed by a culture of instant gratification. Where Marcuse had championed Narcissus against Oedipus in *Eros and Civilization* (Marcuse 1966: 159–71), he now argued that this would result in a consumer-driven hedonism which would foster narcissistic personalities, not autonomous individuals. As Douglas Kellner points out, Marcuse's potential today lies in the unresolved tension between his Romantic anti-capitalism and a materialist research programme that is yet to be concluded (Kellner 1984: 372–5). These latter lie, as Morton Schoolman proposes, in Marcuse's philosophical anthropology of the hidden radical potentials in the dispositions of modern individuals (Schoolman 1980: 351, 356).

Summary of key points

Critical Theory

- Frankfurt School Marxism endorses the opposition between reification and totality, but refuses the idea of the proletariat as identical subject-object of history. Instead, it aims at an interdisciplinary materialist research programme that is reflexively aware of its own social position in class society and is committed to practical emancipation.
- Frankfurt School Marxism involves a dialogue with non-Marxist theoretical and philosophical sources, such as Weber and Husserl, as well as anti-Enlightenment conservatives such as Nietzsche and Schopenhauer. Probably the most important non-Marxist influence is Freudian psychoanalysis, which sets up the Frankfurt School's suspicions towards labour practice as a model of human activity.

Social-theoretical positions

- In general, Frankfurt School Marxism holds that twentieth-century society has become a form of state capitalism, characterized by economic planning, bureaucratic management, cultural industries and conformist personalities, within which the individual is increasingly constrained to adapt to an administered society.
- Alongside considerable potential for authoritarian personality structures, the administered society promotes forms of individuality

that are dependent on authority, particularly through its industrial standardization of culture. Art has become a question of light entertainment rather than a representation of human possibilities, and with the exception of dissonant modernism, has lost its critical edge.

Philosophical implications

- Modernity depends upon a reification of reason itself, known as instrumental rationality. The principle of universal equivalence operating in commodity exchange (the reduction of material qualities to abstract quantities due to the monetarization of social relations) expresses itself through reason as an operation of classification, systematization and formalization, with the ultimate aim of the reduction of life to something calculable.
- Alternatives to instrumental reason may exist in unconscious instinctual forces linked to the life drive (Eros) or the most anticommercial forms of modernist art, which express the final inability of the natural human being to completely adapt to a repressive society, and are therefore the reservoir of hope in an otherwise grim situation.

five

Structural Marxism

Structural Marxism burst upon the radical 1960s as an aggressively polemical intellectual revolution, announcing that "theoretical anti-humanism" had finally arrived to claim possession of the vast continent of history discovered by Marx. Resolutely rejecting historical teleology, it constructed its bridgehead on the declaration that "history is a process without a subject or a goal" (Althusser 1976: 99), within which human beings acted only as bearers of structural functions. Bitterly resented, and generally misrepresented, Structural Marxism was one of the most fertile and inventive of the twentieth century's efforts to generate a renaissance in historical materialism, based around a principled rejection of the Hegelian legacy in Marxist historiography. Impressed by French psychoanalyst Jacques Lacan's structuralist-influenced "return to Freud", his compatriot, philosopher Louis Althusser, went for the same sort of angular recasting of social theory. The key to Marxism, Althusser maintained, was Marx's radical break with most of the things usually attributed to him, especially the proletariat as historical subject, the dialectical method and the base-and-superstructure model. Undeterred by the bewilderment and dismay that these declarations generated, Althusser's "return to Marx" proceeded apace, with a startling series of hitherto completely unknown categories – "structural causality", "imaginary relations", "absent cause", "epistemological break" – unveiled as the central discoveries of Marx.

Although the Structural Marxists agreed that social formations consisted of economic, political and ideological levels, they refused to accept that Marx had thought that the economic level always acted as the foundation for the other levels. The intention here was to conceptualize the relative autonomy of politics and ideology from economics, thereby avoiding vulgar Marxist economic reductionism. Seeking an alternative terminology to the base-and-superstructure metaphor, Althusser and co-thinkers described these as "structural instances", or "regional structures", rather than levels, and Althusser pointedly described the Marxian concept of the social formation as a "totality of [structural] instances articulated on the basis of a mode of production" (Althusser & Balibar 1970: 207 note 205). Accordingly, the research programme developed a concept of social formations as complex structured wholes and called for the development of regional theories of the economic, political and ideological "instances" for all of Marx's modes of production. Alongside Althusser, Étienne Balibar, Roger Establet and Jacques Rancière worked on the central categories of this structural rethinking of historical materialism, while, elsewhere, Nicos Poulantzas, Christine Buci-Glucksmann and Ernesto Laclau considered politics, Göran Therborn and Michèle Barrett investigated ideology, and Pierre Macherey and Terry Eagleton researched aesthetics. Always somewhat coy about their relation to the then-fashionable structuralism of figures such as Claude Lévi-Strauss, the Structural Marxists are best considered to be not structuralists, but structural-functionalists, operating with a novel form of functionalist methodology. Most recently, Robert Resch has produced a superb reconstruction of the entire programme that influences my presentation of Structural Marxism, and developed an innovative conception of agency from the Structural Marxist perspective (Resch 1992).

Unjustly, Althusser and co-thinkers have been accused of obscurantism and Stalinism. In truth, their insistence on the scientific status of Marxism mandated constant theoretical revision, with the consequence that they were anti-dogmatic. Their political stance within the powerful European communist parties was in opposition to the Stalinist leadership, for *theoretical* anti-humanism must not be confused with *practical* anti-humanitarianism (Elliott 1987). In fact, making a clear distinction between social science and political consciousness, Althusser and co-thinkers consistently advocated socialist humanism as the ideology of the communist movement (Althusser 1969: 221–47), at a moment when the political prospects for European socialism briefly flowered. It must not be forgotten that this was not an intellectual game, but a very serious political project with potentially dangerous consequences for theoretical mistakes. The conjuncture of the 1970s, reminiscent of the 1930s, was utterly different to today's situation of widespread apathy and bipartisan consensus on neoliberal governance. From the worldwide student revolts of 1968 onwards, a wave of mass mobilizations spread across Latin America and Asia, in the context of the Vietnam War. As military dictatorships supported by America and its NATO allies mushroomed in these areas to prevent the spread of left-wing governments, popular sentiment in Europe itself shifted to the Left. Before long there were massive protests against existing military regimes in Greece, Portugal and Spain, and support for the alliance of socialist and communist parties in France and Italy climbed sharply. The communist parties in western Europe decisively distanced themselves from the brutal repression happening in eastern Europe, especially in Czechoslovakia, and announced the advent of "Eurocommunism", a non-reformist sort of liberal socialism that intended to win power through parliamentary democracy. As centrally involved with the left wing of Eurocommunism, many of the Structural Marxists made an important contribution to this political strategy.

Theoretical practice and complex structures

For Althusser and co-thinkers, the break with Hegel's teleological conception of history involves a critique of economic reductionism. As we have seen, the classical interpretation of Marx's "1859 Preface" regards the superstructures as a space of ideological and political contingency, as opposed to the historical necessity acting through the economic foundation. Superstructural transformations only happen as a delayed result of infrastructural evolution, and politics and ideology are merely the forms in which historical agents become conscious and contest (accelerate or retard) this process. Accordingly, the teleology of classical Marxism fundamentally depends upon the idea that the historically necessary evolution of the economy is reflected in society as a whole "in the last instance". Althusser ridicules this simplification of society and history:

> The economic dialectic is never active *in the pure state*; in History, these instances, the superstructures, etc. are never seen to step respectfully aside when their work is done or, when the Time comes, as his pure phenomena, to scatter before His Majesty the Economy as he strides along the royal road of the Dialectic. From the first moment to the last, the lonely hour of the "last instance" never comes. (Althusser 1969: 113)

The economy never acts on its own, outside the global structure of social relations in which it is embedded, and to think otherwise is to think metaphysically, that is ideologically. Economics, politics, law and ideology always reciprocally influence one another, and Marxism, for Althusser, is the science of the totality of these structured interactions. In order to think through his complex alternative, Althusser freely appropriates structuralist theory, in particular the history of science produced by Gaston Bachelard and the structural anthropology of Claude Lévi-Strauss.

Bachelard supplies the idea that sciences emerge from non-scientific ideologies (e.g. Marxism from Hegel) through radical intellectual ruptures involving the formalization of concepts (Lecourt 1975). Sciences then develop through a series of further "epistemological breaks" that are reminiscent of the notion of paradigm shifts advocated by Thomas Kuhn. What Althusser calls "theoretical practice" involves the production of conceptual generalizations: the ideological raw materials which are the data of experience (Generalities I) are transformed through logical formalization and conceptual testing (Generalities II) to produce rigorous models of a theoretical object-domain (Generalities III; Althusser & Balibar 1970: 11–70). Althusser proposes that there is just such an epistemological break between the Hegelianism of the young Marx and the scientific socialism of the mature Marx. Accordingly, the significance of the shift from alienation to exploitation is that it marks the transition from ideological simplification to a theory of social complexity.

Lévi-Strauss provides a model for how a theoretical anti-humanism can yield startling insights into society. Where theoretical humanism concentrates on agents' interpretations of social practices, for instance asking Caduveo Indians about the meaning of their facial tattoos (they symbolize sub-group membership), theoretical anti-humanism locates social practices in the total functional context of the network of social relations. From this perspective, the Caduveo Indians' facial tattoos perform the ideological function of providing a medium for sub-group differentiation in a way that preserves the unity of the lineage structure (i.e. "tribal" unity; Lévi-Strauss 1968: 245–68). Structuralism breaks with the ideological image of the social formation as an organic totality ("society") that can be grasped by its individual members, and Althusser's central claim is that Marx arrived at just such a conception of society long before structuralism.

Althusser and co-thinkers therefore maintain that the fulcrum of "Marx's immense theoretical revolution" is not the base-and-superstructure model, but the structure of the social formation as a complex whole (Althusser & Balibar 1970: 182–93). Behind the some-times baroque terminology of Structural Marxism is an idea of singular brilliance. With the notion of extra-economic coercion in past societies, Marx had implied that the social relations determining exploitation in non-capitalist modes of production did not necessarily reside in the economic "base" of the social formation. Lapidary expressions, such as the quip that "the Middle Ages could not live on Catholicism, nor the ancient world on politics" (C1: 82), actually suggest that ideology and politics, respectively, are dominant regions of social life in feudalism and antiquity. Indeed, it appears that the key to the difference between ancient, feudal and capitalist modes of production actually reduces to the question of whether the economic, the political or the ideological dominates in the social formation. In the terminology of Structural Marxism, the social formation consists of (at least) three "structural instances", or "regional structures" – the economic, the political and the ideological. By "structure" is meant a functionally defined ensemble of many institutions and practices, and the complex structure of the social formation is the set of relations between these regional structures. The key to this is the question of which one of them is the dominant structure in the social formation, or "structure-in-dominance", because it is where the social relations are housed that make the exploitation of labour possible. This can be depicted abstractly by representing eco-nomics, politics and ideology with a letter (e, p, i) and rendering the structure-in-dominance in bold type:

Capitalism: **e**, p, i
Antiquity: e, **p**, i
Feudalism: e, p, **i**

But what is it that assigns to economics, politics or ideology the role of a structure-in-dominance? For Althusser, the intellectual epicentre of Marx's theoretical discovery is that the crucial connection that per-forms this "articulation" of economics, politics and ideology *itself resides in the economy*, in the set of relations governing the labour process. Unsurprisingly, this connection is the one between the productive forces and the relations of production, which Structural Marxism describes (with some terminological complications that are unimportant here) as a connection between the division of labour and property relations (Althusser & Balibar 1970: 212–14).

According to Althusser and Balibar, then, "the economy is determi-nant [only] in that it determines which of the instances of the social structure occupies the dominant place" (*ibid.*: 98–9, 224). The structure-in-dominance "distorts" the relational social field by imposing a hierarchy of effectiveness on the other structural instances, making some weak and others strong. It also transforms logically autonomous regional structures into *relatively* autonomous regions (Althusser 1969: 201–2). Certainly, the economic is dominant in capitalism, but this is a historical peculiarity. For Althusser, it is a characteristic of economic reductionism to believe in the eternal "primacy of the economy", based on the mistaken notion of the permanence of the structural dominance of the economic region (*ibid.*: 213).

Consequently, Marx *is* proposing "economic determination in the final instance", but this does not mean that the economic instance is the dominant instance in all social formations. That only *looks* like a paradox or a provocation because of the enormous intellectual hold that Marx's architectural metaphor has exercised on the radical imagination. According to Poulantzas's summary:

> By *mode of production*, we shall designate not what is generally marked out as the economic (i.e. relations of production in the strict sense), but a specific combination of various structures and practices, which, in combination, appear as so many instances or levels, i.e. as so many regional structures of this mode. ... Furthermore, the fact that the structure as a whole is determined in the last instance by the economic does not mean that the economic always holds the *dominant role* in the structure. The unity constituted by the structure-in-dominance implies that every mode of production has a dominant level or instance, but the economic is in fact determinant only insofar as it attributes the dominant role to one instance or another. ... Therefore, what distinguishes one mode of production from another and consequently specifies a mode of production is the particular form of articulation maintained by its levels: this articulation is henceforth referred to by the term *matrix* of a mode of production.   (Poulantzas 1973: 13–15)

Instead of the image of economic base and politico-ideological superstructure, then, the relation between mode of production and social formation is that of a *structural matrix* that determines the *asymmetrical relation* between structural levels of the social formation, by assigning to one instance the role of *structure-in-dominance* (Althusser & Balibar 1970: 319).

Mode of production and social formation

Structural Marxism's position is impossible to grasp if we insist on retaining the classical Marxist model of base-and-superstructure. Rather, the Structural Marxist concept of the mode of production and social formation yields the topology depicted in Figure 3.

The Althusserian problematic involves the effort to "rethink the idea of historical causality in terms of the matrix effect of a structured whole on its elements" (Resch 1992: 79). It does this primarily by conceptualizing causality not as something happening between entities, but as the consistency of a field of relations (Callinicos 1976: 52). This is possible because of Althusser's interpretation of "determination in the last instance" not as a historical thesis, but as a structural thesis in abstraction from historical development (Benton 1984: 17–18). The structural matrix of the mode of production is a principle of articulation connecting economics, politics, law (suppressed for clarity in the diagram) and ideology. There are several consequences of this position.

First, Structural Marxism focuses on social reproduction from a structural-functionalist perspective, which means that it concentrates on the structural mechanisms that maintain the basic functions of every social formation. These functions are the production of material life (economic structures), the maintenance of the unity of the social formation (political structures) and the provision of socialized individuals, or social subjects (ideological structures). These structures are integrated into a "complex whole" (Althusser & Balibar 1970: 188), because subordinate regional structures provide the material requirements, or "conditions of existence", for the structure-in-dominance. For instance, the capitalist mode of production is defined by the articulated combination of the wage relation (capitalist relations of production, namely the extraction of surplus value) and mechanized production (capitalist productive forces). The absence of extra-economic coercion means that the

Social formation: complex unity of a structure-in-dominance

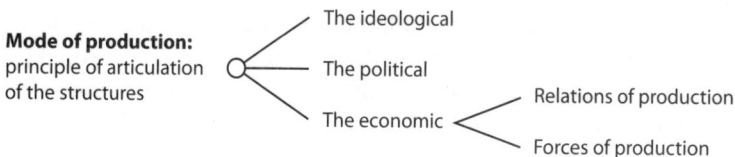

Mode of production: principle of articulation of the structures

- The ideological
- The political
- The economic
  - Relations of production
  - Forces of production

Figure 3 The structure of the complex whole (based on Jameson 1981: 36).

economic instance is the structure-in-dominance. But the accumulation of capital depends upon the reproduction of certain conditions of existence in the political (the institutional separation of politics and economics through the nation state), the juridical (contractual legal relations) and the ideological instances (the ideology of possessive individualism and the "isolation effect" of an ideological split between citizenship and class). Accordingly, in capitalism core regions of the political, juridical and ideological instances function as "conditions of existence" for the dominant, economic instance.

Second, the operation of this system of functionally defined and differentially related structures is what Structural Marxism describes as "structural causality". The best way to grasp structural causality is through Althusser and co-thinkers' polemic against the idea that the mode of production is the same as the economic structure. On the one hand, in a way, the mode of production is nothing more than a shorthand description of which regional structure is the structure-in-dominance. Accordingly, Althusser insists that the mode of production is the "absent cause" of the social formation, "present only in its effects". This is a striking, polemical formulation designed to combat the idea that the mode of production is some*thing* that can be localized in the social formation (e.g. His Majesty, the Economy). The mode of production is "immanent in its effects" within the social formation rather than located somewhere else. This means that "the whole existence of the structure consists of its effects, in short, it is merely a specific combination of its peculiar elements [and] is nothing outside its effects" (*ibid.*: 188). On the other hand, the mode of production performs an explanatory role, insofar as it is a specific combination of the division of labour and property relations that determines which regional structure is the structure-in-dominance. That is what is meant by saying that the mode of production acts as a matrix of constraints, or a structural "skeleton", by assigning a location and function to the structural instances, and defining their limits of variation consistent with the social reproduction of the complex whole (Hindess & Hirst 1975: 14–15).

Third, Structural Marxism focuses on the *relative autonomy* of the regional structures in the social formation. The relation between regional structures, their provision of conditions of existence for the structure-in-dominance, means that none of them can be sealed compartments. Instead, the general tendencies of economic development are influenced by developments in the political, juridical and ideological instances, and conversely, the developmental dynamics of the political, juridical and ideological instances are distorted by economic tendencies. On the

Structural Marxist conception, over time, the inter-relation of relatively autonomous regional structures is not automatic, so there is always potential for dysfunctionality between structures, and therefore socio-political crisis. Therefore, we pass from the deterministic universe of high structuralism and enter a *probabilistic* universe, where the exertion of structural constraints sets the probability of smooth social reproduction, on the lines of the concept of "structural selectivity" (Resch 1992: 309–14).

The complexity of the materialist dialectic

The relative autonomy of the regional structures means that a general theory of the social formation demands (at least) specific knowledge of economics, politics, law and ideology. Knowledge of society cannot be simplistically deduced from economic laws, as economic reductionism attempts to do. Indeed, Structural Marxism maintains that the distinct tendencies of the relatively autonomous regional structures results in uneven development in the social formation. "Unevenness is internal to the social formation", Althusser claims, "because [of] the structuration in dominance of the complex whole" (Althusser 1969: 213), and this results in different rates of historical change in the various structural instances.

For Althusser, the social formation is uneven and heterogeneous, consisting of the distinct evolutionary rate of different structural elements, which therefore have "differential histories". This concept of the "complex whole" is set up against the "homogeneous temporality" of both Hegelian dialectics and classical Marxism (Althusser & Balibar 1970: 99–100, 104–5). Ideological structures, for instance, are notorious for their glacial rate of development in relation to economic changes, producing the politically problematic "time lag" between economic crisis and class consciousness that we have already remarked upon several times in previous chapters. The differential rhythms of the discrete structural instances imply that the synchronic field of the social formation (the unity of a conjuncture) includes several distinct temporalities, destroying the unified present of the expressive "*Zeitgeist*". It is therefore necessary to theorize the specific historical temporality of every structural instance and its distinct social contradictions and rate of development (*ibid.*: 100). Instead of the homogeneous development of the entire social formation in a unified temporality, Althusser affirms that in a complex whole "it is no longer possible to think the process of development of the different levels of the whole in the same historical time" (*ibid.*: 99).

The notion of differential temporalities connects to another innovation of Structural Marxism, which is to think about the social formation as including many subordinate structures from other modes of production. Obviously, this is particularly important when considering semi-colonial countries, but it has wider application, for the metropolitan countries also include many structural remainders of vanquished modes. Because the concept of structural articulation extends "all the way down" into the regional structures of economics, law, politics and ideology (and others, such as aesthetics), the structural instances are potentially extraordinarily complex. They consist of internally complex, regional structures that form the organizing matrices for ensembles of institutional apparatuses, where the relative unity of a structural instance is determined by regionally dominant "substructures" (Poulantzas 1973: 115). If you like, this is the Structural Marxist equivalent to Trotsky's concept of "combined and uneven development", but it also includes the possibility that regional structures include substructures that anticipate a post-capitalist mode of production. The limit to the "higgledy-piggledy" nature of the regional structures in a complex social formation is the core areas of these, which provide the conditions of the existence for the structure-in-dominance – these must function smoothly, or risk social crisis.

Concepts of structural causality, relative autonomy and differential temporalities mean that, for Structural Marxism, historical development is a contingent sequence of disjunctive modes of production and not a logical series (a conceptual ascent) or the realization of a teleological principle. The best way to consider this idea of the unevenness and complexity of historical change is to regard the regional structures as composed of different sorts of practices, thus bringing together structure and practice with the rejection of historical teleology. Althusser specifies that "all the levels of social existence are the sites of distinct practices" (Althusser & Balibar 1970: 58); as Resch explains, "social structures are realized, reproduced and transformed through rule-bound yet open-ended *practices*" whose model is transformations effected by the labour process (Resch 1992: 36). Social practices are – as Resch explains – "rule-governed but open-ended" practices whose effect on the structure is potentially transformative (*ibid*.: 216–21, 309–18). In capitalist social formations:

> All practices are viewed by Structural Marxists as unevenly developed or "contradictory" [and] it is reasonable to generalise the contradictions in the various instances as follows. (1) In economic practice, contradictions exist between relations

of cooperation and exploitation within the labour process (the forces of production) and economic ownership (the social relations of production) … and these contradictions are manifest in the antagonistic class interests of the labourers and the exploiters of labour power, and take the form of struggles over control of the means of production (economic class struggles, the politics of production). (2) In political practices, contradictions exist between relations of representation and relations of hegemony, expressed in the antagonism between the "power bloc" – those classes and class-fractions that effectively control the institutions of collective social organisation – and the "masses" – other classes and class-fractions within the social formation lacking this institutional control. (3) In ideological practices, contradictions exist between relations of qualification (relations of empowerment that enable individuals to become effective social subjects) and relations of subjectification (relations restricting individuals to certain roles and specific capacities). (*Ibid*.: 37)

The social formation is conceptualized in terms of different sorts of local struggles happening, on the basis of contradictory practices, as it were, "all over the place". Althusser's concept of "over-determination" is intended to unify these otherwise discrete struggles, lending them the significance of *class* struggles. Now, over-determination is a term of art from Lacanian psychoanalysis that describes the way in which something happening at one level can be the effect of an intersecting multiplicity of causes originating at several other, different levels. Althusser insists that this is not just the pluralist idea that everything has multiple causes, because "the structure articulated in dominance that constitutes the unity of the complex whole [is reflected] within each contradiction" (Althusser 1969: 206). Frankly, that explanation is as clear as mud. Poulantzas's sometimes difficult idea of "social class" is an effort to specify exactly why the totality of economic, political and ideological practices represents *class* practice and *class* struggle. It therefore clarifies what is actually meant by over-determination.

Social classes and class practices

There is an essential preliminary step, though, for Structural Marxism's radical reconceptualization of the mode of production has implications for the very concept of class. In classical Marxism, classes are entities formed in production relations, that is economic classes, which have political interests and ideological representations of their social identity. But Poulantzas thinks of classes as effects of the structural whole, rather than positions in economic production alone, so that classes are the result of a "triple determination" by economic, political and ideological structures (Poulantzas 1973: 64). Although "the economic place of the social agents has a principal role in determining social classes", politics and ideology are part of the "objective determination" of class location (Poulantzas 1975: 14). He rejects the classical approach as a mere sociological aggregate of occupational positions and dismisses equation of class with class-consciousness, that is a social identity conditioned by ideological unity, as the idea that individuals are somehow assigned class "number plates" (Poulantzas 1973: 202). Although the economic determination of waged, productive labour is primary, political determinations of supervisory role and ideological determinations of educational qualification participate in the definition of the proletariat and other strata. The basic effect of this argument is to acknowledge that the proletariat, defined as unskilled manual, non-supervisory workers who produce surplus-value directly, is a tiny minority of the population. It is surrounded by a vast ensemble of "social categories" (e.g. the intelligentsia) and "social strata" (e.g. the labour aristocracy), who make up the new middle strata, the vast majority of the population in the industrialized democracies. The capitalist class, meanwhile, is likewise fragmented into numerous "autonomous fractions", so that no fundamental class of production in modern society can possibly become hegemonic except through a social alliance.

What Poulantzas calls *social* class is not a different set of persons alongside his economically, politically and ideologically defined classes and strata. Rather, it is an effort to describe the class significance of the antagonistic field of social practices and local struggles at any moment in a social formation. This is potentially confusing, and best imagined as a mobile "superstructure" of antagonistic relations arising on the "foundation" of the objective determination of class location by the complex whole. If the regional structures of the social formation are driven by practical antagonisms – labour versus ownership, masses versus power bloc, empowerment versus subjectification – then at any time there is a global relation of forces across the complex whole, resulting from the social struggles happening at a vast multiplicity of points. Social class describes the overall opposition resulting from this situation. But how does this work?

According to Poulantzas, the field of conflicts over practices – a field traversed by the political conflicts of social classes – is distinct from the complex structure of the social formation. Indeed, it seems that the field of practical struggles, the arena of the "lived experience" of structural conditions which he confusingly describes as "social relations", rises up as a superstructure on the infrastructural basis of the social formation. "Social classes do not present themselves as the effect of one particular structural level ... i.e., as the effect of the economic structure on the political or ideological". Instead, they "manifest themselves ... entirely as the global effect of the structures in the field of social relations which, in class societies, themselves involve the distribution of agents/supports to social classes" (Poulantzas 1973: 64). For Engels, historical events happen as the result of a "parallelogram" of forces, representing the sum of many individual actions in a conjuncture. The historical event is the "resultant", irreducible either to the intentions of agents or the contextual determinants forming the terrain on which the event happens. It is in this context that Engels speaks of economic determination in the last instance. But we have seen that Structural Marxism interprets this as a structural thesis and not as an historical explanation. The concept of social class as the effect of the totality of social practices is the Structural Marxist replacement for Engels's idea, designed to preserve the claim that class struggle is the motor of history, without relapsing into the economic reductionist version of this hypothesis. To use a metaphor that Poulantzas employs, the complex whole of the social formation provides the terrain on which social agents, whose action is limited but not automatic, move, and in their movement, these agents transform or maintain that terrain:

> Social class is a concept which shows the effect of the ensemble of structures, of the matrix of a mode of production ... on the agents which constitute its supports: this concept reveals the effects of the global structure in the field of social relations. ... Social classes do not cover structural instances but social relations: these social relations consist of class practices, which means that social classes are conceivable only in terms of class practices. [These] relations consist of class practices in which social classes are placed in *oppositions*: social classes can be conceived only as class practices, these practices existing only in oppositions *which in their unity constitute the field of the class struggle.* (Poulantzas 1973: 67, 86)

That is rather convoluted, to say the least. I am going to clarify it with another metaphor. The terrain of a structural region creates many potential sites of conflict. But some of these conflict sites are critical to the survival of the structure-in-dominance, because they are locations that provide its conditions of existence. The terrain of a structural region therefore sets up a game of "capture the flag" (that is preserve or alter the social practices that reproduce the conditions of existence of the structure-in-dominance), which players in various conflicts are involved in whether they know it or not. The presence of the "flag" polarizes social conflict happening on the terrain of a regional structure. The sum total of the balance of forces in struggles for the economic, political, juridical and ideological (and other) "flags" has a class significance, because social reproduction and therefore the preservation of a mode of production is in question. Accordingly, there is a strategic–relational tension across the practical struggles on the terrains of the social formation, and the distribution of forces to either side of this antagonistic "game" is what social classes are. Social class, as an effect of the structured multiplicity of contradictory practices, is therefore inseparable from class struggle, although what this means is very different from the classical picture. Not only do the shifting fortunes of the struggle over social practices (the class struggle) alter the boundaries of social classes, but despite the effect of structural determinations in fixing the horizon of the class struggle, social class interests cannot be mechanically deduced from the structure. Instead, Poulantzas conceptualizes social class interests as formed within the "horizon of action" of possible structural transformations and therefore fundamentally determined by the material possibilities for new articulations in the political conjuncture (*ibid.*: 64).

Social class is therefore not fundamentally a new, broader definition of class as a set of structural locations that define material interests, as in the classical picture. Rather, it is a (terminologically confusing) description of how historical change is really the effect of class struggle, that is an effort to explain what over-determination actually means. The idea of social class mandates a political summary of the balance of forces involved in social struggles across the social formation at any moment, that is a summary of the conjuncture, in terms of the forces for structural transformation versus the forces for social reproduction. In this context, Poulantzas speaks of the capacity to introduce new structural elements in a strategic-relational field of contestation. Ultimately, the strategic stake here is the introduction of elements of a post-capitalist mode of production into the complex whole, with the effect of breaking up the unity of the capitalist social formation. This provides a new definition of socialist strategy that does not rely on social classes as "subjects of history", and which therefore seeks to defend the idea of class struggle as the dynamic of history without reintroducing historical teleology. Historical change happens as a result of a myriad of interventions in localized contexts on the basis of "lived experience", that is as social practices in the *habitus*, or social space, of individuated subjects (Resch 1992: 322–5).

The specificity of the political

Social class, it has to be said, never really caught on as a contribution to social theory. Instead, acknowledgement of the need for social alliances in contemporary capitalism went hand-in-hand with the recognition that the structural location of individual agents was potentially very complex indeed. Classes were not just economically, politically and ideologically fragmented. They were also impacted by a variety of other structural determinations, such as race and gender. Perhaps for this reason, Structural Marxism increasingly confronted the question of socialist strategy on the terrain of politics and ideology, in the context of institutional struggles and popular alliances. Structural Marxists such as Christine Buci-Glucksman of Italy (Buci-Glucksmann 1980) and Ernesto Laclau of Argentina (Laclau 1977) were ideally placed to rethink the Marxist conceptualization of the capitalist state as an internally complex regional structure, with its own historical development and practical contradictions. But it is Poulantzas's *Political Power and Social Class* (1973) that determines their approach, and his *State, Power, Socialism* (1978) that best defines the strategic consequences flowing from this.

According to Poulantzas, the state is central to "the sense of the cohesion of the ensemble of the levels of a complex unity, and is the regulating factor of its global equilibrium as a system" (Poulantzas 1973: 45). In other words, the social function of the regional structure of the political, within the *general* theory of historical materialism, is to secure the unity of the social formation (*ibid*. 37–56). Although politics, functionally defined, is everywhere, a dimension of every social practice, the political structural instance – the state – is the key to maintaining social reproduction. Political struggles therefore tend to condense on the terrain of the political instance, which in the capitalist mode of production takes the institutional form of the nation state, and is defined by the regional contradiction between relations of representation and relations of domination (Resch 1992: 37, 308–64). The maintenance of the structural integrity of the social formation means protection of the structure-in-dominance. Therefore, every state is a *class* state insofar as maintenance of the social formation means protection of its defining property relations (Poulantzas 1973: 54).Turning to specifically capitalist social formations, Poulantzas investigates the peculiarity of the capitalist state, namely its institutional separation from economics. Within the *particular* theory of the capitalist mode of production, the relative autonomy of the political instance from the economic is a consequence of the absence of extra-economic coercion in capitalist production (*ibid.*: 123–41). To develop this *regional* theory of the relative autonomy of the state, Poulantzas requires an analysis of the effects of the state in unifying the power bloc and isolating economic from political struggles (*ibid.*: 190–94). The "isolation effect" requires that the capitalist state is not the instrument of the dominant class, but instead, as a national-popular state, appears as the neutral-universal instance where hegemonic leadership is exercised. Consequently, both the state form and its regime of government incorporate concessions to a vast network of popular struggles and accommodate the shifting balance of forces within the hegemonic alliance itself. Finally, Poulantzas shifts to the *conjunctural* analysis of specific class political practices within the institutional apparatuses of the state (*ibid.*: 229–53). This movement – from abstract functions to concrete structural analysis – introduces economic and ideological determinants of the state into the regional theory (*ibid.*: 130–41) and investigates the practices of social classes (defined as complexes of economic, political and ideological determinants in a relation of forces) on the strategic terrain of the state institutions (*ibid.*: 195–224).

Poulantzas argues that state power is, in the *final* analysis, class power (*ibid.*: 99–121), and that – as he later expresses it – the state apparatus represents the material condensation of a balance of social forces (Poulantzas 1978: 123–62). This seeks to combine a strategic-relational concept of political power, as the capacity to act in opposition to a social antagonist (to make a difference, that is to introduce a new structural element), with the Marxist concept of the social whole (Jessop 1985: 115–47). Because of its functional role in maintaining the unity of the social formation, the state condenses power. The state constitutes the "strategic point where the various contradictions fuse" (Poulantzas 1973: 43). One consequence of this thesis is that the multiplicity of social struggles are *in the final analysis* class struggles, because the function of the institutional apparatuses of the capitalist state is to unify and condense social protest into specifically political oppositions. The specificity of the political therefore refers to two things: a non-instrumental theory of the state and the idea that politics is site of social transformations. Poulantzas concludes that:

> it is from this relation between the state as the cohesive factor of a formation's unity and the state as the place in which the various contradictions of the instances are condensed that we can decipher the problem of the relation between politics and history. This relation designates the political struggle as the "motive power of history". (*Ibid.*: 45)

Against this intellectual background, *State, Power, Socialism* argues for non-reformist structural transformations within a strategic-relational, that is social class, perspective on politics. The state is grasped as an institutional ensemble (including executive, legislative, juridical and ideological arms) that can be broken apart by popular mobilizations and strategic transformations. Accordingly, the state is not "smashed", but simultaneously dismantled and rearranged, through a combination of parliamentary legislation, sweeping democratization of the state bureaucracy, popular organs of political participation, and radical transformations of the army and police that would include the replacement of elite specialized bodies with the populace under arms.

Ideological interpellation

Probably the most influential innovation within Structural Marxism is Althusser's reconceptualization of ideology. Althusser rejects the critical conception of ideology as false consciousness and proposes that, instead, "ideology represents the imaginary relationship of individuals to their real conditions of existence" (Althusser 1971: 162). Maintaining that *no* society, including communism, can dispense with an ideological instance, he describes ideology as a "system of representations" or "world outlook" (Althusser 1969: 231–2). Ideologies can be true or false, he claims, but in all cases they are the opposite of science, because of their subject-centred character, designed to recruit agents to a worldview rather than to explain the world scientifically as a "process without a subject or a goal". A prime example of a true ideology in this sense is in fact the left-wing Hegelianism of the young Marx, with its proletarian subject of world history and historical teleology (*ibid.*: 51–86).

But in actuality, this is a more complex idea than it appears, for "Imaginary" is a term of art from Lacanian psychoanalysis that is roughly coextensive with the Freudian concept of the ego. For Freud, a lot of the ego is in fact unconscious, and the implication is that ideology is not "false consciousness", but an unconscious naturalization of the individual's learnt perception of the world. Indeed, in his initial formulation of the theory of ideology in *For Marx*, Althusser immediately qualifies his description of ideology as a system of representations by saying that these representations are "profoundly unconscious" (*ibid*.: 233). In reality, ideology is *lived experience*, that is the way in which the socialized ego makes elementary sense of the phenomenal world through commonsense ideas and habituated perceptions. In particular, in the lived experience of everyday routines, individuals "recognize" one another as, say, free persons with basic rights, or God's creatures cast in the image of their Creator, and this set of perceptions seems to them as natural as their own egos seem unified. Psychoanalysis argues that these assumptions are the result of socialization, fundamentally dependent on the internalization of an image of authority into the self, in the form of the superego, which becomes the voice of conscience, policing the ego's conformity to social norms. When Althusser says, then, that ideology generates social subjects and fits them to functional roles, this means that ideology operates at the most basic levels of personality formation, long before it is explicitly codified as a philosophical statement, or "world outlook". This perhaps clarifies what is at stake when Althusser claims that "what is represented in ideology is therefore not the system of real relations which govern the existence of individuals, but the imaginary relation of those individuals to the real conditions in which they live" (Althusser 1971: 165).

Initially, Althusser had proposed that ideology, as the commonsense construction of lived experience, was the "cement" that maintains social reproduction, and it seemed to emanate from everywhere and nowhere. This position effectively theorises social subjects as mindless drones of the reigning social order and prevents the emergence of social agents capable of initiating revolutionary transformations of the structure (Benton 1984: 96–107; Hirst 1976: 385–411). The events of May 1968, when student protests triggered a general strike in France that brought the government down, catalysed Althusser's abandonment of this bias towards the automatic reproduction of the social formation.

In his celebrated essay on "ideological state apparatuses" (or ISAs) in *Lenin and Philosophy*, Althusser (1971: 127–86) reconsiders the problem. He investigates the formation of socialized individuals through their recruitment (or "interpellation") by ideologies, which are propagated through institutions. Althusser's ISAs essay proposes that ideology inserts biological individuals into forms of social subjectivity with different types of political agency. He contends that "ideology has the function (*which defines it*) of 'constituting' concrete individuals as subjects" (*ibid.*: 171; emphasis added). Althusser claims:

> Every human cannot be the agent of a practice unless he takes the form of a subject. The "subject form" is in fact the form that the historical existence of every individual, every agent of social practice, takes: for the relations of production and reproduction necessarily involve ... ideological social relations which, in order to function, impose on every individual agent the form of a subject. (Althusser 1976: 95)

A human person (a biological individual) is not an *agent* without an imaginary relation to the real conditions of existence, which is to say, without a socialized ego. Social practice requires a socialized subject and this socializsation takes the form of ideological "interpellation". "Concrete subjects only exist insofar as they are supported by a concrete individual [and] ideology ... transforms the individuals into subjects (it transforms them all) by that very precise operation ... called interpellation" (Althusser 1971: 174). Althusser likens this process to the hailing of a person by the police ("hey, you!"): as the person spins around and "recognizes" himself or herself as hailed, they at once become an individual citizen and subject themselves to the discipline of the state.

For Althusser, despite the advent of modernity, religion remains the exemplary instance of ideological interpellation. The discourse of religion creates social subjects by positioning them within a body of representations whose major doctrine is that "humanity is made in the image of God" (Althusser 1971: 178). With the rise of modernity, what Althusser calls the "School–Family couplet" replaced the church as the major locus of subject formation and so social subjects "recognize" one another in the image of the liberal distinction between public citizen and private person. This alters the *content* of ideological representations, but not their *form*, which remains paradigmatically religious. As Alex Callinicos explains, "ideology is the way in which men and women are formed in order to participate in a process of which they are not the makers, and ideology performs this function by giving them the illusion that history was made for them" (Callinicos 1976: 70). In this context, Althusser defines ideology as both recognition (it is "obvious" that we are subjects and recognize one another on this basis) and misrecognition (of the structural conditions of the public/private distinction; Althusser 1971: 172, 183).

The ambition of this reconceptualization is to explore the political implications of ideological struggle: at a stroke, social reproduction becomes something politically contested (Benton 1984: 96–107; Resch 1992: 208–13). In effect, Althusser tries to accommodate the existence of bourgeois and proletarian ideologies, transforming the conception of a dominant ideology into the thesis of a *hegemonic* ideology. Although Althusser only discusses the dominant ideology and the state apparatuses, the implication is that this theory is a contribution to the formation of an anti-capitalist social alliance. The idea is that in opposition to possessive individualism, communist militants will promulgate a socialist humanist ideology through such institutions as schools and universities, trades unions and social movements, thereby recruiting to the revolutionary movement.

Ideological state apparatuses

The idea of a hegemonic ideology confronted by counter-hegemonic ideologies connects, in Althusser's treatment, with a determined effort to break with the conception of the "ruling ideas" as a free-floating body of representations lacking an institutional location. Althusser proposes in the second major thesis of the ISAs essay that "ideology has a material existence" (Althusser 1971: 165). Breaking with the distinction between ideas and action, Althusser proposes to "talk of actions inserted into practices … governed by the rituals in which these practices are inscribed, within the material existence of an ideological apparatus" (*ibid.*: 168). Because religion is the paradigm of ideology, Althusser turns to the cynical discussion of religion by French philosopher Blaise Pascal, for whom religious beliefs are the result of indoctrination, rather than conversion. Pascal's formula, "kneel down and you will believe" – in other words, participate in the institutional ritual and religious faith will follow – indicates, as far as Althusser is concerned, the real nature of ideological convictions. He argues that ideology is the result of a process of conformity to institutional routines and habituated practices. Ideologies are forms of social subjectivity that belong to the agency required to perform socially normal functions, rather than being primarily doctrinal abstractions or grand ideals. Accordingly, Althusser proposes that ideas themselves are "material actions inserted into material practices governed by material rituals which are themselves defined by the material ideological apparatus from which derive the ideas of the subject" (*ibid.*: 169). The talismanic repetition of "material" is designed to banish "ideas" and replace them with institutionalized practices of subject formation (*ibid.*: 169), for "there is no practice except in and by an ideology [and] there is no ideology except by the subject and for subjects" (*ibid.*: 170).

Despite the centrality of the educational system to ideological inculcation, what Althusser calls ideological state apparatuses are not restricted to the sphere of the state and its semi-governmental organizations. To the contrary: the major illustrations of the concept of the ISAs offered by Althusser, aside from universities and schools, are drawn from the "private" sphere of civil society. These include the church, trade unions, the family, the mass media, political parties and cultural practices. Following Gramsci, Althusser contends that the political hegemony of the ruling class can be functionally differentiated into the RSAs ("repressive state apparatuses", which function predominantly by the exercise of coercion, namely police, army and the apparatus of punishment) and the ISAs, where the dominant ideology is institutionalized in a multiplicity of state and non-state locations. Althusser specifies that:

> (1) all state apparatuses employ both ideology and repression, but the distinction between ISAs and RSAs relates to the relative proportions present in the different apparatuses; (2) the ISAs have a relative autonomy and a dispersed multiplicity as opposed to the unified consistency of the RSAs; (3) the sole unity of the ISAs is secured by the dominant ideology.
> (*Ibid.*: 149)

Althusser's conception of ideological state apparatuses tends to suggest that despite the diversity of ideological practices and institutional sites, ranging from the education system to the church and family, the "ideological state apparatuses" are unified by means of the dominant ideology. The reason why these are said to be "state" apparatuses, however, is not particularly clear. Althusser appears to be collapsing civil society into the nation state in a way that is not really very helpful. What is clear, however, is that the intent of this discussion is to support the Eurocommunist "long march through the institutions" (Anderson 1976: 33–7). It advocates the capture of the various "state" apparatuses of an ideological kind and their re-functioning, from forums for the dominant ideology into vehicles for counter-hegemony. Nonetheless, ideology and politics tend in the ISA's essay to collapse into one another: ideology becomes an appendage of the state while the hegemonic class acquires a monolithic aura (Resch 1992: 36).

By contrast, Göran Therborn drops the confusing ascription of ideology to the state, introducing a new opposition between "ideological apparatuses" and "ideological counter-apparatuses". He maintains that contradictions within the process of subject-formation spring from the requirement that ideology must generate a correspondence between two processes. Individuals are "subjected" to a social arrangement through the inhibition of drives and the formation of capacities. They are also "qualified" to perform certain roles in social life that can include critical reflection and transformative action. When subjection and qualification fail to correspond, Therborn argues, "the effects of a contradiction between subjection and qualification are opposition and revolt, or under-performance and withdrawal" (Therborn 1980: 17). The ensemble of structural determinations, exerted by economic and political relations, over-determines the contradictions of the interpellation process, so that the contradiction between subjection and qualification is not isolated from contradictions of domination and exploitation (ibid.: 45–6). The concept of material contradictions in the ideological apparatuses, and the existence of socio-political antagonisms between ideological apparatuses and counter-apparatuses, lends theoretical substance to the claim that the material existence of ideology enables conceptualization of ideological class struggle (ibid.: 86). Second, and perhaps more interesting, Therborn recasts the characterization of ideology so that it goes beyond a description of how subjects are fitted to functional roles. In a chapter entitled "The Ideological Universe: Dimensions of Human Subjectivity", he proposes that ideology has both historical–social and existential–personal aspects. Where the former category is well understood in Marxism, under the heading of "class ideologies", the latter, which are essential for subjects' experience of the world as a meaningful space for personal development and social action, have yet to be fully grasped by historical materialism. Religion is the key example of an existential ideology providing an explanation of "the meaning of life, death, suffering, the cosmos and the natural order" (ibid.: 23). Gender is another, and although Therborn has been highly active in the investigation of this field, we now turn to the striking contribution of Michèle Barrett for an example of how Structural Marxism handles women's liberation.

Women's oppression and structural articulation

The advantages of Structural Marxism are on display in Barrett's *Women's Oppression Today* (1980). Her fundamental claim is that the nuclear family represents a survival from pre-capitalist modes of production that is both ideological and economic in character. What Barrett describes as the ideological–economic unit of the "family-household" is structurally articulated to capitalist regional structures, in a classic instance of the Structural Marxist interpretation of combined and uneven development. But she insists that this articulation is historically contingent, shaped by social struggles in the nineteenth century, and that the insertion of the pre-capitalist family-household into capitalist relations has modified its structure and functioning at both economic and ideological levels.

Barrett arrives at this position on the basis of an exhaustive review of two major debates in socialism and feminism. The first is the "domestic labour debate", concerned with the question of why a gender-segregated division of labour, which assigns women to domestic labour and to a relatively unskilled and underpaid segment of the labour market, exists in capitalism (Barrett 1980: 152–86). In general (at least in the 1970s and 1980s), female domestic labour and the socialization of children is unproductive (i.e. non-value producing) work that reproduces the labour power of the male breadwinner. Women entering the labour force must often continue to perform these tasks even as they work for a wage or salary, and female wages continue to be only about 66 per cent of the male wage in a similar industry. But the conclusion that Barrett draws from this debate is that it cannot be definitively demonstrated that privatized reproduction of labour power through the family unit is a necessary consequence of the combination of private property and wage labour. Capitalism could equally well be organized on the basis of the commercialization of domestic labour and child-rearing services, with women in full employment and without a gender-segmented labour market. She therefore argues that the current situation is the consequence of historical factors, and specifically of the way in which the pre-capitalist family-household was integrated into capitalism.

Up until the eighteenth century, the family-household was a unit of economic production as well as essential to the reproduction of the labour force. Capitalism reorganized economic production on the basis of private property, creating public, waged labour, and split this off from the residual private, domestic labour in the reproduction of the workforce, which continued to be done in the family-household unit. This had contradictory effects. On the one hand, it reduced the available supply of wage workers, by excluding half of the potential labour pool, and this resulted in the ability of mainly male trade unions to successfully struggle in the nineteenth century for wage rises. From the perspective of an individual entrepreneur, then, the persistence of the privatized reproduction of labour power through the family-household structure is irrational, because relatively expensive. On the other hand, though, this gender segregation divided the working class, with the trade unions often vigorously campaigning to keep women in the home on the basis that female workers undercut the male breadwinner. Many socialists reinforced this politically regressive line, not least through the invisibility of domestic labour as a theoretical category of importance in the analysis of the division of labour. From the perspective of the capitalist class as a whole, then, the persistence of the family-household structure has extraordinarily beneficial political effects in dividing and disorganizing united resistance to capitalism.

The second debate concerns the question of "capitalist patriarchy", the hypothesized existence of a dual structure in contemporary societies that combines capitalist economic exploitation with masculine domination organized culturally. Barrett does not for a moment doubt that male dominance exists or that it involves not just material privileges for men, and the assumed universality and neutrality of masculinity as the paradigm of what is human, but also a series of extremely negative ideological stereotypes. These extend all the way down, from the cultural denigration of femininity as inferior and the disgraceful exploitation of women in the cultural industries, to the internalization of negative associations around feminine sexuality in the socialization of boys and girls. But she argues that a dualist framework naturalizes the division between male–public and female–domestic labour. It also fails to explain the *interconnections* between capitalist exploitation and masculine domination. Radical as it might sound, "capitalist patriarchy" continues to frame the question of the division of labour in male-centred terms and neglects the functional integration of the nuclear family into capitalist societies.

Barrett's alternative takes advantage of Althusser's reconceptualization of ideology as institutionalized rituals that have the effect of generating forms of social subjectivity. The family, she proposes, is foremost an institutionally organized set of social practices whose effect is *gender*, the culturally defined roles of and hierarchical distinction between masculine and feminine. By allocating these culturally determined characteristics to individuals who are sexually male or female, familial ideology reproduces the gender segmentation of the division of labour and the cultural privileges of masculinity. It also naturalizes these by making it appear that they are automatic consequences of reproductive biology. Barrett takes up Althusser's suggestion that under capitalism, the central ideological structure is the "School–Family" apparatus. She contends that "the oppression of women, although not a functional prerequisite of capitalism, has acquired a material basis in the relations of production and reproduction of capitalism today" (Barrett 1980: 249).

Furthermore, Barrett maintains, following Althusser, the ideological naturalization of cultural gender roles is deeply unconscious. Although sharply critical of Althusser's limited technical understanding of psychoanalysis (Barrett 1993), she agrees with his underlying approach. "Gender identity and the ideology of the family", Barrett proposes, in line with psychoanalytic conceptions of the self, "are embedded in our very subjectivity and our desires at a far more profound level than 'false consciousness'" (Barrett 1980: 226). Gender ideology has a sufficiently deep hold on individuals' sense of themselves to manage to perpetuate deep divisions, despite the relatively "sex-blind" operations of the market. Barrett concludes that:

> These divisions are systematically embedded in the structure and texture of capitalist social relations in Britain and they play an important part in the political and ideological stability of this society. They are constitutive of our subjectivity as well as, in part, of capitalist political and cultural hegemony. They are interwoven into a fundamental relationship between the wage-labour system and the organization of domestic life, and it is impossible to imagine that they could be extracted from the relations of production and reproduction of capitalism without a massive transformation of those relations taking place. Hence, the slogan "No women's liberation without socialism; no socialism without women's liberation" is more than a pious hope.
> (*Ibid.*: 254–5)

Structural Marxism and Eurocommunism

What has been described as the Eurocommunist "long march through the institutions" involved the effort to capture positions in the state, universities and media, as well as labour parties, trades unions, social movements and church groups, in order to transform these institutions. Most of the leading thinkers of Structural Marxism in the 1970s were members of the mass-based communist parties of France, Italy, Spain and Greece, and many of them supported the shift in these parties from Stalinist politics to the politics of Eurocommunism. The Eurocommunist movement represented an effort to rethink socialist strategy as a prolonged, democratic struggle for "structural reforms", rather than an insurrectionary surge. The "historic compromise" with parliamentary democracy that this reflected involved the acknowledgement that liberal conceptions of liberty, equality and rights represented not just mass ("false") consciousness, but historic gains for the popular masses, not lightly to be thrown away. The Leninist strategy of popular insurrection against the bourgeois state was replaced by a policy of protracted democratic contestation for electoral hegemony (Antonian 1987: 117–35). Socialist transition was reconceptualized as an entire historical stage of "advanced democracy", characterized by the shifting equilibrium between social forces struggling around a new social order (Claudin 1978: 122–65).

The Eurocommunist idea of socialism was that of a "revolution in liberty", that is an extension and deepening of democratic processes through the democratization of society, and a revolution that would preserve negative liberty even as it strove for positive freedom. Substantively, Eurocommunism involved three major elements:

1. The *transformation of the vanguard party* into a mass formation capable of participating in alliance politics with equal partners in a democratic front.
2. The *democratization and decentralization of the state*, through the extension of parliamentary control over the state-apparatus, linked to the *abandonment of the dictatorship of the proletariat* for *liberal socialism*.
3. Abandonment of the *command economy* for *market socialism*, conceptualized as a democratically planned mixed economy including workers' self-management (Boggs 1982; Carrillo 1978; Claudin 1978).

The strategy of Eurocommunism during the 1970s embraced the full implications of democratic politics including the negotiated formulation of joint programmes representing political compromises and therefore rejected the popular front led by the proletarian party. Instead, it advocated the norm of regular alternation of governing parties involved in political competition as part of a multi-class transitional strategy (Napolitano 1977).

Within the Eurocommunist movement, the left-wing opposition – including theoreticians such as Althusser, Balibar, Buci-Glucksmann (Buci-Glucksmann 1980) and Poulantzas (Poulantzas 1978) – promoted the strategy of combining democratic politics with mass mobilizations (Antonian 1987). For many of the Structural Marxists, the communist parties had not developed a democratic political practice that might recognize the legitimacy of representative democracy while avoiding the trap of piecemeal parliamentary reformism. But radicals were not able to develop forms of participatory democracy supported by a mass movement that might counter-balance the potentially conservatizing effects of participation in liberal-democratic governments (Poulantzas 1978; Weber 1978). Although the left Eurocommunists (especially Fernando Claudin, Pietro Ingrao, Lucio Magri, Rossanna Rossanda, Nicos Poulantzas and Étienne Balibar) struggled for their theoretical alternative and political strategy within the Eurocommunist movement, the right retained a solid majority throughout (Antonian 1987: 87–102).

By the mid-1980s, Eurocommunism had conclusively failed to realize its potential. Structural Marxism, meanwhile, was in deep difficulties. Leading members experienced insanity or committed suicide (Althusser, Poulantzas), and many drifted away intellectually under the impact of the post-structuralist critique of the concept of structure as a whole. The Structural Marxists never resolved the central problem with the entire programme, its persistent normative deficit perfectly expressed through the contradictory call for theoretical anti-humanism and practical humanism. The problems with transforming moral and political values into reflexes of the social structure hardly need restatement. In effect, this is likely to result in a cynically manipulative relation to practical struggles, or, at best, a wretched consequentialism of the "greatest good for the greatest number". Not surprisingly, Structural Marxism only had a very weak response to the rise of the New Philosophy in the 1980s, a right-wing movement in thought promoting the idea that everything beyond a militant defence of human rights leads automatically to the Stalinist Gulag. The collapse of historical Communism and the disintegration of the communist parties lay on the horizon, alongside the transformation of most politicians in the world into miniaturized versions of Margaret Thatcher. Marxism as a whole was about to become something that you provided a good alibi for, rather than something you contributed fresh ideas to.

Summary of key points

Theoretical revolutions

- Theoretical anti-humanism involves the structural-functionalist perspective on individuals as "bearers" of social roles, in a complex functional differentiation of institutions whose effect is to ensure social reproduction, that is the maintenance of the social whole.
- From this perspective, "history is a process without a subject or a goal": historical change happens because of structural mutations, which occur as a result of dysfunctionality creeping into the relations between institutions as a consequence of the complexity of the social formation.
- The centrality of the Marxist concept of social practice modelled on the labour process is retained, in the context of a radical rethinking of social structure designed to highlight the "relative autonomy" of Marx's economic, political and ideological "levels" of society.

Social complexity and differential histories

- Instead of the base-and-superstructure model, the social formation is conceptualized as a totality of structural instances, or regional structures linking a multiplicity of functionally related institutions, articulated by the mode of production.
- The mode of production assigns to one of the structural instances (the economic, the political, the ideological) the role of structure-in-dominance, while other instances provide its conditions of existence.
- Although the structural instances are inter-related by the effects of the structure-in-dominance, they each have their own defining practices and determinate contradictions, and they evolve according to different internal dynamics with a distinctive "temporality", or rate of development.

Class politics and class struggle

- The relation between an internal rate of development within a structural instance and the interfering effects of the structure-in-dominance and other structures on this particular evolutionary path is thought of descriptively in terms of "over-determination", which under capitalism means the displacement into ideology or the condensation into politics of economic antagonisms.

- "Social classes" (with shifting boundaries) are the result of a balance of forces that can be summed up across the entire social formation, based on the state of play around contested practices in each of the structural instances, in a global antagonism between struggles for social reproduction versus struggles for social transformation.

- "Social classes" are not to be confused with the idea of classes of production, defined as structural locations in the social formation, which are said to have economic, political and ideological determinants of identity.

State politics, ideological hegemony and revolutionary strategy

- The political instance is defined as the ensemble of institutions dedicated to the maintenance of the unity of the social formation, centred on the state as the apparatus where power is concentrated and legitimized. Nonetheless, the nation state under capitalism is not theorized as a monolithic unity, but rather as itself an ensemble of institutions (executive, legislative, juridical and ideological) susceptible to fracturing under popular pressure.

- Ideology is radically redefined through the description of lived experience as an "imaginary relation" to social structures. Ideology depends on the internalization of institutional rituals during an individual's socialization, transformation of the "ideological state apparatuses" the key to ideological hegemony.

- Ideology as an unconscious relation to social structures is illustrated by the gender division between men and women, produced by the family structure, a legacy of pre-capitalist modes of production that has been articulated into capitalism at the levels of economics (through domestic labour) and ideology (through gender roles).

- Socialist strategy is reconceptualized as a protracted struggle for "advanced democracy" in capitalist social formations, during which progressive forces strive to transform existing structures into post-capitalist institutional arrangements.

six

Analytical Marxism

The reconstruction of Marxism essayed by a loose collective of thinkers in the US and the UK since the 1970s is best described as "analytical Marxism". This is a designation that captures members' allegiance to an "analytically sophisticated Marxism", based on "wholesale embrace of conventional scientific and philosophical norms" (Wright *et al.* 1992: 5). Possible alternative nomenclatures include the movement's colloquial name, NBSMG – the "Non-Bullshit Marxism Group" – and "Rational Choice Marxism", a label based on the adherence of a majority of these thinkers to particular techniques of social scientific modelling (Roberts 1996: 3). The idea of no-nonsense Marxism gives a sense of the impatience of these thinkers with bewildering talk about dialectical contradictions and relational–strategic class oppositions, but it perhaps lacks a bit of specificity. Rational Choice Marxism, meanwhile, designates with all the specificity one could desire a set of methodological strictures based in the research strategies of analytical philosophy, the search for sociological microfoundations based on methodological individualism, the modelling techniques of game theory and the mathematical approach of neo-classical economics. But it rules out too much, for it excludes important analytical contributions that are methodologically holistic, albeit based on a "wholesale embrace of conventional scientific and philosophical norms". It also overlooks those who modify the central postulate of Rational Choice approaches, that people are basically "rational, self-interested optimizers", in the direction of descriptive realism.

Analytical Marxism, then, is a movement that seeks to reconstruct Marxism by re-examining ideas about labour practice, social structure and the historical process, using a series of methods that define the cutting edge in non-Marxist social and economic science in the English-speaking world. Analytical Marxism is "the view that Marxism should, without embarrassment, subject itself to the conventional standards of social science and analytical philosophy". This "implies a rejection of the thesis that Marxism as a social theory deploys a distinctive methodology that differentiates it radically from 'bourgeois social science'" (Wright *et al.* 1992: 108). Instead of the sorts of positions that defined the Marxist Renaissance, which advocated a specific method as the core of histori- cal materialism, even as they redefined the relations between its terms, "Marxism should be distinguished from other social thought not by its tools, but by the questions it raises" (Roemer 1988: 176). Gerald Cohen, Jon Elster, Adam Przeworski, John Roemer, Elliott Sober, Erik Olin Wright, Andrew Levine, Allan Buchanan, Alex Callinicos and Philippe van Parijs are among the contributors to this strand of Marxist thought, whose political positions range from "revolutionary democratic social- ism" through to "left-wing libertarianism" (Roberts 1996: 3).

Restricted historical materialism

In his introduction to Marx, which is in fact an introduction to the analytical reconstruction of historical materialism, Jon Elster takes aim at three methodological fallacies:

> The first is methodological holism, the view that in social life there exist wholes or collectivities, statements about which cannot be reduced to statements about the member individu- als. The second is functional explanation, the attempt to explain social phenomena in terms of their beneficial consequences for someone or something, when no intention to bring about these consequences has been demonstrated. The third is dia- lectical deduction, a mode of thinking that is derived from Hegel's *Logic* and that does not lend itself to brief summary.
> (Elster 1986: 21)

It is ironic, then, that analytical Marxism was launched by G. A. Cohen's remarkable *Karl Marx's Theory of History* (1978), already discussed in relation to classical Marxism. This is a work that aggressively locates its reconstruction of Marx in the space of holistic functional explanation, although it rejects the Hegelian vision of history in the young Marx. Instead, Cohen bases himself on the mature Marx's "1859 Preface" in order to derive and defend a frankly determinist theory of historical progress. Cohen's determinism is holistic because it argues from the class locations specified by economic structures to the behaviour of individuals. It also engages in functional explanations, explicitly proposing the functional relationship between productive forces and relations of production as the explanatory ground for historical change (Cohen 1978: 36 note 31, 160).

That Cohen's position catalysed the formation of a current that some have described as Rational Choice Marxism, then, might seem extremely strange. But it can be explained by two features of Cohen's argument. The first is extraordinary methodological clarity combined with frank preparedness to state exactly what he means, freely and fearlessly accepting the risk of falsification and rebuttal. "Overnight", writes Elster, Cohen's work "changed the standards of rigor and clarity that were required to write on Marx and Marxism" (Elster 1985: xiv). The second is that Cohen's holism and functional explanation are not grounded in the standard way, through broad descriptive claims about social reproduction. Instead they depend upon a set of daringly precise hypotheses about human nature, which are expressed as claims about rational behaviour. For the analytical Marxists, what was impressive about Cohen's position was this approach, reasoning about historical cases from clearly stated first principles. But the Augean Stables of historical materialism had been cleansed of dialectical mystification, they felt, only to have the accumulated muck replaced with functionalist obfuscations and an implausible determinism. Cohen had hit upon the wrong set of first principles in his attempt to reconstruct the broad insights and emancipatory intentions of Marx. But that was something that the right method would soon correct.

Analytical Marxists have broadly taken two paths towards methodological rigour. The first is to scale down the pretensions of classical Marxism by defending a "restricted historical materialism" supported by a "weak technological determinism" (Wright *et al.* 1992: 94). The second is to drastically shrink the scope of economic determination of political and ideological processes down to a handful of key areas. Nonetheless, this explanatory programme still has traction, if and only if a set of mechanisms can be identified connecting the economic foundation to the specific areas of the political and ideological superstructures. For Wright, Sober and Levine, the problem is not the basic intuition of classical Marxism concerning historical development and social structure, but its deterministic and totalizing scope. Their criticism of Cohen's classical determinism – the "Development Thesis" – is to advance logical and anthropological objections to the idea that there is a trans-historical human interest in the reduction of effort through technological innovation. Furthermore, they contest the classical conflation of explanation with determination.

From their perspective, the productive forces cannot be defined outside their social application, with the consequence that they cannot be held separate from legal forms of property. This means commitment to a relational definition of the productive relations and productive forces, which ruins efforts to locate the productive forces in natural history. Moreover, Levine and co-thinkers point out, technological innovation means productivity improvements, and it is not obvious that every human being will have an interest in this under all circumstances. Specifically, although exploiting classes should have a strong interest in innovation, exploited classes might not benefit in terms of a reduction of effort at all. What is stake for the direct producers is not the production of a fixed quantity of things, but their labour time and therefore the expenditure of human effort. They reason that the exploited have no significant interest in regression, but no particular interest in advance either. The consequence of this analysis is that the productive forces do not so much advance, as mainly fail to regress: technological development is "sticky downwards" (Wright *et al.* 1992: 78–9). In the final analysis, this episodic tendency of the productive forces to ratchet upwards depends on the balance of class forces, and centrally it depends on the advent of periods of instability in which rising classes have an interest in revolutionary solutions to the problems of stagnation.

The clear implication is that the path of development for any society is historically contingent, rather than determined necessarily by a tendency operating in – or below – the base. To this end, Levine and co-thinkers propose the analysis of variant "historical trajectories" (*ibid.*: 61–88), disclosing "multiple routes into the future" (*ibid.*: 90). Furthermore, they argue, the notion that functional explanation of the relation between the economy and the superstructure leads to a plausible "determination in the last instance" by the foundation is not credible. Classical Marxism conflated definition of the effects of one region of social life in restricting the set of possible actions in another region of social life, with a cosmological vision of society as a set of empirically modulated appearances of a class essence. To be credible, Marxism must define the restricted areas of the ideologico-political superstructure that are functionally dependent on the economy. It must do this through identifying a set of mechanisms of structural selectivity that connect the economy to small regions of politics and ideology. The economic foundation, then, to use an architectural metaphor, has some pylons emerging from it into the actual building – nothing more. Marxism should not try to claim that the entire edifice of society is somehow determined by its material foundation, but restrict itself to the plausible claim to explain *how* and *where* that building is connected to its economic substructure.

Alex Callinicos would certainly not accept Levine and co-thinkers' divorce of radical politics from the Marxist theory of history. But he does accept something rather like weak directionality and restricted causation. He is wary of functional explanations, however, and argues that Marxism lacks a fully satisfactory account of historical agency, of "making history". As Przeworski has explained, the problem with historical materialism is that "Marxism was a theory of history without any theory about the actions of people who made this history". Specifically:

> Marx was the last thinker who simultaneously viewed behaviour as rational, strategic conduct, and sought to explain how people acquire their historically specific rationality, including preferences. (Przeworski 1985: 95)

Marxism describes all action twice, once as a set of routine performances with unintended consequences and once as a set of strategic deliberations based on material interests. What Callinicos seeks to do is to close the gap between structure and agency without recourse to functional explanation. His position seeks to explain how agents' historically specific rational calculations of their own material interests generate a set of unintended effects. The connection is the theory of ideology (Callinicos 1988: 134–77), which explains the formation of collective agents. A common identity forms around a representation of shared interests (*ibid*.: 134). Describing his methodological collectivism as "classical historical materialism" rather than analytical Marxism (*ibid*.: 90), he maintains that this explains the influence on structure on agency. But he commits what for proponents of methodological individualism is a central fallacy, the ascription to aggregations of individuals of a collective subjectivity. History on his account is made by what another tradition would call "class subjects", whereas, the rejoinder would probably run, in reality it is made through recurring patterns of individual action without these persons necessarily having a single identity.

Rational choice and methodological individualism

For Elster, Przeworski and Roemer in particular, then, methodological individualism is the remedy for dilemmas of agency and structure. It is a radical cure, however, because it involves dropping even weak directionality and restricted forms of functional explanation. From the perspective of rational choice Marxism, there is a bad synergy between methodological collectivism, historical teleology and functional explanation. As far as Elster is concerned, methodological collectivism involves the postulation of meta-subjects, that is the ascription to groups (e.g. classes and nations) of the properties of individuals. These are supposed to act on and in society, as if they possessed the desires and beliefs that motivate action, together with the conscious ability to reason about the most efficient means to the ends shaped by these desires and beliefs. The threshold between the postulation of collective subjects and the invocation of historical teleology is porous indeed. As soon as the collective subject is treated as if it were an actually existing, ontologically primary entity (and not an aggregation of individuals), its "intentions" begin to shape a discussion of its "actions". For instance, "Humanity was for Marx what Spirit or Reason was for Hegel – the supra-individual entity whose full development is the goal of history, even though it is not endowed with the qualities of an intentional agent who could bring about that goal" (Elster 1985: 116). Such talk is merely disguised, rather than eliminated, in functional explanation, where actions are explained with reference to the actual benefits for such collective subjects. Functional explanation appears to avoid recourse to intentionality. But Elster argues that either the supposed functional "goal" of the action is a disembodied "intention" of the collective subject, or the claim is internally contradictory, proposing to explain intentional action by social agents with reference to unintended effects (*ibid.*: 28).

The sorts of things that functional relations and collective agents seek to clarify – namely why groups of individuals acting intentionally realize consequences that are not in their interests – can only be scientifically investigated by proposing an explanatory mechanism for patterns of behaviour. Since what is to be explained is a gap between motivations and consequences, the only intellectually rigorous mechanism that can be proposed must involve the intentional actions of individuals, especially when they act in similar ways in the absence of a coordinating framework. Methodological individualism, Elster insists, is not the exclusive property of neo-classical economic theory and neo-liberal political philosophy (*ibid.*: xiii), but can be used to investigate the "specifically Marxist contribution" to social science, the explanation of "aggregate phenomena in terms of the individual actions that go into them" (*ibid.*: 4).

Elster insists that there is nothing right-wing about this. Methodological individualism is *methodological*, not ontological. Its individuals are not the isolated bourgeois of classical economics or the selfish individualists of neo-classical economics (*ibid.*: 6). The sort of individual involved depends on the assumptions made by the theory, and Elster's assumptions would appear to be that individuals are historically and socially formed. Such individuals get involved in what he calls a "fallacy of composition" (the cognitive mistake of transposing what is true for a part onto claims about what is true for the whole) when they act without a mechanism of coordination. For instance, for every individual capitalist, cutting wages raises profits. But for the capitalist economy, generalized reductions in wages produce crises of under-consumption. A similar argument applies to the tendency of the falling rate of profit as the effect of individual reasoning about technological innovation. Elster thinks that these sorts of "aggregate phenomena" are best explained using methodological individualism.

The use of game-theoretical modelling can further clarify the sorts of "aggregate phenomena" that rational choice Marxists are thinking about, and how they think about them. Game theories involve the postulates of rational choice theorems about individual action. These reduce to the idea that individuals act strategically and reason instrumentally: individuals possess beliefs and desires, which lead them to formulate preferences; individuals rationally maximize the satisfaction of their preferences; individuals do so based on the selection of the best means to these ends, from a set of feasible alternatives. A "game" is then a situation involving complex strategic interdependencies among rational optimizers, and the "prisoners' dilemma" is its elementary cell form. Analytical Marxists typically use examples such as the situation where two employees believe that their firm is about to downsize by making one of them redundant, but have no opportunity to communicate effectively with one another to plan joint action. Each knows that if they both take strike action, the employer will fold, and staffing levels will be maintained. But if only one of them strikes, she will probably be the one sacked, while the other will most likely retain her job, with some probability that the employer will then demand higher productivity. If both do nothing, a redundancy is highly likely. Although it is in both their interests to strike, neither will in fact take that action under these circumstances. Uncertain about the decision of the other, each of them reasons that it is rational for the individual to let the other person take all the risks. The free-riding individual will reap possible benefits without incurring negative consequences. Thus they both do nothing, and the consequence of their rational, strategic action is an unintended, suboptimal outcome for each. The functionalist would maintain that dividing the working class (through competitive socialization, possessive individualism, and ideologies of race and gender) benefits the capitalist class. The methodological individualist would reply that she has actually demonstrated a micro-foundational mechanism that explains the phenomenon, without reference to functional teleology. Roemer believes that this approach can explain labour market behaviour, Przeworski thinks that it can clarify party-political strategies and Elster believes that collective action can be explained through game theories.

Exploitation and inequality

The application of methodological individualism's analytical techniques to classical Marxism leads to a fairly thorough demolition of Marx's positions, beginning with the rejection of the labour theory of value and terminating in a dismissive critique of the tendency of the falling rate of profit. As Marcus Roberts points out, this is beautifully illustrated by Elster's index entry for "labour theory of value" in *Making Sense of Marx*:

> labour theory of value, 127–41; ill-defined because of the heterogeneity of labour, 130–1; plays no role in the determination of equilibrium prices an rate of profit, 133–8; cannot explain the possibility of exchange and profit, 138–41; does not provide a criterion for the socially desirable choice of technique, 149–51; does not explain the actual choice of technique under capitalism, 144–6; ill-suited to the analysis of balanced economic growth, 143; inconsistent with the Marxist theory of class, 325 n 3; constitutes a weakness in the theory of exploitation, 167, 202–3; vitiates the theory of fetishism, 98–9; vitiates the critique of vulgar economy, 503; rests on obscure Hegelian foundations, 125–6.   (Elster 1985: 554; Roberts 1996: 155)

Even an unmarked grave would be more dignified. Elster notes that *Capital* appeared just before the end of classical economics and argues that Marxist economic theory never came to grips with the neo-classical revolution of the 1870s. Noting that there are, despite this, advanced contemporary variants of Marxian economics, he quips that "it is possible to be obscurantist in a mathematically sophisticated way, if the techniques are applied to spurious problems" (Elster 1986: 60). These pseudo-problems are basically coextensive with Marx's central concepts. Elster's assumption is that "like most classical economists, Marx tried to explain price formation by a labour theory of value" (*ibid.*: 64). On this basis, the labour theory of value is faulted for failure to consider the heterogeneity of labour and inability to convert values into prices, among other cardinal sins. The first problem has to do with natural talent: Marx considers skilled labour as unskilled labour plus education and training (i.e. human capital), but allegedly cannot deal with forms of skill that are not produced as commodities; the latter has to do with the notorious difficulties caused by the fluctuation of prices around values (Elster 1985: 130, 135). Given that "later Marxists have offered a deduction of prices from values that is formally correct", the real killer is the heterogeneity of labour, because this "prevents the labour theory of value from even getting off the ground" (*ibid.*: 131). It does so because it is said to affect the determination of the value of labour power. Mind you, this conclusion is enigmatic, because Marx's theory deals not with concrete labour, but with abstract labour; the point being that natural skill differentials go unrewarded in a mode of production that systematically reduces qualitative distinctions to quantitative differences.

At any rate, in complete agreement with the idea that the fundamentals of Marxian economics are up the spout, Roemer produces a "general theory of exploitation" that uses game-theoretical models to generate some interesting results. He argues that exploitation means having to work longer than is socially necessary when others work less than is socially necessary, and qualifies this by linking it to the existence of realistic alternative possibilities.

> I propose that a group be conceived of as exploited if it has some conditionally feasible alternative under which its members would be better off. … Formally, this amounts to specifying a game played by coalitions of agents in the economy. A coalition can either participate in or withdraw from the economy. To define the game, I specify what any particular coalition can achieve on its own if it withdraws from the economy. Given these specifications, if a coalition can do better for its members by "withdrawing", then it is exploited.
>
> (Roemer 1982b: 276)

Exploitation means being *economically or politically compelled* to work longer than necessary when other work options exist (historically speaking). Presumably, "withdrawal" means not strike action, but the construction of (for instance) a market socialist economy, or perhaps subsistence production. The effect is to locate exploitation in historically possible alternative sets of economic relations. Operating with this definition, Roemer demonstrates that, beginning from unequal material positions, privileged commodity-producing agents can manage to exploit underprivileged agents in the absence of wage contracts and labour markets. On the other hand, allowing wage contracts but distributing starting resources equally produces non-exploitative labour markets. Finally, he shows that by allowing wage contracts and labour markets, and allocating differential endowments to rational agents, the model generates classes and exploitation. The labour theory of value is redundant and "the heresy is complete: not only does exploitation emerge logically prior to accumulation and institutions for labour exchange, but so does the articulation of exploitation into classes" (*ibid.*: 265).

What's more, the implication of this position is that class formation is historically contingent. That means that class locations cannot be derived from property relations alone, but also depend on variables such as skill and organization. Based on the work of Wright, statistical correlations between class, income and consciousness appear to be empirically robust: "agents *choose their own class* positions – not willingly, but under constraint, as a consequence of optimizing, given their initial endowments" (Roemer 1988: 80). Consistent with the postulates of Rational Choice theory, Roemer thinks that class is the unintended collective result of individualistic reasoning given differential endowments of capital stock. As Roberts comments, "Roemer's principal objection to capitalism appears to be not so much that unequally endowed individuals would choose capitalism, but that, being unequally endowed, they would have no choice but capitalism" (Roberts 1996: 169). According to Roemer's modelling, then, exploitation emerges as a consequence of the unequal distribution of capital assets in the original position of rational agents, which implies that *inequality*, rather than wage contracts, is the real problem that socialists should tackle. Domination in the workplace, for instance, might be a moral or legal abuse, but it is irrelevant to the question of an historical alternative to capitalist exploitation in socialism:

> Domination at the point of production, so often a concern of Marxism, is only distantly related to the concern with

exploitation. The essential injustice of capitalism is located ... in the property relations that determine class, income and welfare.

(Roemer 1988: 107)

It is therefore crucial not to confuse socialist society with industrial democracy. According to Roemer's analysis, the catastrophe of historical Communism arose from three factors: state ownership of firms, central allocation of goods rather than market mechanisms, and political dictatorship (Roemer 1993: 89). His alternative is to combine democratic politics and market allocation with a system defined in terms of "institutional guarantees that aggregate profit are distributed ... equally" (*ibid.*: 89). His argument is that before Marx, public ownership was regarded as an instrument for securing egalitarianism, and that equality rather than nationalization is the core of socialist politics. The principal problem with historical Communism was motivational, and it lay in the false assumption that after a reform of human nature, individuals would serve the public good rather than private interests (*ibid.*: 93).

Roemer poses the central task for conceptions of socialism in terms of "a system of property rights and an economic mechanism which perform significantly better than modern capitalism", but which preserves both efficiency *and* equity (*ibid.*: 93). He suggests that market socialism must not plan the basket of consumer goods or allocate these centrally, although labour and consumption markets would require regulation. The real innovation in his conception of market socialism is that it would be a "coupon economy", where although "citizens would be allowed to trade their stock in mutual funds for stock in other mutual funds, they would not be free to liquidate their portfolios" (*ibid.*: 96).

In *A Future for Socialism* (1994), Roemer further develops this model of market socialism, designed to preserve the efficiencies that capital markets make possible, but eliminate exploitation, through the equitable distribution of productive assets. The idea is elegant: two ideal economic models are set up, with identical principles of operation and identical starting points. Both are equipped with parliamentary democracies that the rich can influence politically, but one of them has a regulated economy in a sense to be discussed. In both, there are rich and poor, represented by the distribution among the population of "units of the good" (e.g. money). In the capitalist system, individuals trade units of the good and invest in productive assets, as usual. The socialist system is the same as the capitalist "except that", under socialism, "prices of stock are now denominated in [government-issued and legally regulated] coupons, not in units of the good" (Roemer

1994: 65). Citizens can freely trade units of the good, but not government coupons; coupons can only be used for investment purposes, leading to dividends paid in units of the good; a regulation prevents any individual from owning productive assets in excess of their initial allocation of coupons, which is 1,000 coupons to every individual. Result: the capitalist system generates exploitation through concentration of productive assets; the socialist system prevents exploitation emerging; and "the poor (who in this specification constitute 95% of the population) are better off in the market-socialist equilibrium than in the capitalist equilibrium, regardless of the degree of influence the rich have in the elections" (*ibid*.: 73).

Politics and ideology

Some critics engage in sarcastic dismissal of Roemer – "fascinating, professor" – which is unhelpful. Marx and Engels's vision of socialism was, after all, just as abstract, and a good deal less practical. There are, however, pointed, substantive criticisms of Roemer's basic approach that can be made, about the sorts of individuals involved in these models, the relation of the models to historical situations, and the connection between exchange and production (Wood 1990). The deepest problem would appear to be that Roemer's innovative approach to socialist politics depends upon a quite novel definition of exploitation. This makes politics a question of the rational evaluation of historical alternatives rather than a response to perceptions of injury or something based around legitimate moral grievances.

The rational choice approach acknowledges that there is a distinction between agents calculating rational alternatives based on playing the game according to the rules, as opposed to global judgements on the fairness of the current rules of the game. Thinking about exploitation and inequality involves the contemplation of "conditionally feasible alternatives", that is counter-factuals. Clearly, the jump from the agent's perspective to the global decision to withdraw from the current game is the analytical equivalent to the problem of class membership and class consciousness. The attainment of class consciousness is mainly presupposed by Roemer, in order to treat political economy as a zero sum game, where any rational agent can grasp the stark historical choice between capitalism and socialism. Indeed, for Roemer, "historical materialism … claims that history progresses by the successive elimination of forms of exploitation which are socially unnecessary in the dynamic sense" (Roemer 1982a: 271). In other words, Roemer believes that a definition of exploitation based on consideration of "conditionally feasible alternatives" can intersect with historical materialist explanations of epochal shifts between modes of production. But who are the agents of these transformations and how do they manage to operationalize their rational calculations of feasible alternatives? And what happens when they reasonably believe that, rather than there being no *imaginable* alternative to exploitation, there is no *viable* way out, and settle for improving their lot under current arrangements?

The first question first. Wright, as we saw in Chapter 1, initially adopted an approach to the definition of class boundaries based on the idea of contradictory class locations, defined in terms of a hierarchy of determinations (exploitation relation, supervision functions, independence in work process). In light of some difficulties with this position, in *Classes*, Wright embraces Roemer's theory of exploitation, with the consequence that classes are now straightforwardly defined in terms of effective control of productive assets (Wright 1985: chapter 3). He proposes that the advantage of this position is its explanatory purchase on phenomena of income differentials and social attitudes, and much of *Classes* is devoted to empirical corroboration of the link between these things and exploitation-defined classes. Significantly, however, Wright's efforts to refute Elster's declaration that "the centrality of class in social conflict cannot be upheld" (Elster 1985: 394) reduce to the assertion that property relations are central to material existence, and so must play a determining role (Wright 1985: 97–8). Recognition that the link might be indirect, from the existence of classes to the formation of characteristic beliefs, which then determine the sorts of grievances that motivate social conflict, is ruled out, at least for Wright, Roemer and Elster, because of their rejection of all variants of the theory of ideology.

Analytical Marxism's sharp criticism of the concept of ideology is a consequence of its focus on rational calculation as the basic explanation of social action. The most economical formulation of the objection is Roemer's: "one cannot use exploitation as an explanation of class struggle unless it is perceived by the workers as an injustice that they wish to erase [but that is impossible to do] if one simultaneously wishes to claim that capitalist relations obscure relations of exploitation" (Roemer 1988: 85). Class consciousness, then, is a question not of removing ideological false consciousness, but of accurately weighing historical alternatives under conditions of systematically imposed fallacious reasoning. Elster, highly critical of Marx's theory of ideology, presents this in terms of "cold", structural mechanisms whereby, in a decentred economy, fallacies of composition regularly arise. Marx's major methodological contribution turns out to be an insight into the social conditions behind the common but mistaken belief that "causal relations valid locally … retain their validity when generalised to a wider context" (Elster 1985: 19, 487). In more colloquial terms, "ideology" reduces to the problem that rational agents, rather than seeing that conditionally feasible alternatives are historically imaginable, decide that the most reasonable thing for them to do as individuals is to free-ride on collective action while attempting to join the exploiting class. Class consciousness can then be reframed: "Elster's proposal is to understand class solidarity as a transformation of the preference orderings characteristic of the free-rider problem (the prisoners' dilemma payoff matrix) into an assurance game" (Wright *et al.* 1992: 123). An assurance game is defined by agents' conditional altruism (a preference for altruism conditional upon an assurance that others will not free-ride), which depends on shared information, and therefore political organization.

Now the second question. Przeworski in effect argues against the poet John Milton's great rebel, that rational beings will not declare it "better to reign in Hell, than to serve in Heaven". The assurance game of social solidarity might generate collective action, but nothing can guarantee revolutionary success. Indeed, a moment's reflection is sufficient to convince a rationally self-interested optimizer that the construction of a socialist society must involve a protracted transition period, during which some experiments with new political and economic arrangements might well fail. Better to play a different style of game than to opt out; and given that Analytical Marxism regards Marx's crisis theory as completely false, there is no reason to suppose that the standard rules will change suddenly. The most effective strategy under those conditions is to strike a reasonable balance between excessive industrial militancy (which leads to retaliation) and utter compliance (which leaves workers "free to lose"):

> Unless the capacity to institute socialism is organized economically, politically and ideologically with the capitalist society, wage-earners are better off avoiding crises and cooperating in the reproduction of capitalist accumulation.
>
> (Przeworski 1985: 165)

On Przeworski's analysis, the reform strategies of social democratic parties are rationally determined responses to the economic and political constraints of capitalism. *Capitalism and Social Democracy* has, perhaps inadvertently, a classically tragic structure: its protagonist, social democracy, confronts a perfect dilemma. Given that "universalism is the ideology of the bourgeoisie", and that the common interest is necessarily defined in terms of the continuation of capitalism, social democracy has no prospect of generating democratic socialism (*ibid*.: 21). On the one hand, the working class is too small to form an electoral majority alone; on the other hand, building electoral coalitions with middle-class voters necessarily involves dilution of class politics into non-class populism. There is a certain tragic dignity to this presentation of the social democratic parties rending themselves, setting up and then tearing down the welfare state. Certainly, it would be a callow Marxism indeed that would refuse to acknowledge the contribution of social democracy to working-class politics, or denigrate the historic achievement that social rights represent. But it is an unusual Marxism that with satisfaction declares of this no-win, no-exit situation that things have turned out about as well as could have been hoped for, under the circumstances (*ibid*.: 239).

Marxism and justice

Recent efforts of Analytical Marxism have focused on the normative foundations of market socialism. As Cohen says, if domination depends on the distribution of property, not exploitation at the point of production, then "the question of exploitation resolves itself into the question of the moral status of capitalist private property" (Sitton 1996: 85, Cohen cited). Valuably, the analytical approach has inspired some important reconstructions of Marx's underlying normative convictions and their retrieval from his confusions on the question of justice. Rodney Peffer, for instance, reconstructs Marx's moral theory as:

> recommending the promotion of one or more types on non-moral good – freedom, human community and self-realization – [where] the criterion of right action is not simply the maximization of the non-moral good. This type of moral theory holds that there are other right-making characteristics of actions, rules for actions and/or social policies and actions, for example treating people as ends in themselves … or respecting others people's rights. (Peffer 1990: 80–81)

According to this interpretation, Marx is a mixed-mode deontologist, that is someone who thinks that the basis of freedom is moral autonomy, but who denies the pertinence of the fact/value distinction and holds that autonomy makes possible a perfectionist account of political justice. The other way to go is to suppose that Marx holds a teleological ethics based in an ideal of human flourishing. From Elster's perspective, Marx's most enduring contribution is the idea of "self-realization through creative work", amounting to an ethical individualism (Elster 1985: 521, 527). This is a valid ideal, but one that should be implemented with caution, specifically in relation to a viable distributive principle (*ibid.*: 522). Elster thinks that Marx held an ill-defined distributive theory of justice based on a contribution principle (proportional receipts for individuals' social contribution through the labour process), but rejects it as a serious normative position (*ibid.*: 516–17). The "needs principle" outlined in the "Critique of the Gotha Programme" is better, but in the absence of the requisite social arrangements, Rawls' "difference principle" would at least provide for social equality (*ibid.*: 230). It is interesting and significant that Elster and Peffer converge, from different perspectives, on the claim that a modified Rawlsian position on justice, based in the value of equality, is the most defensible Marxist theory of justice today (see Peffer 1990: 364–5).

According to Rawls's signature work, *A Theory of Justice*, "justice as fairness" will result from a social contract, struck between rational agents who determine distributive principles for society based on a hypothetical agreement. Individuals situated behind a "veil of ignorance" regarding what sorts of things they will possess and what sorts of values they will hold in the future society, he argues, will agree on two basic principles. The Equality Principle states that "each person is to have an equal right to the most extensive scheme of equal basic liberties compatible with a similar scheme of liberty for others" (Rawls 2003: 53). The Difference Principle provides that "social and economic inequalities are to be so arranged that they are reasonably expected to be to everyone's advantage", while its other part, the equal opportunity principle, stipulates that these inequalities be "attached to positions and offices open to all" (*ibid.*: 53). As Allen Buchanan demonstrates, the only way to fully grasp socially concerned political liberalism is to recognize that "Rawls' work incorporates basic Marxian themes" (Buchanan 1982: 161) within a defence of the welfare state, based on universal principles of distributive justice. Many standard Marxian objections to this position fail, because, once we consider the requirements of the social context, or circumstances of justice needed to support such principles, it is fundamentally not a defence of actually existing capitalism, but instead an argument for a mixed economy combined with sweeping social reforms.

Rawls is closer to social democracy than to the parties that claim to be liberal today; but then, social democracy is a form of political liberalism inflected through social concerns derived from Marxism.

Now, there are three basic ways that Marxists can respond to the challenge of this highly progressive form of liberalism:

1. Refuse to elaborate an alternative conception of justice on grounds that the whole problem only arises under conditions of scarcity, which means that Marxism is a *critique of justice*. Marxists who adopt this line have to be extremely confident about the elimination of scarcity in the society of abundance, which is difficult once classical Marxist economics and the classical conception of communism are abandoned. Its proponents also fairly quickly discover that not only does justice remain rather pressing during any envisaged transition period, but also that distributive justice remains necessary after the transition to communism, because it concerns reconciliation between individuals who hold differing conceptions of the good life. Rawls's distributive principle *does not* reduce to the distribution of things; it also concerns the problems that arise in a value-pluralist environment. To cope with these difficulties, Marxists who adopt the "critique of justice" line tend to be consequentialists, that is they believe that ethics consists of maximizing some good for the greatest number of individuals. Peter Singer's utilitarian interpretation of Marx is an excellent example. Consequentialism can be a difficult position to sustain intellectually, however, because of its tendency to license conclusions that offend basic moral intuitions (it tends to support ideas about the sacrifice of individuals for the greater good), and it has had disturbing applications in the history of "actually existing socialism".

2. A second option is to promote Marx's own ethical individualism as something that gets us "beyond justice". According to Roemer, his approach does not "locate the historical materialist imperative in considerations of justice", because it is founded on the distinctively Marxist conception of self-actualization (Roemer 1982a: 275). This would appear to mean the following. Where theories of justice – and especially that of Rawls – concern equality in distribution, a self-actualization theory assumes material abundance, and therefore the supersession even of egalitarian arrangements, and investigates the forms of human flourishing. Again, this reasoning misunderstands what is meant by "distribution",

reducing it to the allocation of things, and neglects the ways that a theory of distributive justice also concerns conflicts between individuals who hold different conceptions of self-actualization. Unless it is held that everybody will rationally agree on a single conception of human flourishing, the need for distributive justice does not vanish just because the moral foundation for the theory shifts from deontological to teleological grounds, and the resulting normative political philosophy is framed in perfectionist terms.

3. The third option is to argue an alternative model to Rawlsian "justice as fairness". One way to go is to claim that deontologically based liberal conceptions of right contain internal potentials for their own self-transcendence in the direction of substantive equality, especially once the social undermining of autonomy that capitalism involves is eliminated. This broadly Hegelian strategy is the one adopted by Critical Theory (see next chapter). Another way to go is to propose that the central problem with Rawlsian liberalism is that the Equality and Difference principles provide for, respectively, equality and inequality. This is the route taken by G. A. Cohen in his late work. For Cohen, radicalization of the Equality Principle leads to the rejection of the Difference Principle (Cohen 2008: 7); serious investigation of the moral principles and considerations of justice behind the Equality Principle mandates the conclusion that substantive, and not merely formal, equality is the desired outcome. Cohen's central task is "rescuing the *concept* of justice" from the social facts of capitalism, by arguing that Rawls is wrong to exclude the ethos of society from his definition of the basic structure of society that considerations of justice are said to be capable of reforming (*ibid.*: 229–73, especially 261). The ethos of a just society, one characterized by substantive equality, would be egalitarian, and this is what socialism means today.

According to Roemer, in light of the sorts of arguments that both he and Cohen marshal, the value of equality criticizes as unjust the capitalist distribution of productive assets and supports public ownership, which means that "the goal of socialism is best thought of as a kind of egalitarianism" (Roemer 1994: 125). The egalitarian programme developed by thinkers such as Cohen is based on a perception of "the greatness of Rawls" (Cohen 2008: 11). Political liberalism is without question one of the great achievements of the modern world, and Rawls is its current summit: facile dismissals by Marxists of "liberal-democratic capitalism" are a real sign of political immaturity. The task of socialism is not to smash the noses off the classical statues, but to arrive at a higher set of social arrangements. Nonetheless, as Alex Callinicos notes, because egalitarianism bases itself *at least* on market socialism *in opposition* to the Difference Principle, there is a real and substantive distinction between it and liberalism (Callinicos 2000: 52).

From the perspective of Analytical Marxism, an extremely serious effort has been made not only to reconstruct the emancipatory impulse of Marxism and basic insights of Marx, but also to move this programme decisively into the mainstream of political philosophy, where it can no longer be ignored. But the thing is that Marx failed to hold up his end of the arrangement, providing what proved to be an extremely fallible set of claims: "Marx was almost never right; his facts were defective by the standards of modern scholarship, his generalizations reckless and sweeping" (Elster 1986: 3). Under these conditions, the meaning of socialism changes, but the orientation to egalitarian social arrangements does not. To the contrary, it has received a more precise direction.

Nonetheless, there remains something bloodless about this sort of socialism. The methodological assumption of the rational utility-maximizer might generate interesting economic models, but it does not have sufficient descriptive depth to capture the human condition. Marx considered human beings as creative, social animals and developed a rich theory of the flourishing of historical societies, which is why he cites the poets alongside the political economists. The basic difference between Marxism and liberalism, when it comes to the conception of justice, is that Marxism rejects as a mutilation of the human condition the reduction of human beings to socially isolated, rationally maximizing consumers of utilities. Human nature is creative and social, characterized by historically generated material needs and deeply situated psychological desires for free self-expression and full personal realization, Marx asserts. Moral autonomy and the social contract, with everything that follows from them, such as human rights, political liberty and social equality, represent invaluable historical and intellectual contributions to a just society. But the atomizing effects and vested material interests that flow from capitalist political economy directly undermine the political participation, social solidarity and affective reciprocity necessary to make them effective realities. In political liberalism, precisely because of its failure to truly confront these issues, moral autonomy and the social contract become the fronts for massive inequality; the virtue of equality becomes an empty sham – equality before the law under conditions of the naturalization of inequality – and the political community is depopulated of virtuous citizens, even by realistic, modern standards.

Faced with the insufficiency of Marx's conceptual apparatus today, the alternative theoretical decision could of course have been to reconstruct the richness of historical materialism using valid contemporary philosophical methods, rather than to expose its impoverishment using the methodological tools of its fiercest critics. But that would require a very different set of philosophical and political convictions, to which we turn in the next two chapters.

Summary of key points

The analytical approach

- Cohen's defence of functional explanation and technological determinism set new standards of argumentative rigour, but subsequent Analytical Marxists have adopted methodological individualism and rational choice theories.
- Rational choice methodology involves the assumption that the individual is a rational maximizer of utilities, and applies this to modelling social situations through game theories developed from the prisoner's dilemma.
- The central concern of Marxism shifts from the labour theory of value to new concepts of exploitation and ultimately to a concern with inequality in the distribution of productive assets.

Praxis, structure and history

- Practice is reconceptualized as making rational choices among feasible alternatives based on a set of preferences that flow from the assumptions governing the game in question.
- Weak historical materialism involves only those political and intellectual conditions directly connected to the economic model in question; historical explanation involves regarding epochal changes as decisions between sets of alternative economic models.
- The state remains central to coercion and distribution, but a social democratic approach to parliamentary participation is often adopted, alongside models of market socialism based on public ownership of productive assets.

The question of justice

- Socialism becomes a question of normative arguments in support of historically feasible alternative arrangements, which means that justice becomes a central concern.
- Engagement with Rawlsian liberalism leads many Analytical Marxists to define themselves as egalitarians, who support substantive equality and public ownership and criticize liberal ideas that defend inequality as beneficial to society.

seven

Critical Theory

Although Critical Theory represents a reconstruction of historical materialism in general, it is particularly focused on reactivating the legacy of Frankfurt School Marxism, albeit under dramatically altered historical and intellectual circumstances. This situation has mandated a thorough critique of their predecessors, so that despite sometimes being described as the "second generation of the Frankfurt School", influential thinkers such as Jürgen Habermas, Axel Honneth, Albrecht Wellmer, Claus Offe and Seyla Benhabib are best thought of as embodying a distinctive new approach.

- The historical circumstances concern preserving the emancipatory impulse of Western Marxism in the context of, initially, the post-war reconstruction of liberal capitalism, and now, neoliberal forms of globalization with illiberal implications. The experience of the fascist dictatorships in Europe had made abundantly clear just how limited the left-wing dismissal of human rights and parliamentary democracy, as the superficial, ideological façade of the bourgeois state, really was. The new Critical Theorists in the 1960s, beginning with Habermas's groundbreaking analysis of the *Structural Transformation of the Public Sphere* ([1962] 1991b), initiated a retrieval of democratic theory for progressive ends, with a strong normative component. Critical of the social-democratic welfare state for its bureaucratization and commodification of social relationships, they have tended to advocate a civic republicanism based on political participation through "deliberative democracy". This approach, which stresses public debate and democratic will-formation, positions contemporary Critical Theory as a vigorous critic of imperialist aggression, authoritarian governance and social exclusion. But it is founded on a set of historical experiences which suggest that acceptance of the false idea of an inevitable transformation of liberal democracy into fascist totalitarianism is profoundly disabling.

- The intellectual conditions relate to philosophical engagement with a critique of the intellectual roots of fascist ideology, in irrationalist and authoritarian currents in German thought. Critical Theory sought to decisively shift the centre of gravity of central European philosophy in a progressive direction, especially through participation in the "linguistic turn" towards a social conception of reason. For the Critical Theorists, the core of a principled and consistent rejection of Romantic, anti-Enlightenment strains in both left-wing and right-wing German philosophy resides in a philosophical understanding of the emancipatory potential of modernity. The key to this is recognition that modern rationality is internally complex rather than monolithically simple, together with a critique of the Enlightenment's limited understanding of its own implications. They demonstrate that the dominant, epistemological problematic of Enlightenment thinking, grounded in the subject-object relation, is only a part of the wider field of rational subject-subject agreements, or "intersubjectivity". Critical Theory thereby critiques the catastrophic perspective of a "tragedy of enlightenment", with its implicit hostility to modernity, together with Adorno and Horkheimer's paradoxical total critique of reason by means of reason, as a limited response to the problems of Enlightenment philosophy.

Yet the *questions* posed by the Frankfurt School are regarded as the right ones. It is for this reason that the leading thinker of Critical Theory, Jürgen Habermas, has been moved to maintain that he is "the last Marxist", someone "fiercely determined to defend [historical materialism] as a still-meaningful enterprise" (Habermas 1992: 464, 469). An interdisciplinary, materialist research programme, one that aims at an emancipatory critical theory with a practical intent, must seek to unite the critique of domination with the question of a meaningful existence, in the context of a focus on human suffering. To this end, Habermas in particular has reconstructed the relations between practice, structure and history in historical materialism, in the context of a thorough critique of classical Marxism. Practice is recast in terms of two distinct forms of activity, corresponding to the subject-subject and subject-object distinction, as communicative interaction and instrumental action in the labour process. This dualism then informs a distinction between the society as a space of communicative participation, or "life-world", and the society as a functionally differentiated social system grounded in the division of labour. As outlined by John Sitton and David Ingram in studies that inform this chapter, Habermas accepts that the notion of social complexity alters contemporary theory's relation to the radical tradition (Sitton 2003), but holds that a proceduralist concept of reason can preserve the emancipatory thrust of the ideal of a rational society (Ingram 1987). In particular, Habermas advocates the idea that the evolution of society, involving a ramifying differentiation of functional subsystems, such as economics, administration, juridical, media and so forth, is conceptually independent from the evolution of normative structures in cultural processes. Multiple evolutions within a dynamic environment take the place of teleological development, and the lack of a "centre" to society means the abandonment of revolutionary utopias involving transformations based on the state.

Differences with the Frankfurt School

The subtitle of Habermas's highly influential *The Structural Transformation of the Public Sphere* (1991b), "an inquiry into a category of bourgeois society", indicates that it implicitly operates against the background of the Marxist theory of history. Specifically, it works in tension with the theory of instrumental reason developed by Adorno and Horkheimer, whose tragic dialectic of enlightenment suggests that liberal democracy inevitably succumbed to manipulative forms of technocratic political management. For Adorno and Horkheimer, Enlightenment rationality necessarily mutated into neo-positivism, the theory that an isolated individual seeking to adapt to external reality must formulate falsifiable hypotheses on the basis of the totality of inert facts. This position translates in the social sciences into the idea of a value-neutral scientific sociology that bases itself on evidentially grounded explanatory and descriptive theories, which can then be used to managerially control social processes. In the "positivism dispute" in Germany in the 1950s and 1960s, Habermas, who was Adorno's research assistant, takes the side of the Frankfurt School's founders in critiquing this sort of "technocratic ideology". Although he supports the idea of an evidence-based social theory, Habermas attacks the absence of social and historical contextualization in neo-positivism, and its idea of value-neutrality when speaking of intersubjective agreements (Wiggershaus 1994: 567–8, 584). He believes that technocratic ideology, as evident in neoliberal politics, neo-classical economics and functional systems theory, is now the most important form of contemporary ideology, having replaced political liberalism (McCarthy 1996: 1–16). But Habermas refuses Adorno and Horkheimer's identification of logical reasoning and propositional argumentation with neo-positivism, together with their reduction of Enlightenment reason to means–ends rationality. In particular, Habermas does not think that the modern idea of democratically steering society on the basis of reasoned public debate is mere false consciousness, a socially necessary illusion masking a quasi-totalitarian administered society.

Accordingly, in *Structural Transformation*, Habermas argues that rational debate about the general interest, through open discussion of public concerns, secretes an egalitarian ideal. The process that he calls "democratic will-formation" took shape during the eighteenth century in a network of forums, or "sphere" of public debate, based around (in-principle) open arenas including the media and parliament. Civil liberties, political rights, the free press, together with coffee houses, literary journals, parliamentary parties and the like, were the institutional locus for the articulation of ideals of liberty, equality and solidarity. Although the "public sphere" thus constituted was undermined by the contingent reality of class inequality, the practices of open dialogue and democratic will-formation have an emancipatory potential. The idea that the social contract is based on rational consent grounded in open dialogue and that it invests individuals as the authors of the laws that they must obey is the foundation of modern notions of liberation. The public sphere mediates the social existence of individuals, linking their private interests and domestic lives to their public participation in the political community as citizens, and it provides a mechanism by which collective agreements can direct the administrative apparatus, or "public authority" (Habermas 1991b: 30). According to the ideal of inclusiveness, transparency and rationality that founds the public sphere, elaborated in the political philosophy of the Enlightenment's thinkers, no individual should in principle be excluded from public deliberations in the political community. In practice, however, the ideal of the public sphere clashed immediately with the realities of bourgeois society, not only in the exclusion of persons on grounds of class, race and gender, but also in that the institutions supporting democratic will-formation were quickly commercialized and bureaucratized.

Having outlined the egalitarian ideal of the public sphere, Habermas in the second half of *Structural Transformation* turns to the corporatization of the media, and to the entrenching of the special interests of the powerful groups in class society through the professionalization of politics and its mutation into a form of public relations exercise. Together with the highly conservative implications of technocratic ideology, which seeks to maintain the status quo by efficiently directing society in the interests of system imperatives belonging to the capitalist economy and state bureaucracy, these changes have inverted the function of the public sphere. He speaks in this connection of a "re-feudalization" of the public sphere, where the corporate media and parliamentary parties join with technocratic experts and wealthy interest lobbies to transform rational will-formation into a sort of courtly performance among the powerful, aimed at manipulating democratic legitimacy (Habermas 1991b: 231–2). At the same time, the transformation of citizens into consumers in late capitalism drives individuals back into "civic privatism" and undermines their democratic citizenship (*ibid.*: 141–80). Meanwhile, the role of the bureaucratic administration in steering complex economic and social processes (discussed below) means that the state can less and less afford the "luxury" of democratic deliberation (*ibid.*: 181–235).

Habermas's endorsement of the ideal of democratic will-formation and his location of the public sphere in a complicated historical dialectic governed by complexity and contingency, together with his implicit claim that there is a contradiction between parliamentary democracy and capitalist society, suggest a major disagreement with Adorno and Horkheimer. Indeed, this sets the scene for some signature differences between Critical Theory and what I have called Frankfurt School Marxism. Against the sometimes sweeping generalizations of the first-generation thinkers and their implicit reliance on an inverted version of Hegel's historical teleology, second-generation Critical Theorists are concerned with the empirical texture of social processes in open-ended developments, and are almost allergic to the "philosophy of history" as a totalizing gesture. Deeply involved in dialogue with philosophical methods and social theories that do not originate in Marxism, the Critical Theorists tend to interpret a multidisciplinary research programme in terms of interventions into other debates, rather than recruitment of various research findings into a potentially monolithic vision of an administered society. Habermas proposes that the wellspring of the difference lies in Adorno and Horkheimer's acceptance – despite their forceful criticisms – of the model of rationality based on the isolated subject contemplating its object of knowledge. The identification of reason as a whole with supposedly baleful "instrumental rationality" springs from this source. In their search for an alternative to commodity reification and instrumental reason, the first generation of the Frankfurt School was led by this definition of rationality to valorize non-propositional (and sometimes irrational) modes of thinking as the alternative to the Enlightenment. Instead of the dead-end of that approach, which ultimately terminates in a Romantic anti-capitalism, Habermas refuses to accept that instrumental manipulation of objects, guided by the criterion of successful efficiency, exhausts the concept of reason. He proposes instead to consider the internal differentiation of modern thought, within which instrumental rationality would be only one component of reason, legitimate in its sphere of competence but problematic when applied globally (Habermas 1984: 339–99).

Critique of historical materialism

In a series of articles in the 1960s and 1970s, Habermas generates a reconstructive critique of historical materialism premised on a firm rejection of the natural-scientific version of Marxist orthodoxy represented by Engels and then Stalin. There is a core reason why Habermas's specific objections to a raft of positions – the theory of instrumental reason, the administered society and what he calls Adorno's defensive cultural and political "strategy of hibernation" (Habermas 1979b: 43) – must lead back to a general critique of Marx. This concerns the normative foundations of emancipatory social theory, because Marx's evolutionary schema for historical progress through the advance of the productive forces fatally compromises the practically oriented criticism of capitalism in light of universal moral claims. Adorno's "instrumental reason" tacitly accepts this framework, even if it inverts its position on labour. The historical materialist theory of social evolution transforms the standpoint of normative critique into a superstructural "reflection" of developments in production. According to Habermas, the dialectic of forces and relations of production must be reformulated and the reductive relation between base and superstructure completely abandoned (Habermas 1970: 113–14, 1973: 168–9). "The development of the productive forces", he writes, "triggers but does not bring about the overthrow of relations of production and evolutionary renewal of the mode of production". But, he instantly adds, "even in this formulation the theorem can hardly be defended" (Habermas 1979a: 146).

According to Habermas, Marx employed two different sorts of arguments in his critique of capitalist political economy (ibid.: 130–77). On the one hand, advancing productive forces generate a sequence of modes of production, characterized by specific class struggles that provide the dynamic for the internally motivated transformation from lower to higher stages of society. The decline of a mode is accompanied by social disintegration, that is "the common ruin of the contending classes" (MESW: 36), together with historically created but socially unsatisfied human needs, which point the material interests of the exploited classes in the direction of a struggle that transcends that socio-historical stage. What this means is that the foundation for emancipatory critique rests upon an evolutionary logic, which renders specific propositions in historical materialism unfalsifiable at the cost of making the whole theory invalid after the first failed revolution. On the other hand, Marx criticizes capitalism for its failure to realize equality, liberty and solidarity, pointing out that these values are the ones actually held by the majority of the population. In his concrete historical analyses of specific political struggles, Marx acknowledges the importance and independence of cultural and intellectual factors. What this suggests is that the independent development of normative standards, in the form of moral consciousness, is only linked to social evolution, rather than a dependent variable appended to it. Consequently, in Knowledge and Human Interests (1968) and Communication and the Evolution of Society (1971), Habermas sets out to theorize the distinct processes of social evolution and normative development, and to clarify the possible connections between them.

Habermas argues that the two sorts of approach employed by Marx – social evolution and normative critique – were conflated, because of a collapse of reason into instrumental manipulation modelled on labour practice. Actually, this problem is the signature of the "philosophy of the subject" that, from the Enlightenment onwards in Western thought, had based its reflections on the model of the isolated subject seeking knowledge about conceptual and material objects. René Descartes and Immanuel Kant are the most important placemarkers for the predominance of the subject-object problematic in the "philosophical discourse of modernity", and Habermas is well aware that Hegel and Marx's work represents a critique of the philosophical and social implications of their approaches. But Hegel and Marx's critique miscarried, because Hegel's collective subject, supposed to expressively generate the historical and social totality through alienation and then rediscover itself as the result of a long series of struggles, merely transposes the subject-object relation onto the relation between the world spirit and the ethical life of a socio-historical totality (Habermas 1972: 7–24). Marx decoded Hegel's world spirit and ethical life as the economically exploited classes and the politico-cultural superstructures, without challenging the terms of the basic model (*ibid.*: 25–42). For a vanishing moment, the young Hegel glimpsed the possibility of conceptualizing the collective subject in terms of a set of agreements arrived at through open debate between subjects who, instead of instrumentalizing one another as manipulable objects, regard the other as another subject worthy of historically defined forms of moral respect (Habermas 1973: 142–69). But this became quickly subordinated to the young Hegel's equally important insight – anticipating Marx – that the totality of subject-object relations creating the historical world for the collective subject was founded on labour.

Marx and Hegel, in other words, missed an opportunity to conceptualize a distinction between the subject-object rationality of labour practice, oriented to instrumental success and guided by efficiency criteria, and the subject-subject rationality of "interaction", oriented to reaching mutual understanding and guided by agreement based on the force of the better argument. Marx, accordingly, presupposes but does not thematize the communicative dimension of interaction, as in, for instance, his insistence that labour is *social* labour mediated by language. This remains an insight which never crosses the conceptual threshold into a theory of normative development – that is, pre-eminently, the development of universalistic forms of moral consciousness – that would run alongside Marx's theory of social evolution through technological progress. There are two important consequences of Habermas's argument about a significant gap in Marx's position (*ibid.*: 1–40, 195–252). The first is that the theory–practice relation in Marxism is generally grasped in instrumental terms, reducing social theory to political strategy and severing the connection between social theoretical claims and intersubjectively recognized forms of truth. The "test" of Marxist social theory becomes historical practice, which means success in revolutionary strategy. Therefore, Marxist social research has languished in an empirically under-developed backwater, insufficiently attuned to the complexity of society and dogmatically oriented to an "all-or-nothing" form of falsification which militates against the refinement of hypotheses. The second consequence is that historical materialism lacks the dimension of self-reflexive critique. Instead of reflection on the status of its own truth claims, and especially its own normative foundations, classical Marxism tends to reduce these to effects of social evolution.

Legitimation crises in late capitalism

The reconstruction of historical materialism around the distinction between labour and interaction, together with a reconceptualization of social structure and historical evolution through dialogue with mainstream sociology, does not mean abandonment of the traditional Marxist focus on linking crisis potentials of the capitalist system to the normative convictions of social agents. For both Habermas and associated thinker Claus Offe, the twentieth-century rise of the interventionist state in the context of monopoly capitalism is an irrevocable development, but it is not one that fundamentally solves the basic crisis dynamics of the system. Although they reject the labour theory of value and the falling rate of profit, Offe and Habermas support a conventional definition of the working class as waged labour and the state as an administrative institution separate from the economy, which is characterized by a monopoly of violence and a foundation in constitutional law based on property forms. In *Contradictions of the Welfare State* (1984) and *Disorganized Capitalism* (1985), Offe deals with the financial and political burdens on capitalism of post-war social welfare and economic planning. Offe holds that capitalism is characterized by a basic contradiction between economic anarchy and the socialization of production that happens through state intervention and economic planning (Offe 1984: 15, 48). Under conditions of the decline of liberal ideology as a justification for the system, especially the disintegration of the "achievement principle" of just rewards for hard work linked to possessive individualism, and the management of class conflict by arbitration commissions, a political sea change happens. The technocratic ideology of successful growth and material prosperity re-politicizes the "private sector", making capitalist disorganization a social concern, at the same time that there is a shift "from conflict over group interest to conflict over general rules, and from the definition of claims to the definition of legitimate claimants" (Offe 1985: 231). Politics becomes a question of the rationality of the administrative sub-system, that is class conflict becomes latent, manifest only through issues of the effective steering of the economy. In *Legitimation Crisis*, Habermas accepts the broad thrust of this sort of argument, despite endorsing the labour theory of value and the falling rate of profit:

> Economic growth takes place through periodically recurring crises because the class structure, transplanted into the economic steering system, has *transformed the contradiction of class interests into a contradiction of system imperatives.*
>
> (Habermas 1975: 26)

That Habermas subsequently drops the categories of classical Marxist economics for an analysis substantively identical to Offe's therefore has no impact on his general position.

Habermas's innovation is to identify two additional forms of crisis tendency, beyond economic crises and their displacement into rationality crises of the administrative sub-system, that are invisible in the classical analysis. These crisis types are "legitimation crises", affecting society's consensus agreement on the just exercise of political authority, or legitimacy of the administration, and "motivation crises", affecting individuals' dispositions to engage in work performances, cooperate socially and support prevalent cultural values. Legitimation and motivation crises arise within the socio-cultural sub-system, which operates according to a different logic from that of the economic and political sub-systems (Figure 4).

Habermas's position is best grasped as a left-wing reply to Daniel Bell's neoconservative thesis on the "cultural contradictions of late capitalism". According to Bell, there is a contradiction between late capitalist

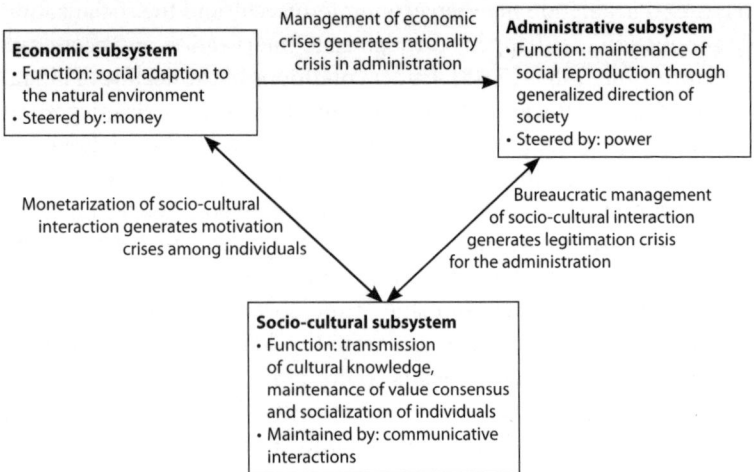

Figure 4 Rationality, legitimation and motivation crises in late capitalism (based on Habermas 1973: 49).

multinational corporatism and bureaucratic administration, arising in economics and politics, and the forms of governance and types of personality needed to make the system work. Western societies face a crisis of governance because of an excess of democratic expectations that is incompatible with system imperatives of economics and administration. Furthermore, consumer hedonism and modernist culture have undermined the work ethic, generating a motivational crisis affecting labour performances and sparking an anti-authoritarian counterculture. For Bell, the solution is to depoliticize the administration in order to unload democratic expectations, through radical economic deregulation, and to combine this with a return to religion in order to generate conformist personalities that have been re-oriented to the work ethic. For Habermas, by contrast, emerging legitimation and motivation crises point to the need for a radical democratization of administration and economy, together with an expansion and deepening of modernist culture. The emancipatory potentials of modernity have been choked, because the economy and the administration, with their anonymous and amoral imperatives, have colonized the socio-cultural system and the public sphere. Consumer hedonism is certainly a problem, but a modernist anti-authoritarian culture and a set of highly democratic expectations are part of the solution.

More theoretically, Habermas's fundamental point is that "disturbances of system integration endanger [the] continued existence [of a social formation] only to the extent that social integration is at stake, that is when the consensual foundations of normative structures are impaired so that society becomes anomic" (Habermas 1975: 3). Social integration through interaction is different to system integration through the anonymous media of money and (bureaucratic) power. The consensual coordination of action among social agents, or social integration, cannot be accomplished via the interventions of money and power. These areas of social life depend on communicative interaction rather than success-oriented efficient action and they cannot be made more effective through functional differentiation. Accordingly, the socio-cultural sub-system simply does not behave in the same way that the economy and administration do, which is why the monetary manipulation of consensus formation and the bureaucratic production of values and motivations *always* deepens the crisis rather than resolving it. The notion of crisis tendencies concerning the normative justifications for legitimate orders and personal motivations corrects the bleak perspectives of the "total system" advanced by Adorno and Horkheimer (Habermas 1987a: 130).

Communicative action versus strategic action

In the first of the two massive volumes of *The Theory of Communicative Action* Habermas deepens and extends the perspective developed in *Legitimation Crisis*, together with his reconstructive critique of historical materialism. His fundamental strategy is to develop the distinction between labour and interaction, which implicitly underscores the opposition between crises of system integration (economic crises: economics; rationality crisis: administration) and crises of social integration (motivation crises: culture; legitimation crises: society), into a distinction between strategic action and communicative action. Accordingly, Habermas defines strategic action and communicative action as the two different modalities of the social coordination of action regulating the economic and political sub-systems and the socio-cultural system respectively:

- Strategic action involves the instrumentalization of social cooperation: strategic action is coordination of action by means of "influence", where influence means the employment of inducements other than reasons – such as money, force or status – to gain the required pseudo-consensus for action (Habermas 1984: 332–3). Strategic action operates legitimately in sub-systems steered by generalized media (money – economics; power – administration). It is illegitimate when it enters areas of value consensus, personality formation and cultural knowledge, either as direct manipulation through money and power or as indirect manipulation through distorted communication, such as appeals to prejudice or false representations of material interests.
- Communicative action involves the coordination of action through "consent", based on the linguistic process of reaching understanding in dialogue, operating in the socio-cultural sub-system (Habermas 1984: 94–6). Consent means understanding of the justifications for action, and it presupposes the rationality of participants and their unforced agreement. Communicative action therefore means not just the existence of dialogue, but the process of rational justification and reasoned argument, which in turn entails the legitimacy of dissent and therefore reciprocity between participants.

From this perspective, ideology means "systematically distorted communication", that is forms of self-deception in which norms and values are protected from rational scrutiny by their acceptance as common convictions "beyond question". This happens because they have taken on the function of legitimating forms of strategic action, and debate is selectively controlled by power interests in the public sphere and bureaucratic administration (Habermas 1987b: 346). Note that this is different from forms of pseudo-consensus resulting from the strategic manipulation of debate through influence or concealment of real interests, because it refers to the effect of *system pressures* on individuals' conception of their own values and interests.

Habermas then reconstructs the pragmatics of speech involved in communicative action, in order to clarify how universal normative standards, which can be agreed upon by all rational persons, represent a critical perspective on the crisis tendencies of late capitalism. To set this up, Habermas turns to Weber. Instead of interpreting of rationalization as reification (e.g. Adorno), Habermas interprets reification as an effect of unbalanced rationalization.

According to Weber, modern, formal rationality generates a secular society characterized by the separation of cultural value spheres (science, morality, art) into distinct expert specializations, which develop independently of one another by following up the particular logic of their subject matter. Habermas describes this process as "cultural rationalization" and holds that it is progressive. For Habermas, the division of modern reason into the distinct cultural value spheres follows from the structure of speech itself. This involves two steps:

1. The programme of "universal/formal pragmatics" involves rendering explicit "from the perspective of those participating in discourses and interactions ... the pre-theoretical grasp of rules on the part of competently speaking, acting and knowing subjects", by means of an analysis of what counts as rational action under certain conditions (Habermas 1987a: 297–8). For Habermas, rational action entails plausible belief, since making an action intelligible for a community involves the actor providing reasoned arguments for their belief regarding a situation in the world. For Habermas, the dialogical justifications that agents provide one another for their conduct leads to the intersubjective construction of psychological, social and natural reality, through the building up of situation definitions regarding the world. Rationality is seen as grounded in the intersubjective process of reaching agreement through dialogical justifications. In this process, agents manage to cooperate because they share rationally agreed situation definitions – and therefore a common world – so that argumentative

justification (rational action) generates at once individual autonomy and social solidarity.

2. Argumentative claims presuppose a belief in states of affairs in what Habermas calls the objective, social and subjective worlds. Just as instrumental transformation of nature is justified with reference to states of affairs in the objective world, moral conduct is justified with reference to states of affairs in the social world and self-expression is justified with reference to states of affairs in the subjective world of the speaker (Habermas 1984: 75–101). Specializations in the different validity claims about the objective, social and subjective worlds yield the differentiated value spheres of natural and social science, morality and law, and art. The rise of expert cultures, specialized in one of the value spheres to the exclusion of the others, reinforces the autonomy of value spheres and the decentring of the modern worldview. A major consequence is that rational agreement is now a procedural question rather than a substantive one, because the sort of reasons varies according to the kind of validity claim. Speech acts "can always be rejected under each of the three aspects: the aspect of the rightness that a speaker claims for his action in relation to a normative context (or indirectly for those norms themselves); the truthfulness that the speaker claims for the expression of subjective experiences to which he has privileged access; finally, the truth that the speaker, with his utterance, claims for a statement (or for the existential presuppositions of a nominalized proposition)" (Habermas 1984: 307).

The totality of these different sorts of argument Habermas calls "communicative reason". There is a neat "triplicity" to Habermas's schema that flows from his somewhat Kantian, approach. This can be laid out in a table that I will explain below (see Table 1).

According to Habermas:

- Cognitive claims about the objective world are valid if they represent the truth about states of affairs, argumentatively redeemed through propositional logic and experimental falsification. Knowledge springing from these arguments forms the (natural and social) sciences and is deposited in the everyday lives of individuals as formal cognitive operations and verified hypotheses.
- Normative claims about the social world are valid if they represent guidelines for right conduct that can be agreed upon by all

Table 1. Communicative reason and cultural rationalization (based on Habermas 1984: 23).

Referential world	Dimension of communicative action	Validity claim as part of communicative reason	Cultural value sphere = institutionalized learning process	Structure-forming effect of expert knowledge
Objective	Cognitive	Truth	Science	Formalized cognition (formal-operational hypothetical attitudes to objective nature)
Social	Normative	Rightness	Morality	Normative universality (post-conventional moral discourses on the social world)
Subjective	Expressive	Truthfulness	Art	Post-traditional motivations (reflexively critical relation to cultural need-interpretations)

affected, argumentatively redeemed through universalistic moral reasoning. Knowledge springing from these arguments forms the moral basis for modern legislation and is deposited in the everyday lives of individuals as post-conventional moral discourses, such as utilitarian ethics and formal-universal ("deontological") morality.
- Expressive claims about the subjective world of modern individuals are valid if they represent interpretations of human needs and cultural values that a community can accept as authentic, that is as a truthful expression of desires and feelings that lead to healthy

forms of individual self-realization. Knowledge springing from these arguments forms modern art and is deposited in the everyday lives of individuals as post-traditional motivations, that is as a set of attitudes that enables modern persons to select a lifestyle for themselves in the context of pluralism.

To summarize, on Habermas's interpretation, each of the value spheres operates according to a distinctive logic, of cognitive (science), normative (law and morals) and expressive (aesthetic) reasoning, governed by the particular procedures by which their defining validity claims of truth (cognitive), rightness (normative) and truthfulness (aesthetic) are articulated symbolically and redeemed argumentatively. Because these domains are institutionalized as specialized forms of inquiry, liberated from religion, protected from the pragmatic pressures of everyday communicative action, and shielded from the intrusive predominance of one another's validity claims, they can develop expert knowledge about the objective, social and subjective worlds (respectively). Ideally, this flows back into the everyday existence of modern individuals through processes of translation, resulting in the release of rational potentials into cultural knowledge, social integration and socialized personalities. The intention here is to specify why it is that modernity is an advance on pre-modern community, because it leads to differentiated, secular knowledge and expanded possibilities for individual self-realization.

Habermas is now in a position to specify exactly how universal normative standards, which can be agreed upon by all rational persons, represent a critical perspective on the crisis tendencies of late capitalism. The Habermasian "ideal speech situation", or "unconstrained communication", is intended as a counterfactual ideal (or ideal normative standard) that is latent in modern communicative action but everywhere prevented from realization by commodification and bureaucratization. Engagement in reasoned argument, Habermas explains, presupposes that participants are implicitly committed to the force of the better argument alone and that they must reach consensus in order to cooperatively act. Another consequence is that the conditions of existence for this debate can legitimately be contested, so that the existence of exploitation and oppression necessarily call into question the validity of any argumentative consensus. Implicitly, then, participants in rational debate subscribe to the ideal of an open, democratic community that is not disfigured by any inequalities which would prevent participation in decision-making. In other words, what it is to be human, and especially what it is to speak in the modern world, carries with it the ideal of emancipation from domination and existence in a meaningful social world (Habermas 1984: 398). Habermas formalizes this as follows:

1. Every subject with the competence to speak and act is allowed to take part in a discourse.
2. (A) Everyone is allowed to question any assertion whatsoever; (B) Everyone is allowed to introduce any assertion whatsoever into the discourse; (C) Everyone is allowed to express their attitudes, desires and needs.
3. No speaker may be prevented, by internal or external coercion, from exercising their rights as laid down in (1) and (2) above. (Habermas 1999: 89)

Against this background, Habermas outlines a programme for post-conventional moral and legal representations called "discourse ethics", designed to spearhead the reconstruction of society within a democratic framework. Discourse ethics goes beyond deontological morality, because it allows speakers to consider generalizable interests as well as universal principles, consequences of action as well as norms of conduct. Among other things, Habermas intends this as a foundation for legislation that would set a normative ceiling on the forms of strategic action that can happen in the economy and administration. Having defined the conditions for rational discourse (above), he sets up "D", the Discourse Principle, as:

D: Only those norms may claim to be valid that could meet with the consent of all affected in their role as participants in a practical discourse. (*Ibid.*: 197)

On this basis, he defines "U", the Principle of Moral Universalisability, as:

U: For a norm to be valid, the consequences and side-effects of its general observance for the satisfaction of each person's particular interests must be acceptable to all. (*Ibid.*: 197)

Such a moral criterion is perfectly compatible with social complexity and democratic politics, but it does not reduce politics to morality (Habermas 1996: 110). Habermas's position takes a process of societal rationalization in economics and administration that has run out of control, and confronts it with the democratic implications of a process of cultural rationalization that has yet to fulfil its potentials. Habermas therefore suggests that the problems of modernity spring from the institutionalization of strategic action (instrumental reason in its social application), to the exclusion of communicative action. In keeping with the investigation of legitimation and motivation crises, the problems of modernity emerge at the level not of system integration but of social integration – the central faultline in modern social conflict is system versus lifeworld.

System versus lifeworld

In the second volume of *The Theory of Communicative Action*, the "lifeworld" is a highly generalized replacement for Habermas's "socio-cultural system" from *Legitimation Crisis*, but it remains the locus of the crisis tendencies in contemporary capitalism. According to Habermas, society is only a "system" when regarded from the perspective of an observer interested in the functional differentiation of social actions. Society is a "lifeworld" when regarded from the position of a partici-pant, that is from within the performative attitude adopted by speaking subjects in the generation of consensus. Whereas the efficiency of the system depends on adaptation to the system's environment, based on survival needs, the coherence of the lifeworld depends upon cultural reproduction, social integration and personal socialization. Habermas proposes that modern existence involves a dialectical relation between cultural rationalization – the emergence of a new consensus within the meaningful whole of the lifeworld – and social rationalization – the increasing complexity of a system composed of functional sub-systems. Because of the "selective rationalization" of modernity – that is the pre-dominance of strategic action and instrumental reason – system and lifeworld are in conflict.

Habermas proposes that everyday life happens through a network of communicative actions (the mutual negotiation of situation definitions) taking place against a background of unquestioned presuppositions. Accordingly, coherent social reproduction requires the consistency of the cultural framework of everyday life. The reproduction of the life-world involves (1) transmission and renewal of cultural knowledge – cultural reproduction; (2) maintaining the solidarity of individuals as members of a community through providing legitimation for institu-tions – social integration; and (3) the formation of personal identities that can form life histories and have motivations for participation in social life – personal socialization. Thus the reproduction of the lifeworld is also the reproduction of the structural components of the lifeworld, culture, society and person (Habermas 1987b: 137–8). Against the notion that society is solely a system operating through subjects who are mere bearers of a process, Habermas insists that society fundamentally consists of conscious participants who take part in a coherent, symbolically-structured form of everyday life. The symbolic structures of everyday life, he maintains, "are reproduced by way of the continuation of valid knowledge, stabilization of group solidarity and socialization of responsible actors" (*ibid.*: 137).

In line with hermeneutic theories, Habermas defines the lifeworld as a "culturally transmitted and linguistically organized stock of interpretive patterns" that make shared definitions of worldly situations and therefore rational consent to social cooperation possible for participants in social life (*ibid.*: 136). Consonant with this hermeneutic conception of the lifeworld, Habermas specifies that it consisis of the pre-theoretical and pre-reflexive horizon of pre-understandings (background assumptions) that supply the context against which actions are intelligible. The lifeworld is the global context of knowledge and beliefs that must be assumed by actors as the horizon of expectations for their action: "everyday communicative practice is not compatible with the hypothesis that everything could be entirely different" (*ibid.*: 132). Problematic situations make us aware of some of the background assumptions that guide our conduct, and these assumptions lose their certainty – in Habermasian terms, the assumptions that are thematized (highlighted) generate the situations within which the horizon can be glimpsed *as a horizon*.

The lifeworld is reproduced as a coherent whole when social actors can connect new situations with existing or renovated cultural interpretations, legitimate orders and personal histories (*ibid.*: 140–41). In other words, social integration happens when social actors are able to connect emergent social conditions with action norms governing pre-existing situations, that is with a raft of cultural meanings, legitimate values and personality types. People have to know what is happening, what to do and who they are during major social change. Lack of answers to any of these questions generates disorientation, especially when the collective generation of new answers – through political debate and social mobilization – is systematically blocked by a commodified culture and a mediatized democracy. Thus a crisis in the lifeworld results in failure of interpretive schemes (loss of meaning), loss of legitimacy (legitimation crisis) and anomie (motivation crisis).

- *Culture.* Seamless cultural reproduction means the adaptation of existing cultural frameworks to new situations and therefore the insertion of social actors into institutional roles with the sense that their participation is meaningful and valid. Cultural reproduction means the maintenance of, or innovation within, interpretive frameworks, leading to cultural knowledge that is relevant to new situations.
- *Society.* Effective normative integration reinforces the cultural norms and ethical values that legitimate the social order as just, and maintains the sense of personal relevance to social actors of their social obligations. Normative regulation happens when individuals believe that they have a moral duty to other members of their society and that their participation will be rewarded in proportion to their deserts.
- *Person.* Operative socialization generates personality structures capable of coping realistically with new situations, increasing the capacity for innovatively interpreting and integrating new knowledge (culture) and increasing the likelihood of motivations for actions that conform to social norms. (Habermas 1987b: 141)

A persistent crisis of social integration can therefore be characterized at the levels of culture, society and person. These are marked by: (1 – **culture**) cultural disorientation caused by loss of meaning, as existing interpretative schemes cannot explain new cultural conditions – *problems of relativism*; (2 – **society**) an erosion of solidarity and the rise of alienated/anomic individualism, because new situations cannot be reconciled with the existing normative regulation of social groups – *a crisis of legitimation*; and (3 – **person**) decline in personal responsibility linked to broken generational continuity and the waning of historicity, leading to an increase in psychopathologies and to a disconnection between generalized competencies for action and personal responsibility – *the spread of anomie and pathological narcissism* (*ibid.*: 142–3).

The rationalization of the lifeworld foregrounds the contingency of cultural traditions, social relations and individual biographies. "The further the structural components of the lifeworld and the processes that contribute to maintaining them get differentiated, the more interaction contexts come under conditions of rationally motivated mutual understanding, that is of consensus formation that rests in the end on the authority of the better argument" (*ibid.*: 145). The key point here is that Habermas reconceptualizes the Weberian notion of cultural rationalization as a progressive rationalization of the lifeworld, in order to propose a sort of syllogism. (1) The process of redefining cultural knowledge, social norms and personal identities through rational argument, which happens as new situations emerge, leads to an increasingly rational way of life. (2) The tendency of late capitalism to crises of social integration (interpretive, legitimation and motivation crises) is the result of new, post-traditional forms of culture, society and personality being blocked by system imperatives. (3) Therefore, late capitalism is irrational insofar as it generates "cultural contradictions" that could be rationally solved, by altering the balance between system and lifeworld. Nonetheless, Habermas does not advocate a *transparent* society along lines of Enlightenment rationalism: although rationalization of the lifeworld is permanent unless deliberately turned backwards by a willed suspension of disbelief, the lifeworld remains a sort of conservative ballast within the persistence of reflexivity (Habermas 1984: 70). A background of pre-reflexive consensus is essential to the conduct of everyday life, for reflexive debate about all social conduct would be exhausting and impossible.

According to Habermas, the economy and administration are not coordinated through communicative action, but are "steered" by means of "media" such as money and power. For Habermas, "media" turn linguistic coordination of action into coordination through quantitative values or qualitative performances. Correspondingly, the social practices of agents engaged in media-steered sub-systems ("mediatized") become predictable performances, within arenas that are normatively neutral and governed solely by efficiency. Consequently, he (eventually) proposes that economy and state are domains of strategic action, with a normative ceiling set by legislation reflecting a value-consensus emanating from the lifeworld (Habermas 1996: 55–6, 78–9).

- Economy: according to Habermas, the mediatization of economy and politics reduces the burden on communicative action in the detraditionalized lifeworld. The real abstraction of monetarized systems bypasses the processes of consensus-oriented communication, because the market functions as an information system, so that strategic agents can control the actions of others at a distance through price movements (Habermas 1984: 185). The automatic coordination of strategic actors and the efficient reproduction of material conditions are accomplished by the same mechanism. The law of contracts makes an area of social life in which individuals can relate strategically – meaning that the burden of legitimation for strategic action in the economy passes from the economic subsystem to the legal system, whose legitimacy subsidizes the entire network of contracts (Habermas 1996: 187–8).

- Politics: according to Habermas, disequilibria in the economy are managed by the bureaucratic administration that is mediatized by "power". The legally constituted authority of the administrative personnel results in a predictable hierarchy of qualities (degrees of authority) that relate to scientifically specified organizational performances, political decisions and manipulations of public loyalty (Habermas 1987b: 346–53). It seems to me that "power" is a qualitative medium where "money" is a quantitative medium – administrative legislation specifies the qualitative authority of state officials and describes their performances in ways that are predictable, rather than calculable numerically. Once again, this is a domain of strategic action sanctioned by law, whose legitimacy underwrites the entire network of performances.

For Habermas, the contradictions of capitalism have been so successfully managed that a continuous rise in living standards and new social cleavages have displaced class conflicts. The opposition between system and lifeworld constitutes the new shock front in social conflict (Habermas 1987b: 345).

The colonization thesis and the public sphere

Habermas explores the conflict potential of modern life at the end of *The Theory of Communicative Action* and in *Between Facts and Norms*. According to him, social reproduction must happen in both dimensions of social existence – system and lifeworld. Functional integration of the sub-systems of the social system is essential for the material production of life and the reproduction of social existence. But the normative reproduction of the lifeworld is crucial for social cohesion and personal motivation. For Habermas, the problem is that functional (system) integration depends increasingly on a technocratic society with a managed democracy, whereas normative (social) integration tends towards legitimation through public deliberation and self-reflexive social practices.

The result is the intrusion of system dynamics into the processes of the lifeworld, which Habermas describes as the "internal colonization" of the lifeworld by the system (Habermas 1987b: 332–73). The imperatives of system dynamics, driven by money and power, lead to the management of system disequilibria, such as economic stagnation or political crises, through transferring the fallout of these difficulties onto the lifeworld. In short, irrationalities of capital accumulation and bureaucratic domination are shunted onto the lifeworld through legal management of the normative problems that arise when rational agreement fails but processes of the renewal of consensus are blocked. According to Habermas, this happens through "juridification", the recasting normative relations as legal relations. For Habermas, legal relations are two-sided: both the missionaries of media colonization (as "juridification") and the pacemakers of normative social evolution (as the legislative control of social life based on deliberative democracy; Habermas 1996: 29, 40). (1) Legal relations carve out arenas for strategic action by formalizing relations between persons and making performances predictable. (2) But legal relations also impose a normative ceiling on strategic conduct, beyond which even actors who regard one another instrumentally cannot go. A clear example of this duality of the law is labour law and industrial relations. The key point is that the juridification of social relations displaces communicative action, and this process is an index of the clash between system and lifeworld.

Instead of normative agreement, juridification makes possible an imposed consensus based on formal performances. The paradigm of juridification is the transformation of citizens into clients of welfare bureaucracies through the expert management of socialization and acculturation, a situation that Habermas describes as "civil privatism". Another instance would be the transformation of communicative relations into monetary values through the legally sanctioned deregulation of market relations in everyday life. The system is driven by internal imperatives to reduce the complexity of its environment by eliminating the risks involved in public debates that aim at achieving consensus. From the lifeworld perspective, however, social relations become formal and abstract, while the state bureaucracy confronts its clients as a monolithic apparatus. According to Habermas, social crisis is managed by the mediatized sub-systems of economy and politics so effectively that crisis tendencies only really emerge in the lifeworld. Internal colonization happens once money and power extend beyond their legitimate domains of application and invade domains of action that require communicative consensus to operate successfully. The results are the characteristic crises of lifeworld structures (crises of loss of meaning, decline of social solidarity (anomie) and rise of psychopathologies). This is the Habermasian version of the reification problematic and the problem of "instrumental reason":

I still explain these pathologies by referring to the mechanism driving capitalism forward, namely, economic growth, but I assess them in terms of the systemically induced predominance of economic and bureaucratic ... rationality, within a one-sided or "alienated" communicative practice.

(Habermas 1991a: 225)

The process of colonization is made possible, because of the incomplete cultural rationalization of the lifeworld. Although traditional interpretations have lost their validity, the decline of the public sphere prevents the dissemination of the cultural resources needed to oppose the encroachments of mediatized systems. Nonetheless, resistance happens, particularly in the form of the new social movements, breaking out "along the seams between system and lifeworld" (Habermas 1987b: 395).

For Habermas, the environmental crisis, together with the decline of social solidarity, that is, a widespread loss of confidence in the legitimacy of institutional arrangements, is the major problem in contemporary society (Habermas 1996: 445). In complex social systems, which require rationalization of the lifeworld to make them possible, social solidarity takes the form of communicatively mediated self-determination. According to Habermas, problems in the monetarized-bureaucratic systems are diverted into culture and person, to protect the already weakened structure of solidarity, as from a system perspective, crises of meaning and anomie (e.g. the widespread dissatisfaction that goes with consumer hedonism and leads to nihilistic relativism) are preferable to crises of legitimation. Nonetheless, Habermas is adamant that the solution to the problems of modernity is not political revolution. He protests that the complexity of mediatized sub-systems is too great for the legislature (whether a parliament or soviet) to direct society consciously, since "no complex society could ever correspond to the model of communicative social relations" (*ibid.*: 326). Because the political is only one sub-system in a decentred system, "democratic movements emerging from civil society must give up holistic aspirations to a self-organizing society, aspirations that also undergirded Marxist ideas of social revolution" (*ibid.*: 372). Although the political sub-system "continues to be the addressee for all unmanaged steering problems", it cannot be imagined as "a macrosubject supposed to bring society as a whole under control and simultaneously act for it" (*ibid.*: 372). Instead, the dream of a transparent society needs to be replaced by the prospect of a self-organizing legal community based on democratic will-formation, in a renewal of civil society that aims to restore the public sphere.

As a consequence, in Habermas's rethinking, the progressive project undergoes a drastic truncation. Habermas rejects state socialism and the planned economy, together with insurrectionary politics and the working class as subject of history. But he also rejects alternatives such as market socialism and versions of democratic socialism that acknowledge the legitimacy of parliamentary democracy and seek to supplement this with social movements and political participation. In the place of the twentieth-century programme stands a modest programme for the renewal of the public sphere and the restoration of civil society, in a republican revival of democratic deliberation in advanced capitalism. The exemplary instance of this political project is the self-limiting democratic revolutions of 1989 (see for instance the Habermas-influenced analysis of 1989 in Arato & Cohen 1992).

For Habermas, the project of the left is to restrain system expansion and protect the social integration performed by the lifeworld. At the same time, the economic and administrative sub-systems must be protected against rash democratic impulses, which under conditions of social complexity might risk a new barbarism. The left must abandon the idea of the proletariat or the state as a macro-subject and the programme of the de-differentiation of society, to articulate a new balance between cultural and societal rationalization. A reinvigorated public sphere must be the epicentre for a practice of democratic will-formation capable of keeping the economy and administration within the right boxes. For Habermas, "only in an egalitarian public of citizens that has emerged from the confines of class and thrown off the millennia-old shackles of social stratification and exploitation can the potential of an unleashed cultural pluralism fully develop" (Habermas 1996: 308). But "throwing off the shackles" seems to involve an impressive broadening of the left project at the cost of a surprising loss of depth. The inspirational programmes of deliberative democracy, post-national governance, a cosmopolitan international order and discourse ethics seem supported by disappointingly modest reforms, including the formation of a critical public with egalitarian expectations, a reinvigoration of the public sphere, equal opportunities supported by participatory rights and a programme of reflexive controls over the public authority (Habermas 1996: 457–62).

The programme of deliberative democracy is the form taken by this effort to reflexively control the economy and administration without resorting to political violence or succumbing to the dream of a rationally transparent totality steered by the revolutionary state. Part of the problem with revolutionary aspirations was that these located renewed solidarity in the radical virtue of "new post-revolutionary men and women", an expectation that was always going to be disappointed in the context of a plurality of values. Habermas holds that a revitalized public sphere, which includes deepened political participation as well as open channels of public debate, is a realistic alternative capable of restoring the decaying solidarity of modern societies. On this basis, Habermas conceptualizes a procedural form of popular sovereignty arising from a radical democratization of society, where public deliberation on the legal system would create a balance between system and lifeworld. This preserves the legitimacy of the legal system by making it responsive to democratic will-formation, correcting the tendencies to legitimation crisis through addressing problems of democratic participation and substantive inequality. At the same time, cultural rationalization of the lifeworld would have to be unblocked, because, according to Habermas:

> even a proceduralized popular sovereignty of this sort cannot operate without the support of an accommodating political culture, without the basic attitudes, mediated by tradition and socialization, of a population accustomed to political freedom: rational will-formation cannot occur unless a rationalized life-world meets it halfway. (*Ibid.*: 487)

Habermas proposes that a deliberative democracy would coordinate constitutional liberties and political rights with extra-parliamentary forms of social activation and democratic citizenship, such as social movements and popular councils (*ibid.*: 299).

Beyond communication

Habermas's approach has been extraordinarily influential in Critical Theory and beyond, partly because he invites critical debate and responds constructively to argumentative challenges. Two of the most important instances of this have been the interventions of Nancy Fraser and Seyla Benhabib, who have questioned the extent of the *critical* part in contemporary Critical Theory. Although, from the beginning, Habermas indicated that Critical Theory would not be a utopian programme in the lineage of Romantic anti-capitalism, he insisted that it reconstruct the framework of historical materialism in line with its emancipatory intentions. Yet Habermas's recent political liberalism and endorsement of the idea of a post-secular society are difficult to square with Marx's vision of a radically egalitarian, post-capitalist society guided by participatory democracy. While neither Fraser nor Benhabib advocates a "return to Marx", their criticisms probe the question of what must be re-naturalized in order to shoehorn Critical Theory into the framework of what we might call a "constructive criticism of actually existing liberal democracy".

The question of gender inequality raises serious concerns with the formalism of Habermas's position. By treating gender roles solely as a question of cultural rationalization (traditional sex/gender roles versus de-traditionalized sex/gender roles), Habermas neglects the whole dimension of the gendered division of domestic labour, labour market segmentation, the gendering of social welfare categories and the lack of political representation of women. Fraser challenges the distinction present in *The Theory of Communicative Action* between norm-free economics and administration and an in-principle power-free lifeworld that includes the nuclear family. She draws attention to the structural bases in the gendered division of domestic work of the roles of citizen, labourer, client and individual, which means that these categories cannot be regarded as self-evidently given (as Habermas does). Centrally, by excluding domestic labour from the definition of social labour, Habermas misses the structural roots of women's subordination and the material bases for de-traditionalized (but still oppressive) masculine gender roles, such as the sole breadwinner (Fraser 1995).

Benhabib takes this further into a critique of Habermas's account of abstract selfhood in his developmental theory, which is based on Lawrence Kohlberg's theory of moral-cognitive developmental stages. For Benhabib, it is crucial to recognize that relations to the abstract, "generalized other" (the sort of universal reciprocity that yields mutual respect and social esteem) are not the only dimension of moral existence. Relations to concrete "particular others" are also crucial for caring and for responsibility to other individuals (Benhabib 1995). In her brilliant *Critique, Norm and Utopia*, Benhabib argues that although Habermas speaks about expressing feelings and interpreting needs, this is separate from normative debate. Thus, Benhabib suggests, not only is the normative dimension of Critical Theory unnecessarily foreshortened into a procedural formalism, but the utopian dimensions of the cultural interpretation of human needs and of concrete sociality are also lost (Benhabib 1986).

Axel Honneth's initial reservations about the Habermasian programme have now evolved into a different approach within Critical Theory, one that goes beyond Habermas but refuses Benhabib's

Adorno-influenced alternative. Somewhat startlingly in the context of a post-metaphysical philosophical approach that embraces the intersubjective turn, Honneth's idea of recognition struggles in late capitalism is built upon a critique of Adorno, Habermas and Foucault – and a return to Hegel. This is easily misunderstood. As Jean-Philippe Deranty points out in his striking critical study *Beyond Communication* (2009), although Honneth's powerful alternative is responsible for the recent interest in applying the Hegelian idea of struggles for recognition in late capitalism, this must not be confused with post-structuralist-influenced identity politics (Deranty 2009: 426–40). Instead, Honneth's "return to Hegel" happened in the wake of Habermas, where "reference to Hegel was a means to a non-Hegelian end, an alternative way to found a critical theory of society whose basic premises were certainly not Hegelian, but materialist" (*ibid.*: 9). Honneth's return to Hegel is a kind of return to Marx, not unlike Habermas's earlier claim to have discovered an underdeveloped conceptual distinction at the mutual root of Hegel and Marx's theories, one with the potential to correct their subsequent mistakes.

From Honneth's perspective, the return to Hegel means he can also correct something highly problematic about the way that Habermas relies on functionalism, namely his upholding of "the theoretical fictions of a norm-free domain of social reproduction (the economy, the administration) and of a power-free domain of social integration (the family, the public sphere)" (*ibid.*: 97). As Honneth specifies in his *Critique of Power*:

> [Habermas's] methodological dualism of "system integration" and "social integration" that was initially only supposed to describe two complimentary perspectives in the analysis of one and the same process of evolution is transformed along the path toward the rationalisation of social action into the factual dualism of "system" and "lifeworld". (Honneth 1991: 294)

These problems – the reification of an analytical distinction into an ontological difference, system/lifeworld, and the supposition that these correspond to the distinction norm-free/normative – are of course related, because they are based on the opposition between strategic action and communicative action.

Honneth's alternative is to think through the way that both work and interaction are permeated by the normative dimension, in order to reconnect the process of the expansion and deepening of moral universality with the process of functional differentiation in complex societies. His claim is that the young Hegel's Jena manuscripts contain the germ of a theory of moral identity that includes interpersonal, legal–moral and cultural–ethical dimensions, before these become reified in the philosophy of right into that famous triad of ethical life, the family, civil society and the state. In a complex argument involving moral psychology and a deep interest in psychoanalysis, Honneth proposes that the components of moral identity are developed by agents in response to their socialization, which involves an internalization of social expectations as to how they treat others, and how they are treated themselves. Describing these as three abstract "recognition spheres" that compose every agent's normative self-relation (i.e. sense of moral selfhood), Honneth discusses these components of moral identity in privative terms, defining them in terms of how they can be damaged. Accordingly, he defines these recognition spheres in terms of:

- "love" as an interpersonal bond founded on the non-violation of the body;
- "respect" as a formal, universalistic relation founded on the non-denial of rights;
- "esteem", sometimes also called "solidarity", as a particular, communal relation founded on the non-denigration of individuals' worth.   (Honneth 1995: 106–9)

Two features of these definitions deserve remark. The first is that these are intended as relational definitions of moral identity based in historically developing forms of ethical life, because the key idea is the *violation of an agent's expectations* through the abuse of their body (beyond what they expect), the denial of rights (relative to the ones they actually have) and the denigration of their worth (in a communal context of hierarchical valuations). As Honneth proposes:

> The sequence of forms of recognition follows the logic of a formative process that is mediated by the stages of a moral struggle. In the course of their identity formation and at their current stage of integration into the community, subjects are … transcendentally required to enter into an intersubjective conflict, the outcome of which is the recognition of claims to autonomy previously not socially affirmed.   (*Ibid.*: 69)

The second feature is that the ambition is to describe social conflict in terms not only of interest clashes, but also of normative grievances. According to Honneth, this generates a chain of struggles whose effect is the extension and deepening of the normative relations of a historical form of life:

> [I]n every historical epoch, individual particular anticipations of expanded recognition relations accumulate into a system of normative demands, and this consequently forces societal development as a whole to adapt to the process of progressive individuation. (*Ibid.*: 83–4)

For Honneth, "the result is a chain of normative ideals pointing in the direction of increasing personal autonomy" (*ibid.*: 84). Following Marshall's political sociology of citizenship, Honneth identifies a cumulative development of in modern rights-claims. The scope of legal recognition has expanded considerably during the last two hundred years. Contemporary discussions distinguish:

- civil rights guaranteeing liberty (negative rights securing life, liberty and property);
- political rights guaranteeing participation (positive rights protecting entry into public life); and
- social rights guaranteeing basic welfare (distribution of basic goods).

For Honneth, this represents an expansion in the scope of rights and their progressive extension into spheres – for instance intimacy and solidarity – previously regulated by other principles. This is because struggles for recognition have resulted in a continuous development in the legally safeguarded capabilities regarded as the minimal basis for democratic citizenship (*ibid.*: 114).

Together, these add up to two extremely serious and important claims. (1) Moral progress, at least in the Western world, has been the consequence of recognition struggles that have successfully claimed expanded rights. These things were not generously handed down by a benevolent liberal capitalism. They were won in struggle. And (2) social conflict is generally triggered by *legitimate normative grievances*, with the implication that protest movements and reform claims are usually justified:

> What motivates individuals or social groups to call the prevailing recognition order into question and to engage in practical

resistance is the moral conviction that, with respect to their own situations or particularities, the recognition principles considered legitimate are incorrectly or inadequately applied.

(Honneth 2003: 157)

This is the "motivational basis of *all* social conflicts" (*ibid.*: 157).

Summary of key points

Differences between Critical Theory and Frankfurt School Marxism

- Critical Theory retrieves normatively grounded forms of democratic theory for progressive purposes, especially around the idea of the public sphere, defined as the "social space generated in communicative action", that is the space of rational debates about matters concerning the general interest.
- Critical Theory introduces a distinction between labour (and instrumental rationality) and interaction (and communicative rationality) designed to prevent the collapse of normative questions into the theory of social evolution that is typical of unreconstructed forms of historical materialism.

Social structure, crisis tendencies and political conflict

- Based on conventional definitions of class and state, class conflict has become merely latent because of the administrative management of economic crises, but this transfers crisis potentials to the nation state, which tends to suffer from rationality crises as the bureaucracy struggles with social planning.
- The administrative system transfers rationality crises onto the socio-cultural system in the form of potential for legitimation and motivation crises based around declining social solidarity and the disintegration of the capitalist work ethic.
- Social structure is best conceptualized in terms of regions of strategic action – the capitalist economy and state administration – where action is coordinated instrumentally, and regions of communicative action – the socio-cultural system, better regarded as the lifeworld – where action is coordinated through rational arguments.

- Political conflict, often represented by the new social movements, breaks out along the seams of the opposition between system and lifeworld because of the unbalanced relation between communicative and strategic action domains, which is ultimately a consequence of capitalist social relations.
- Ideology is recast as systematically distorted communication, that is the internalization of norms and values that have been fixed in place to support system processes and protected from debate by vested interests, into the self-identity of individuals in a form of self-deception.

Political strategy and radical prospects

- The ideal of a deliberative democracy seeks to revitalize the public sphere and restore democratic controls over the economy and administration, without returning to the classical vision of a society centred on the revolutionary state and supported by a virtuous citizenry.
- The concept of recognition struggles supports the normative grievances that underlie social conflict and political movements, locating the root of moral progress and democratic potentials in modern society not in rational arguments, but in rationally motivated political clashes that respond to oppression.

eight

Post-Marxism

The "post" in post-Marxism signifies ambivalence, a politics that is after, but not beyond, Marxism. The diversity of post-Marxism is enormous. On the one hand, for many contemporary thinkers, "the only possible future for Marxism is as one contributing strand among others in the new, post-Marxian field" (Aronson 1995: 111, Fraser cited). On the other hand, Marx has become an essential reference point for most social theory today, so that nobody can really be considered to make a serious contribution to the field without engagement with Marxism. This is the spirit in which (non-Marxist) philosopher Jacques Derrida once wrote that "there will be … no future without Marx" (Derrida 1994: 13). The dispersion and dilution of Marxism is the same thing as the breadth and depth of its influence, and this is to be welcomed. As Stuart Sim argues, however, a distinction can be made between *post*-Marxism and post-*Marxism*:

> To be *post*-Marxist is to have turned one's back on the princi-
> ples of Marxism, [whereas] to be post-*Marxist* is … to attempt
> to graft recent theoretical developments … on to Marxism,
> such that Marxism can be made relevant to a new cultural
> climate. (Sim 1998: 2)

We are therefore concerned with post-*Marxism*, a particular part of the post-Marxian field. That part explicitly essays a reconstruction of Marxism, one designed to retrieve its emancipatory impulse under specific historical and intellectual conditions. The discrediting of socialism with the collapse of historical Communism is only one factor in a raft of developments that problematize Marxism. Significantly, developments in twentieth-century philosophy, and especially the "linguistic turn" and the notion of intersubjectivity, have called into question the foundational assumptions of classical social theory. In this sense, then, we have already been in the midst of post-Marxism with Analytical Marxism and Critical Theory. But for various reasons, these "English" and "German" approaches have chosen against describing themselves in that way. Post-Marxism as the self-designation of a theoretical current and political strategy has been restricted to a particular wing of contemporary thinking. The post-Marxists dealt with in this chapter include some of the most exciting and influential contemporary thinkers, such as Ernesto Laclau, Chantal Mouffe, Slavoj Žižek, Judith Butler, Jacques Rancière and Alain Badiou. Although by no means a unified current, these post-Marxists have in common that they emerged from Structural Marxism under the influence, at least initially, of the philosophy of Jacques Derrida, Michel Foucault and Jacques Lacan. Laclau, Mouffe, Butler and Žižek in particular made efforts at the turn of the millennium to form a coherent tendency around a discourse-theoretical rethinking of concepts of practice, structure and history, and they will be the central focus of this discussion.

Although post-Marxism has been strongly criticized by many Marxists, I am not in agreement with the idea that the new post-Marxian field is just an "ex-Marxism without substance" (Geras 1990: 127–68). Alongside Analytical Marxism and Critical Theory, post-Marxism represents a provocative and challenging effort to reconstruct the project of the left while preserving the emancipatory impulse of Marxism. More activist-focused than other currents, post-Marxists argue that new sorts of social movement built around non-class social antagonisms have marginalized the politics of the class-based left, in both the industrialized countries and the developing world. Meanwhile, mainstream politics has shifted from two-party oppositions between liberal and conservatives, or social democrats and conservative liberals (depending on location), to a bipartisan consensus on economic neoliberalism, authoritarian modifications of parliamentary politics and a communitarian emphasis on national belonging often larded with ethnic prejudices. The world of the great neoliberal consensus is a potentially fragile landscape of post-political technocratic management of social conflict, combined with frequent resort to right-wing populism in order to recruit electoral constituencies. Yet the left has been unable to regain the political initiative, despite the decline in the popular base of the mainstream parties and the massive failure of economic neoliberalism in a global financial crisis. By contrast, around the world, radical right-wing movements are framing a mass-based challenge to the agenda of neoliberalism, through a combination of populist politics with religious fundamentalism.

The response of post-Marxism is complex and various – consistent with the diversity of this current – but fundamentally based on a defence of the ability of the politics of protest to develop into a moment of rupture. Indeed, in some respects the "post-Marxism" label reduces to two things. First, most have replaced Marx's anti-political utopianism with a position that affirms the permanence of politics, understood as the necessity and desirability of those social conflicts that contest social relations through the mediation of the political community as a whole. And second, many find in post-structuralist philosophy an intellectual critique of the operation of thinking in fixed essences ("essentialism") that grounds perspectives of the end of politics. For Laclau and Mouffe, for instance, the key to an anti-essentialist politics of social complexity is to embrace the idea of the Democratic Revolution of Modernity. This is the idea that the modern revolution is centred on democratic politics as the process whereby social relations are contested and modified, in an ongoing process of the constitution of society by participating citizens. Accordingly, Laclau and Mouffe develop an agenda that integrates socialist strategy within the modern framework of democratic politics in order to retain the value pluralism characteristic of political liberalism. According to this conception, the left project involves the extension of the "Democratic Revolution of Modernity" throughout society, completely transforming the classical opposition between socialist and democratic revolutions.

The post-structuralist critique of Marxism

Laclau and Mouffe's *Hegemony and Socialist Strategy: Toward a Radical Democratic Politics* (1985) is a major post-Marxian manifesto. Synthesizing some ideas from post-structuralist philosophy, they perform a deconstruction of Marxism in order to argue the lack of credibility of the classical vision. Laclau and Mouffe propose that Marx's sequence of modes of production, unfolding according to the logic of historical necessity at the level of the economic foundation, was undermined at the level of the superstructures by a series of political contingencies. In a long analysis of the development of Marxism in the twentieth century, they argue that in the face of the increasing fragmentation of the proletariat and the expansion of the middle strata, the political strategy of the communist parties eventually embraced an ideologico-political strategy focused on creating a national-popular bloc. Here, the popular front led by the proletarian party strives to accomplish national reconstruction through achieving an ideological hegemony that forges a new collective subject (Laclau 1990: 120–21; Laclau & Mouffe 1985: 47–92). Although this was effectively a concession that acknowledged the failure of the classical model, Marxists (especially Leninists) none-theless insisted that the creation of national-popular hegemony around the proletarian party made it possible to salvage the classical strategy. Describing this Leninist politics as a "Jacobin imaginary", Laclau and Mouffe reject the effort to save the hypotheses of *State and Revolution*, maintaining that:

> What is now in crisis is a whole conception of socialism which rests upon the ontological centrality of the working class, upon the role of Revolution, with a capital "r", as the founding moment in the transition from one type of society to another, and upon the illusory prospect of a perfectly uni-tary and homogeneous collective will that will render pointless the moment of politics. The plural and multifarious character of contemporary social struggles has finally dissolved the last foundation for that political imaginary. Peopled with "univer-sal" subjects and built around History in the singular, it has postulated "society" as an intelligible structure that could be intellectually mastered on the basis of certain class positions and reconstituted as a rational, transparent order, through a founding act of a political character. Today, the Left is witness-ing the final act of the dissolution of that Jacobin imaginary.
> (Laclau & Mouffe 1985: 2)

For Laclau and Mouffe, Marx's theory was economically reductionist, predicting a progressive social polarization that would lead to the con-frontation between fundamental classes. This engaged a messianic vision of "an absolutely united working class that will become transparent to itself at the moment of proletarian chiliasm" (*ibid*.: 84–5). They propose that Gramsci's theory of hegemony represented the big breakthrough, because this makes possible a move beyond economic reductionism and revolutionary utopianism. As we recall from Chapter 3, Gramsci sug-gests that a fundamental class becomes hegemonic when it articulates its sectoral interests as the general interest and begins to exert "moral and political leadership" (Gramsci 1971: 57–8, 180–82). Gramsci's analyses suggest that fundamental classes struggle for hegemony principally on the ideological terrain, where new political subjects are forged, and his concept of ideology as the social cement that permeates the social formation significantly modifies the base-and-superstructure model. For Laclau and Mouffe, Gramsci explicitly acknowledges the importance of the transformation of social alliances into political subjects (Laclau & Mouffe 1985: 65–71). As they conclude, "intellectual and moral leadership constitutes, according to Gramsci, a higher synthesis, a collective will, which, through ideology, becomes the organic cement unifying a historical bloc" (ibid.: 67). Laclau and Mouffe argue that this represented a practical acknowledgement of the fact that instead of fundamental classes forming social alliances, politics really consisted of the struggle to forge collective unity based on ideological symbols. State power is a consequence of the hegemonic position of a new historic bloc, that is, of a social alliance forming itself into a national political subject, rather than a reflection of the capture of a set of institutions.

Yet Gramsci's historical blocs form around economic classes, and for Laclau and Mouffe, "this is the inner essentialist core which continues to be present in Gramsci's thought, setting a limit to the deconstructive logic of hegemony" (ibid.: 69). Accordingly, they argue that Gramsci reintroduces the classical Marxist dualism between the political contingencies of the hegemonic struggle, operative primarily on the ideological terrain, and the historical necessity guaranteed by the economic structure, which acts to unify the historic bloc "in the last instance". By contrast, Laclau and Mouffe affirm that "there does not exist a constitutive principle for social agents which can be fixed in an ultimate class core; nor are class positions the necessary location of historical interests" (ibid.: 84–5). In a prototypical deconstructive move, Laclau and Mouffe use the subversive potential of a minor category (hegemony) to invert the hierarchy between historical necessity and political contingency that, they claim, constitutes the Marxist paradigm.

After this deconstruction, Laclau and Mouffe maintain, political theory can break with the linked ideas of fundamental economic classes, closed social totalities, revolutionary transformations from the centre of social power and the elimination of social conflict accompanied by the end of politics. Then what appears is an immense proliferation of social struggles that criss-cross the complex, open-ended territory of the social field. Nothing whatsoever pre-determines the political orientation of these struggles, because their strategic-relational connection to global strategies of social change – from the left or the right – is a question of ideological articulation. Further, because these articulations depend on symbolic unification of different interests into a common subjectivity through the ideological cement of a hegemonic representation of the world, politics is radically indeterminate, that is completely open. In this light, they regard the emergence of the new social movements (NSM) in the industrialized countries and the developing world – movements such as land occupations, civic activism coalitions, peace campaigns, anti-nuclear protests, feminism, and so forth – as evidence of the non-class nature of contemporary politics. For Laclau and Mouffe, the NSM continue the fragmentation of the "unitary subject" of classical Marxism and highlight "the plurality of the social and the unsutured character of all political identity" (*ibid.*: 166). The big question for the left shifts from "how can the proletariat win moral and political leadership of social struggles and thereby gain hegemony?" to "what representation of social change can secure a broad social alliance capable of demo-cratically winning power?". Laclau and Mouffe propose that the best frame for responding to this strategic question is to regard the NSM as "a moment of deepening of the democratic revolution" (*ibid.*: 163).

New social movements and democratic politics

Laclau and Mouffe formulate their ideas about the open-ended charac-ter of politics in complex, de-totalized social formations through con-cepts of discourse that draw heavily on theories of ideology framed by post-structuralist linguistics. To see why they do this and to understand what they are getting at, it will be helpful to look at their concrete analy-sis of resistance to capitalism in contemporary society first.

Laclau and Mouffe emerge from Structural Marxism, rather than from classical Marxism. But their analysis proposes that because of its insistence on the unification of social formations through the struc-ture-in-dominance, even Structural Marxism has not grasped the crisis dynamics of contemporary society. According to Laclau, instead of the capitalist mode of production:

> there are global configurations – historical blocs, in the Gramscian sense – in which the "ideological", "economic" and "political", and other elements, are inextricably fused and can only be separated for analytical purposes. There is therefore no "capitalism", but rather different forms of capitalist rela-tions which form part of highly diverse structural complexes.
>
> (Laclau 1990: 26)

They do not deny that there is an anti-capitalist potential in the NSM. What Laclau and Mouffe deny is that political resistance to capitalist relations needs to tap into a fundamental class in order to transform society's dominant structure. Their vision is of hegemonic settlements concluded by dominant social alliances. Such hegemonic settlements do not involve domination so much as *dominance*, secured by distributing power among alliance partners and granting concessions to subordinate groups, which has the effect of fragmenting opposition and disorganizing alternatives. The main mechanism of dominance is the hegemonic ideology, and when this is successfully challenged, the social arrangements of a hegemonic settlement also break up.

Writing in the 1980s, Laclau and Mouffe propose that the NSM are the result of the hegemonic post-war formation encountering structural limits to its articulation of economics, politics and ideology. To clarify this claim, they argue that post-war capitalism involved an interventionist state managing social reproduction through welfare mechanisms and economic production through planned investment. Liberal-democratic ideology in the post-war era was reformulated in terms of equality, which framed wage bargaining and welfare claims as claims to equitable rewards and equal opportunities. At the same time, these social arrangements acted as a motor for the commodification and bureaucratization of social relations, so that "there is now practically no domain of individual or collective life which escapes capitalist relations" (Laclau & Mouffe 1985: 161). On this analysis, the NSM emerged in the 1970s and 1980s in opposition to commodification and bureaucratization, in the context of a refusal to frame the concerns of these movements as equality claims. According to *Hegemony*:

> One cannot understand the present expansion of the field of social conflict and the consequent emergence of new political subjects without situating both in the context of the commodification and bureaucratisation of social relations on the one hand, and the reformulation of liberal-democratic ideology – resulting from the expansion of struggles for equality – on the other. (*Ibid.*: 163)

Laclau and Mouffe's analysis, then, suggests that the NSM need to be analysed from a "double perspective". There is the transformation of social relations characteristic of the post-war hegemonic formation. But in terms of the hegemonic ideology, there is "the effects of the displacement into new areas of social life of the egalitarian imaginary", that is the predominance of liberal-democratic equality claims (*ibid.*: 165):

The fact that these "new antagonisms" are the expression of forms of resistance to the commodification, bureaucratization and increasing homogenization of social life itself explains why they should frequently manifest themselves through a proliferation of particularisms, and crystallize into a demand for autonomy itself. ... Insofar as, of the two great themes of the democratic imaginary – equality and liberty – it was that of equality which was traditionally predominant, the demands for autonomy bestow an increasingly central role upon liberty.

(*Ibid.*: 164)

"It cannot be doubted", Laclau and Mouffe sum up, "that the proliferation of antagonisms and of 'new rights' is leading to a crisis of the hegemonic formation of the post-war period" (*ibid.*: 168).

Next, Laclau and Mouffe seek to substantiate their claim about political open-endedness. They argue that the NSM and their demands for liberty – not equality – can go either way, to the right or the left, depending on the sorts of counter-hegemonic project that they get integrated into. In the context of the aftermath of Eurocommunism in western Europe, we can understand their claim that both right and left want to break up the post-war settlement and replace it with something else (market socialism, free market capitalism). Both formulate this in terms of a "revolution in liberty", rather than a gain in equality (liberal socialism within parliamentary democracy, libertarian capitalism hostile to the "nanny state"). But the left, from Laclau and Mouffe's perspective, remains stuck on the idea of fundamental classes, demanding that the NSM accept proletarian leadership and classical strategy, critiquing them as "middle-class protest politics" when they refuse. The neoliberal new right (Thatcher, Reagan) has the advantage, by contrast, for "its novelty lies in its successful articulation to neoliberal discourse of a series of democratic resistances to the transformation of social relations" (*ibid.*: 169).

The new right is an example of successfully challenging the hegemonic ideology. It links up the claim for liberty by the NSM (and beyond) and uses it to undermine the centrality of equality in the post-war welfare state's ideology. The new right, they claim, articulates liberty to free market economics and a restricted democracy, based on rejecting the "chain of equivalences, equality = identity = totalitarianism" and the affirmation of the sequence "difference = inequality = liberty" (*ibid.*: 174). "We are thus witnessing the emergence of a new hegemonic project, that of liberal-conservative discourse, which seeks to articulate the neoliberal defence of the free market economy with the profoundly anti-egalitarian cultural and social tradition of conservatism" (*ibid.*: 175). Drawing upon Stuart Hall's controversial analysis of Thatcher's "authoritarian populism" (Hall & Jacques 1983) and Allen Hunter's assessment of Reaganite discourse as a "specious egalitarianism" (Laclau & Mouffe 1985: 170), Laclau and Mouffe claim that this demonstrates the "fundamental ambiguity of the social". Nothing, for Laclau and Mouffe, is inherently right or left: there are only relational social antagonisms. The NSM demonstrate the "polysemic character of every antagonism", which exposes "the impossibility of establishing in a definitive manner the meaning of any struggle, whether considered in isolation or through its fixing in a relational system" (*ibid.*: 170).

Discursive articulation, hegemonic strategy, social antagonism

Against the political background of the NSM, Laclau and Mouffe maintain that "only the presence of a vast area of floating elements and the possibility of their articulation to opposite camps – which implies constant redefinition of the latter – is what constitutes the terrain permitting us to define a practice as hegemonic" (Laclau & Mouffe 1985: 136):

> We will therefore speak of democratic struggles where these imply a plurality of political spaces, and of popular struggles where certain discourses tendentially construct the division of a single political space into two opposed fields. (*Ibid.*: 137)

For Laclau and Mouffe, rethinking socialist strategy in this context involves a reconceptualization of praxis, structure and history in terms of discourse, antagonism and hegemony. To do this, they rely upon post-structural linguistics, according to which communicative signs are theorized as related by their differences from one another, and are considered to consist of an arbitrary bond between the "signifier" (material symbol) and the "signified" (ideational meaning). From this perspective, they argue, "every antagonism, left free to itself, is a floating signifier, a 'wild' antagonism which does not predetermine the form in which it can be articulated to other elements in a social formation" (*ibid.*: 171). A floating signifier is a symbol whose multiplicity of possible meanings is in flux, whereas an empty signifier is a symbol that stands in for the totality of possible meanings without itself having a determinate meaning. Laclau and Mouffe's former co-thinker Žižek provides the best description of what this means in its post-Marxist political application. In the struggle for ideological hegemony:

> The multitude of "floating signifiers", of proto-ideological elements, is structured into a unified field through the intervention of [an empty signifier], which quilts them, stops their sliding and fixes their meaning. Ideological space is made of non-bound, non-tied elements, "floating signifiers", whose very identity is "open", over-determined by their articulation in a chain with other elements ... If we "quilt" the floating signifiers by means of "Communism", for example, "class struggle" confers a precise and fixed signification to all the other elements: to democracy (so-called "real democracy", as opposed to "bourgeois formal democracy"); to feminism (the exploitation of women as resulting from the class-conditioned division of labour); to ecologism (the destruction of natural resources as a logical consequence of profit-oriented capitalist production); to the peace movement (the principal danger to peace is adventuristic imperialism), and so on. What is at stake in the ideological struggle is which of the [empty signifiers] will totalise, will include in its series of equivalences these free-floating elements.
> (Žižek 1989: 87–8)

There is something interesting about all this. If we accept Laclau and Mouffe's description of the struggle to articulate the claims of the NSM into a political project, undertaken by the New Left and the New Right in the 1970s and 1980s, then Žižek's description of ideological hegemony seems intuitively plausible. But actually – surprisingly – Laclau and Mouffe categorically refuse the restriction of their concept of discourse to ideology, insisting that "discursive practice" involves the modification of social structures (conceptualized according to a language-based model). They define "articulation [as] any practice establishing a relation among elements such that their identity is modified as a result of the articulatory practice. The structured totality resulting from the articulatory practice we will call discourse" (Laclau & Mouffe 1985: 105).

Laclau and Mouffe suppose that "discursive practices" involve the construction of relations of equivalence and difference whereby the identity of discursive elements is modified. The concept of discourse requires that the practice of articulation "must pierce the entire material density of the multifarious institutions" it operates on (*ibid.*: 109). This means that there is no difference between the construction of a political alliance, the modification of institutional arrangements and the creation of a hegemonic worldview. For instance, "enumerative discourse [the listing of alliance partners] *is* a real force which contributes to the moulding and constitution of social relations" (*ibid.*: 110). They therefore speak of ideological subject-positions, social movements, institutional locations and floating signifiers in the same terms.

There has been a fierce debate about the ontology and epistemology of Laclau and Mouffe's discourse theory, in which the critics have been extremely sceptical towards this transposition of a way of thinking based in ideology critique onto the theorization of social formations considered as a whole (Geras 1990; Miklitsch 1995; Palmer 1990). In response, Laclau and Mouffe have vigorously defended their position (Laclau & Mouffe 1987), although it has to be said that Žižek's theoretical slip from discourse in general to ideology alone is representative of the somewhat uncritical reception of this influential strand of post-Marxism.

At any rate, according to Laclau and Mouffe, the formation of hegemony involves building up a social alliance based on opposition to a social antagonist. On the one hand, the empty signifier unifies a series of disparate struggles by transforming them into neutral differences within a broad identity (e.g. feminism, ecologism, peace, etc. each have their specific claims and domain of action in a broad, popular movement). On the other hand, the empty signifier presents the members of this alliance as all "the same" in relation to their political adversary (e.g. "feminism, ecologism, peace, etc. are all fronts of the communist struggle against the anti-popular capitalist oligarchy and its political henchmen"). The implication is that political subjectivity is formed in a process that renders it inherently *incomplete*, because identity depends on opposition to something held to negate the identity of the subject (e.g. "women's rights, nature, peaceful coexistence cannot exist as such because of the constant threat to them by the capitalist regime"). To concretize the concepts of discursive articulation, hegemony and social antagonism, consider the example depicted in Figure 5.

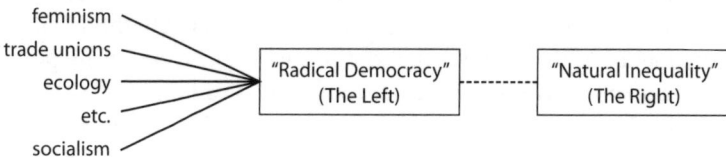

feminism
trade unions
ecology
etc.
socialism

"Radical Democracy"
(The Left)

"Natural Inequality"
(The Right)

Figure 5 The structure of hegemonic articulations (based on Laclau 2000: 303).

Figure 5 outlines a sort of limit case in Laclau and Mouffe's strategic vision. A political alliance of the left has achieved hegemony around the empty signifier of "radical democracy", successfully defining the meaning of the vast majority of social struggles in terms of claims posed within an egalitarian political subjectivity. Between alliance partners, neutral relations of difference exist, determining the various subject-positions, or political identities, within the discursive formation (i.e. the social formation considered as a discourse). But in relation to an excluded element – marshalled around the signifier "Natural Inequality", selected as *the* empty signifier of the political right following Norberto Bobbio (Bobbio 1996: 60–81) – these subject-positions are all equivalent, as parts of the left. The relation of equivalence constitutes a social antagonism, where the social identities in the alliance of the left are decompleted by the existence of the right. Both sides seek to negate the identity of their antagonist by excluding the other while completely defining society.

The most crucial aspect to Laclau and Mouffe's theory is that this social antagonism is ineradicable. Even empty signifiers are still defined by difference, although a signifier that stands in for the totality of possible meanings can only be defined against a meaningless, excluded element. From the perspective of the hegemonic left alliance, then, the right appears as a radical fringe group, a particular interest lacking universal reference. The key point, however, is that the same situation could equally well be diagrammed *from the right*, this time with "natural inequality" as an empty signifier uniting a right-wing alliance and the left as the "meaningless" antagonist. The outcome of this struggle depends upon the contingencies of political interventions, so modern history really consists of the alternation of hegemonic empty signifiers.

Radical democracy, democratic citizenship, social imaginary

Because social antagonism is ineradicable, left-wing politics must become fully democratic, or risk the delusory slide into totalitarianism associated with the "Jacobin Imaginary". Consonant with this position, Laclau and Mouffe propose that the "decisive mutation in the political imaginary of Western societies took place two hundred years ago" with the French Revolution (Laclau & Mouffe 1985: 155). Following Claude Lefort, Laclau and Mouffe propose that the innovation of the French Revolution is representative government, which they describe as "democratic invention" because it involves the shaping of social relations through democratic politics. This depends, conceptually, on a political agreement that the ideal universality of the people, the nation and the state, that is, the sovereign power that unifies society, is a sort of empty place that different groups temporarily occupy following democratic elections (Laclau & Mouffe 1985: 152–9; Lefort 1988: 16–18). Different groups seek to temporarily occupy the place of power with their empty signifiers, thereby generating a hegemonic worldview for a period of time.

What happens in alliance-building, Laclau and Mouffe propose, is that particular demands become unified by empty signifiers, which involves a process of the universalization of the identity of the social alliance in question. Recasting Gramsci's national-popular hegemony in post-structuralist terms, they argue that hegemony can be theorized in terms of the progressive universalization of a subject-position, through the emptying out of the particular contents of a political identity, and its occupation of a locus of formal universality. Laclau and Mouffe describe this as the creation of social imaginaries – that is paradigmatic representations of the world that set limits to what appears to be possible – and argue that the left should seek to construct a new social imaginary rather than to take state power and transform capitalism. We must accept that "the objective of the Left should be the extension and deepening of the democratic revolution initiated two hundred years ago" (Mouffe 1992a: 1).

Accordingly, Laclau and Mouffe propose that the task of the left "cannot be to renounce liberal-democratic ideology, but, on the contrary, to deepen and expand it in the direction of a radical and plural democracy [through] expanding the chain of equivalents between the different struggles against oppression" (Laclau & Mouffe 1985: 176). They reject the idea that a radical democracy would mean the democratization of the entire society, describing this as the "Jacobin temptation" to eliminate antagonism. They insist that the left project must be politically pluralist. Instead of radical democratization of society, then, their project involves the radical democratization *of the left*, together with the democratic radicalization of the forces aligned with post-Marxist currents. They key to this, they argue, is the idea of democratic citizenship, conceptualized in terms of political participation and social contestation. Clearly, the fundamental strategy is based around social movement activism and the permanence of political conflicts as a central part of what democratic politics actually is. The linking of democratic citizenship with radical democracy therefore aims against what Laclau and

Mouffe regard as depoliticized versions of democracy, which think of democratic politics in terms of interest-group negotiations and peak representative bodies (Mouffe 1992b).

At the turn of the millennium, Laclau attempted to form a distinct theoretical current around this redefinition of socialist strategy by engaging Judith Butler and Slavoj Žižek in a debate on political contingency, normative universality and hegemonic strategy. Although Butler remains close to Laclau in broad strategic terms, Žižek upset the party by raising three searching and provocative questions. His intervention was symptomatic of a vigorous re-assertion of radicalism within the post-Marxian field and a decisive shift away from coalition politics focused on the industrialized world, towards a resumption of the left's concerns with the self-emancipation of the oppressed majority of the world's population.

The first probing question was how it was possible that a non-normative, purely descriptive theory of politics as social antagonism, happening between two structurally equivalent social camps, striving for hegemony on the logically arbitrary basis of contending empty signifiers, could possibly issue in a specifically left-wing position. Laclau "oscillates between proposing a neutral formal frame that describes the working of the political field, without implying any specific [political partisanship], and the prevalence given to a particular leftist political practice[:] 'radical democracy'" (Žižek 1999: 174). Lacking normative claims about materially grounded oppression and structurally determined interests, Laclau and Mouffe's theory cannot explain why it leads to *socialist* strategy, as opposed to a Machiavellian recipe that can be equally applied by left and right.

The second pointed question concerned the historical origins and social coordinates of the Democratic Revolution of Modernity. Why is it that *this* revolution creates a formally universal political arena thereafter occupied only by political particulars, yet every subsequent revolution is said to belong to the "Jacobin temptation" and lead only to a "totalitarian erasure of democratic space"? "What about", Žižek asks, "changing the very fundamental *structural principle* of society, as happened with the emergence of 'democratic invention'?" (Žižek 2000: 93).

The third question flowed from this. Why has the political practice of the Left restricted itself to the "critique of actually existing capitalism", based on an identity-political strategy of multiple struggles for cultural recognition? Žižek proposes that proponents of radical democratic politics "as a rule [neglect to mention] the resignation at its heart – the acceptance of capitalism as the 'only game in town', the renunciation of any real attempt to overcome the existing liberal capitalist regime" (*ibid.*: 95).

The post-Marxian field

Against the conceptual background of Laclau and Mouffe's radical democratic post-Marxism, and Žižek's pointed questions about its political implications, we could map out the post-Marxian field by dividing it up into three areas, in order of radicalism. All seek to maintain the spirit of resistance to capitalism, and most connect this to a refusal to reduce democracy to parliamentary lobbying, but none regard revolutionary capture of the state apparatus as a strategic goal for progressive forces.

Marginal subversion

The politics of marginal subversion, best represented by the work of Judith Butler, engages the potential for social role performances to subtly shift from improvisations within the regulations to invention of new regulations. In *Gender Trouble* ([1990] 1999) and *Bodies that Matter* (1993), Butler develops this idea in the context of queer politics and the rights of transgender individuals. Departing from Althusser's theory of ideological interpellation, she rejects the conception of gender as a substantial difference expressing an underlying natural sexual division. Instead, Butler conceptualizes gender as constructed through social rituals supported by institutional power. In line with social constructivism, she proposes that gender identities are cultural performances that construct an individual's sexuality. "Gender", Butler writes, "is the repeated stylization of the body, a set of repeated acts within a highly rigid regulatory frame that congeal over time to produce the appearance of substance, of a natural sort of being" (Butler 1999: 33–4). It follows from this that individuals can disrupt the naturalness of gender by producing cultural performances of gender roles that underline its artificial, constructed character, subversively exposing the way that gender is ideological rather than biological. The concept of "performativity" is intended to highlight the way that ideologically naturalized and culturally mainstream social identities are actually role performances according to a cultural script, one that can, in principle, be altered.

In *The Psychic Life of Power* (1997b), Butler explains why these incremental changes through subversive performances necessarily happen at the cultural and social margins. Every statement of the rules implies a reference to their infraction, through the inherent transgressions built into the "thou shalt not" of the regulations themselves. But the subject's relation to this opposition between regulation and transgression, normality and deviancy, is not one of completely free choice. Instead, transgression involves guilt, while conformity involves a melancholic subjectivity, because it is founded on the loss of an alternative it never knew it had. In her analysis of Althusser, Butler suggests that the ideological effect of "hailing", or ideological policing of the social norms, is not a singular act, but a continuous repetition of ideological interpellations, which means that the subject-citizen is constantly demonstrating their innocence through conformist practices. Her central claim is that "for Althusser, the efficacy of ideology consists in part in the formation of conscience", so that "to become a 'subject' is, thus, to have been presumed guilty, then tried and declared innocent" (Butler 1995: 13, 16). The subject is "driven by a love of the law that can only be satisfied by ritual punishment" (*ibid.*: 24). In the case of gender identity, through a complex argument with psychoanalysis, Butler maintains that that (normalized) heterosexuality emerges from a simultaneous repudiation and preservation of (transgressive) homosexuality, because heterosexuality "requires the very homosexuality that it condemns" (Butler 1997b: 143). Thus social norms, such as what Butler calls the "heterosexual matrix" of the supposed normality of heterosexuality, necessarily conjure up the possibility of marginalized alternatives. In *Excitable Speech* (1997a), Butler suggests "re-signification" (the reclamation of denigration as affirmation) might be one way to activate these marginal possibilities as a political strategy (Butler 1997a: 16).

Permanent protest

The politics of permanent protest, best represented by the work of Jacques Rancière, proposes that real political action involves an unruly disturbance that erupts into the space of technocratic social management. In *Disagreement*, Rancière proposes a fundamental distinction between the ontology of the social field, which is characterized by hierarchical inequality, and the non-ontological status of the political, which is characterized by a radical but formal demand for the principled equality of all men and women as speaking beings (Rancière 1999: 19). Rancière describes the regulation of arrangements that characterize the social field as "the police", and argues that in conventional conceptions of politics as negotiation, consensus and management, what is really happening is the policing of hierarchy (*ibid.*: 28). *Politics*, by contrast, happens when a social group, whose suffering under injustice is generally concealed by the operations of policing, breaks into the space of debate and announces that a wrong has been done. For Rancière, then, "the political", that is politics proper, is *theatrical*: politics involves the entry onto the "political scene" of a hitherto invisible political subject, the "part of no part", the group that does not fit in, whose intervention first and foremost is simply to assert their right to speak, in order to say "no", to disagree (*ibid.*: 45). The relation between the hierarchical social field and the egalitarian field of the political is that of a "twisting", or "torsion", that is a permanent tension, in which the day-to-day operation of the police is constantly endangered by the presence of wrongs. These wrongs can normally be twisted out of sight, because the political is not a thing, but a formal potential for the rebellion of egalitarian subjectivity.

Rancière is thinking of two cases of the political in particular: the nineteenth-century proletariat, which irrupted onto the political stage with socialist demands for radical equality, and the contemporary struggles of "illegal" immigrants in the European Union, a new super-exploited and politically marginalized group. If anything, Rancière suggests, the conditions of immigrants "without papers" is worse than that of the classical working class, because the situation of everyday politics – the police – has today virtually eliminated political dissent. With the advent of "post-democratic" arrangements, through bipartisan consensus on the technocratic management of social problems, the repression of the political – its twisting out of sight – has reached a new level (Rancière 1995: 5–38, 1999: 95–122). The combination of the hidden character of the political, the theatrical nature of political protest and its tendential elimination today explains Rancière's interest in aesthetics. For Rancière, the police determines a "distribution of the sensible", meaning both commonsense and perception, which effectively hides exclusion. Because the political being is the speaking being, to erupt onto the stage and begin to speak – even before anything is actually said – is the political gesture *par excellence*, something that links art's revelation of the invisible to politics' disclosure of unseen and unheard suffering (Rancière 2006: 12–13). Every disagreement is specific and involves particular injustice, which means that Rancière refuses to insert politics within a teleological process of growing equality. Furthermore, Rancière maintains that the sea of suffering cannot be drained, because "the community of equals can never become coextensive with the society of the unequal, but nor can they exist without the other" (Rancière 1995: 84). Accordingly, there is no general emancipation, only a permanent potential for resistance.

Radical rupture

Rancière's anti-ontology of political protest depends upon the assumption of the permanence of the state (and therefore social hierarchy under the police), but it does so on the basis of an ontology derived from Alain Badiou's *Being and Event* (May & Love 2008). The polemics between Badiou and Rancière over equality and universality, anti-ontology and ontology, need not detain us here. What is crucial is that Badiou's ontology is based around the idea of a radical rupture with the status quo that leads up to his conclusion, which is that the communist politics of radical egalitarianism cannot involve the capitalist state (Badiou 2005: 121–8). This conviction is a constant factor despite Badiou's shift from 1970s Maoism to a form of highly radical small-group politics today, one that organizes interventions around questions of immigrant workers' struggles against oppression and exclusion. Badiou's politics of rupture is grounded on a highly abstract ontology based in mathematical set theory that Badiou describes as neo-Platonism, partly in order to vigorously differentiate his position from the linguistic turn. For Badiou, contemporary philosophy, from Anglo-American analytic philosophy through to the post-structuralist aestheticization of reason, is a miserable, conformist form of postmodern sophism, incapable of saying the central thing. This is that neoliberal global capitalism is the ruination of universality into a multiplicity of heterogeneous "language games", a sort of nihilistic atomization of the social bond in the reign of the pure calculability of monetarized social relations (Badiou 1992: 55).

For Badiou, politics only emerges from the incalculable, in the form of an event of rupture with existing arrangements, and political subjects only form by virtue of the positions that individuals take on these unexpected political events. Badiou's ontology is highly formal and logically consistent, up to and including a kind of "formula" for the event, but I shall only deal with it descriptively. It is important to note that Badiou does not think that being is maths, but instead that mathematics describes what can be said about existant things, and that because of some technical issues in higher mathematics, it is possible to demonstrate that *many worlds are possible*, that is that many (ultimately mathematical) descriptions of being can be achieved. According to Badiou, what exists from the perspective of knowledge of a situation (for instance the sociology of a nation) appears to consist of a seamless totality, which describes not only the way that the world is, but also the only way that the world could be. But in actuality, an element always exists that, although it belongs to the situation, does not appear in it because it is denied the status of an existing entity. The event is the discovery that an anomaly belongs to the situation, which instantly renders existing knowledge a nullity and calls forth a radical process of the universal reconstitution of what exists around the site of the event. Politics is the making of worlds, and the paradigm is Marx's discovery that the proletariat is the "unreason of every reason", that is that what Hegel thinks is merely "the mob" is in actuality a new universal class that utterly undoes Hegel's *Philosophy of Right* and prompts instead Marx's *Critique of the Gotha Programme*. Accordingly, Badiou maintains that "every historical event is communist, to the degree that 'communist' designates the transtemporal subjectivity of emancipation, the egalitarian passion, the Idea of justice … an intolerance of oppression, the wish to impose a withering away of the state" (Hallward 2003: 240, Badiou cited).

Enjoyment as a political factor

Žižek's response to the post-Marxian field synthesizes the politics of radical rupture with an eclectic combination of ideas drawn from Hardt and Negri's *Empire* (2000) and Boltanski, Chiapello and Elliott's *The New Spirit of Capitalism* (2007). By inclination disposed to controversial intellectual provocations rather than systematic theoretical development, Žižek is best interpreted as a wake-up call for the left. Although he initially supported radical democratic politics, Žižek now rejects the politics of marginal subversion and permanent protest as nothing more than a hysterical demand for a new master. The left's acceptance of its own marginalization confirms, for Žižek, the psychoanalytic insight that political domination depends upon the internalization of the hegemonic worldview through unconscious attachments to social authority. The left, in other words, is not the equal and opposite of the right, but in the same position as the slave before the master, or the hysterical patient before paternal authority. Therefore, Žižek proposes, the key to a reinvention of left-wing post-Marxist politics resides not in the embrace of anti-essentialist theories, but in an intellectual and emotional break with unconscious acceptance of the invincibility of capitalism.

Žižek conceptualizes these libidinal attachments to social authority through what he describes as "unconscious enjoyment", for him the most fundamental mechanism in political ideology. He synthesizes Althusser's concept of ideology, as an ideological imaginary inculcated through institutional rituals, with Lacanian psychoanalysis, which points to the paradoxical satisfaction in displeasure obtained by neurotic repetition. In psychoanalytic terms, unconscious enjoyment refers to an excess of stimulation that is "beyond [and opposed to] the pleasure principle", the horrifying and disgusting way that the subject "gets off" in their deepest and darkest fantasies. These fantasies circulate around the institutional ritual, which has the force of a neurotic repetition-compulsion, something that Žižek highlights by investigating not how subjects represent their actions to themselves, but what it is that they are actually doing.

What Žižek is driving at is clarified by his pointed analysis of ethnocentric nationalism as the unconscious inverse of democratic politics, for allegiance to the rules of the democratic game implies participation in the institutional rituals of the nation state. But, Žižek claims, the institutional rituals of the nation state are generally based on ethnic exclusions, racist stereotypes and so forth, despite formal political declarations about universal human rights and civil liberties. This obscene, unwritten code:

> represents the "spirit of community" at its purest, exerting the strongest pressure on the individual to comply with its mandate of group identification. Yet, simultaneously, it violates the explicit rules of community life. ... Explicit, public rules do not suffice, so they have to be supplemented by a clandestine, "unwritten" code aimed at those who, although they violate no public rules, maintain a kind of inner distance and do not truly identify with the "spirit of community". (Žižek 1994: 54–5)

Accordingly, Žižek proposes that the ideological cement of any political community is incredibly difficult to dislodge, because it is not only unconscious, but would be denied by every citizen when confronted with the evidence. Yet the exclusionary and vindictive "spirit of community" is the only way to explain the visceral support that the political Right summons when they engage in the politics of scapegoating around immigration, for instance. Žižek believes that this splitting into ideologically sanctioned public law and an obscene unconscious supplement of unwritten codes of group belonging is structural, springing from the emergence of the autonomous subject and the division between public and private spheres:

> When, as a consequence of bourgeois egalitarian ideology's rise to power, the public space loses its directly patriarchal

character, the relationship between public Law and its obscene superego underside also undergoes a radical change. In traditional patriarchal society, the inherent transgression of the Law assumes the form of a carnivalesque reversal of authority: the King becomes a beggar, madness poses as wisdom, and so forth. ... However, once the public Law casts off its direct patriarchal dress and presents itself as neutral-egalitarian, the character of its obscene double also undergoes a radical shift: what now erupts in the carnivalesque suspension of the "egalitarian" public Law is precisely the authoritarian-patriarchal logic that continues to determine our attitudes, although its direct public expression is no longer permitted. "Carnival" thus becomes the outlet for the repressed social [enjoyment]: Jew-baiting, riots, gang rapes ...   (*Ibid.*: 56)

In an extended analysis of the break-up of former Yugoslavia (which Žižek, as a Slovene, personally witnessed), he argues that the basic mechanism at work in the unconscious enjoyment that ballasts ideological hegemony is the fantasy of the theft of enjoyment. At the level of the unconscious fantasy that can be rationally inferred from an analysis of what political subjects actually do in the institutional rituals of their nation state, Žižek claims, it is clear that every citizen unconsciously believes that their way of life is threatened from outside. Žižek insists that "a nation *exists* only as long as its specific *enjoyment* continues to be materialized in a specific set of social practices and transmitted through national myths that structure these practices" (Žižek 1993: 202). In the nationalist fantasy, marginalized groups and external enemies constantly endanger the "spirit of community", in effect threatening to steal the enjoyment that binds the political community. "The late Yugoslavia", Žižek adds, "offers a case study of such a paradox, in which we witness a detailed network of 'decantations' and 'thefts' of enjoyment" leading up to the genocidal events of the Serbian-led war in Bosnia (*ibid.*: 204).

For Žižek, the political implications are straightforward, if extremely demanding. The Left must aim its blow against participation in the institutional rituals of the political community. It must "traverse the fantasy" of nationalism, together with the other unconscious supports of capitalism. The only way to do this, Žižek argues, is to stage an unequivocal identification between the forces of resistance to capitalism and the excluded outsiders who are the targets for ideologically motivated efforts to bind the political community together by scapegoating them. For Žižek, this completely marginalized "part of no part" varies according to circumstance, but in the contemporary world system, it is most of all performed by the untold millions in the slums of the planet and the so-called illegal immigrants in the industrialized countries.

Radicalization of antagonism

Žižek's intervention seeks to radicalize the concept of social antagonism, in order to replace Laclau and Mouffe's horizontal vision of opposed camps striving for hegemony on neutral terrain with a vertical conception of hegemonic struggle reminiscent of Hegel's master–slave dialectic. According to Žižek's interpretation, if the empty (or "master") signifier determines the dominant mode of subjectivity in a discursive formation, then marginal identities have an asymmetrical relation to power. Political competition happens between parliamentary parties and social groups in democratic contestation – liberals versus conservatives, social movements versus bureaucratic administration, and so forth. These all represent efforts to install their demands in the place of power by groups who already have some relation to the ruling or "master" (empty) signifier. Social antagonism is not the same as political competition: in social antagonism, the "slave" is "nothing", a completely excluded element whose identity is entirely negative; this is the part of society with "radical chains", whose emancipation entails the complete restructuring of society. The master signifier, Žižek supposes, divides the slaves from themselves. This negative self-relation (the impossibility for the slave to arrive at self-identity) is positivized in the figure of the master. Hence the slave is the symptom of the master, but the master is the antagonist of the slave. "When we radicalize the antagonistic fight to the point of pure antagonism", Žižek writes, "it is always one of the two moments which, through the positivity of the other, maintains a negative self-relationship" (Žižek 1990: 253).

It has taken two decades of constant research and frenetic publication for Žižek to draw out two analytically distinct sets of possible conclusions from this position (Boucher & Sharpe 2010: 1–28). The first inference is Hegelian: the master–slave dialectic between hegemonic subjectivity and marginalized element triggers a struggle for recognition dynamized by an unconscious desire for full identity, which ascends through a series of stages of increasing inclusiveness, until a more universal form of ethical life is achieved. The Lacanian psychoanalytic twist in this dialectical schema of the struggle for recognition is that the only way to really achieve universality is to renounce the dream of a full identity, that is to abandon the fantasy of a perfectly harmonious society and the associated logic of the "theft of enjoyment" that underwrites it. Reminiscent of existentially inflected forms of Hegelian philosophy, this is a counter-final dialectic that holds open the possibility of social conflict with a progressive potential, refusing to postulate a final form of social utopia. This position is expressed, within the sometimes difficult terminology of Žižek's Lacanian dialectics, in works such as *Tarrying with the Negative* (1993) and *For They Know Not What They Do* (1991).

The other possible inference is anti-Hegelian: the master–slave dialectic is external to the struggles for recognition happening in society, because the revolt of the slave represents a pure, formal universality that cannot be accommodated in the existing political field. The slaves oppose their radical universality to society as a whole, in an insurgent posture that involves a "blank slate" politics of the total destruction of all existing social relations. Writing of the 2006 riots in France, triggered by police repression of and government hostility towards (mainly Muslim) youth in the satellite suburbs of Paris, Žižek maintains that:

> The fact that the violent protesters wanted and demanded to be recognized as full French citizens, of course, signals not only the failure to integrate them, but simultaneously the crisis of the French model of integration into citizenship, with its implicitly racist exclusionary normativeness. … This is why the protesters' demand to be recognized also implies a rejection of the very framework through which recognition takes place. It is a call for the construction of a new universal framework.
>
> (Žižek 2008b: 66)

Žižek's analysis is sometimes clogged with rhetorical provocations, pop-cultural detours and a baroque terminology. Thus, for instance, the revolt of the "singular universal" against capitalism is to be guided by a political theory of "voluntarist decisionism", which is to be combined with "Cartesian mechanism", to generate a "materialist theory of Grace" (Žižek 1999: 114–19). There really are some questions to be raised about the form and substance of these analyses, especially since Žižek's interpretation of Lacanian psychoanalysis can sometimes be challenged (see Boucher 2004; Žižek 2004).

Nonetheless, at its core, Žižek's work is a call to the left to return to the struggles of the oppressed and exploited against domination and exclusion, based on a principled normative universality that utterly rejects post-modern communal particularism and liberal identity politics. He expresses this in quasi-religious terms as a "messianic" injunction:

> Today, more than ever, one has to insist that the only way open to the emergence of an Event is that of breaking the vicious cycle of globalization-with-particularization by (re)asserting the dimension of Universality *against* capitalist globalization. … [W]hat we need today is the gesture that would undermine capitalist globalization from the standpoint of universal Truth, just as Pauline Christianity did to the Roman global Empire.
> (Žižek 1999: 211)

Returns to Lenin

Against this background, Žižek proposes a neo-communist politics based on a (sort of) return to Lenin. He maintains that the biggest obstacles to a left-wing revival are not liberal democracy and global capitalism themselves, but the hesitation of the left based on unconscious psychological attachment to them. His most recent books, *In Defense of Lost Causes* (2008a) and *Living in the End Times* (2010), represent shock therapy for the left, a battery of rhetorical provocations and intellectual challenges designed to bring progressives face-to-face with proof of their hidden complicity with the very thing they claim to oppose. Highly emotive terms such as "revolutionary terror" and "economic collapse" are used to elicit visceral reactions of horror from his (presumably left-wing) readership, which Žižek then confronts with the evidence that these reactions are, in fact, scripted by right-wing defenders of the system. Thus, for instance, Žižek admits that "the true aim of [his] 'defence of lost causes' is not to defend Stalinist terror, and so on, but to render problematic the all-too-easy liberal-democratic alternative" (Žižek 2008a: 6). As we have just seen, Žižek's justification for this drastic intervention is his belief that the contemporary left has become rather comfortable, entrenched in identity-political manoeuvres that accept that capitalism is permanent and liberal democracy is desirable, or frozen into a posture of negation that falls short of efforts to actually transform the state. In other words, in a searing indictment of today's left, Žižek thinks that those who claim to be post-Marx have nothing to say to the wretched of the earth.

According to Žižek, the basic analysis of Daniel Bell is correct: there is a "cultural contradiction" between atomizing effects of consumer hedonism and the social solidarity required to maintain global capitalism and liberal democracy. Advocates of the system have gone two ways. On the one side, the "anti-totalitarians", from the New Philosophy through to mainstream sociology, have declared that any politics beyond a militant defence of human rights leads inevitably to a totalitarian catastrophe based on a nightmarish utopia. The contemporary political blackmail, Žižek insists, is the forced choice between liberal democracy and fundamentalist terrorism, which excludes in advance the radical alternative of an anti-capitalist politics based in a governmental regime that is not parliamentary liberalism (*ibid*.: 4). On the other side, both neoliberals and neoconservatives (including their social-democratic and new-labour clones) are concerned that radical free-market capitalism undermines social solidarity. They address this through "a blend of economic liberalism with a minimally 'authoritarian' spirit of community" (*ibid*.: 2), so that right-wing populism and anti-liberal legislation make constant strides forward. Under conditions where bipartisan agreement between the governing parties has shifted so far to the right that liberal parties, such as the green parties in Europe or Australia, are regarded as "extremists", parliamentary democracy becomes increasingly inflected by authoritarian politics. At the same time, Žižek remarks, the dominant ethos in contemporary society is in the spirit of Francis Fukuyama and his idea of the "end of history": "liberal-democratic capitalism is accepted as the finally found formula of the best possible society, all that one can do is to render it more just, tolerant and so forth" (*ibid*.: 421). There has hardly been an epoch in human history where it has been so difficult to pose the philosophical questions of the good life and the best political regime *as questions*, without a witch-hunt for "totalitarianism" breaking out on all sides.

To break with such a monolithic consensus requires exceptional political willpower, Žižek argues, yet there are signs that the question can at least be raised again of whether capitalism is eternal and liberalism the only possible governmental form for human society. Metaphorically describing these symptoms of impending collapse as the biblical "four horsemen of the apocalypse", Žižek lists the four main antagonisms of global capitalism as:

- ecological crisis;
- new techno-scientific developments, especially genetic science and the bio-technological revolution;
- new forms of intellectual property, which in the context of an information revolution challenge private property in knowledge; and

- new forms of social exclusion, especially the extraordinary proliferation of shanty-towns in the developing world (*ibid.*: 421–7).

The first antagonism looks a lot like an external limit to capitalist
growth, while only the last antagonism yields a minimally plausible
political agent, namely the excluded masses of the "slum planet", whose
emergence is "perhaps the crucial geopolitical event of our times" (*ibid.*:
424). The increasing unrest in these zones of exclusion from global
capitalism signifies "a population living outside state control, in conditions half outside the law, in terrible need of the minimal forms of self-
organization" (*ibid.*: 424). Generating all of these antagonisms, Žižek
insists, is the "zero-level antagonism" between the included and the
excluded, which provides the matrix for integrating all four outriders
of crisis into a conceptually unified theory with a consistent political
strategy (*ibid.*: 428).

In the context of this analysis of global capitalism, it is not surprising
that Žižek's calls for a "return to Lenin" have been inflected through a
rehabilitation of Maoism, for this somewhat impressionistic description
of final crisis and popular opposition is strongly reminiscent of Mao's
ideas about peasant socialism, military strategy and imperialist breakdown. Žižek now argues for an ecological variant of the dictatorship of
the proletariat grounded in the "eternal idea of egalitarian communism",
based on Badiou's presentation of a neo-communist politics:

> In his *Logiques des Mondes*, Alain Badiou elaborates the eternal
> Idea of the politics of revolutionary justice at work from …
> the Jacobins to Lenin and Mao. It consists of four moments:
> *voluntarism* (the belief that one can move mountains, ignor-
> ing "objective" laws and obstacles); *terror* (a ruthless will to
> crush the enemy of the people); *egalitarian justice* (its imme-
> diate brutal imposition, with no understanding for the "com-
> plex circumstances" which allegedly compel us to proceed
> gradually); and, last but not least, *trust in the people* – suf-
> fice it to recall two examples here, Robespierre … and Mao.
> (*Ibid.*: 157)

The joker in the pack is revolutionary terror. This is not the place for
a full analysis of that particular provocation (but see Boucher 2010).
Suffice it to note that the link that Žižek affirms between communist
politics and the Jacobin terror of Robespierre is scripted in advance
by Laclau and Mouffe's radical democratic analysis of Marxism. All
Žižek has done is to invert it from criticism into affirmation, without

contesting its fundamental terms. But it is Žižek who has shown so effectively that this particular idea originates on the "anti-totalitarian" right. By accepting the terms of the antagonist, doesn't Žižek in fact admit defeat in advance?

But in recent works designed for accessibility, Žižek is less interested in provoking the theoretical left than in communicating to a broad audience about the continuing validity of Marxist ideas. Žižek uses his intellectual celebrity status to expose the structural violence inherent in a global profit system that is completely unchecked by meaningful democratic controls or enforceable international regulations (Žižek 2008b). He probes the moral and political responsibility of politicians and economists for the global financial crisis and connects their ideological blindness in a pointed way to the experience of the millions who actually have to pay for the collapse of banking institutions with their jobs, homes and family lives (Žižek 2009). Žižek connects the illegal war against Iraq and human rights abuses in the "war on terror" to massive contradictions in the West, where ideologically it is said to be impossible to do anything wrong in confrontation with an "axis of evil", yet the democracy supposedly being defended is less and less meaningful (Žižek 2002). He performs a blistering philosophical analysis of how neoliberal capitalism, with its promotion of self-interested gratification as the highest good, together with the increasingly authoritarian restrictions on democratic liberties that belong to security states existing in semi-permanent emergency conditions, reduce all values to the value of self-preservation, from which craven perspective of raw survival it appears that anything at all is legitimate against "global terrorism" (Žižek 2005). Finally, Žižek points out that the rapid recruitment of militants from the vast slums around most developing cities, to radical Islam or Maoist insurgencies, happens because of conditions that can be directly attributed to Western imperialism (Žižek 2010). Without for a moment endorsing terrorist atrocities, Žižek has the courage to propose that the destruction of the twin towers in New York is for the contemporary world system the equivalent of the disaster of the Titanic for the world that destroyed itself in the First World War (Žižek 2002: 15). The luxurious but atomized "atonal world" of contemporary individualism has begun to disintegrate as it runs unstoppably onto internal contradictions (financial crisis, marginal revolts) and external limitations (environmental crisis, the rise of Chinese state capitalism), and 9/11 is the symbol of this break-up.

Finally, though, it is Alain Badiou in his *The Communist Hypothesis* (2010) who best summarizes the dilemma of the neo-communist break-out from post-Marxism. Post-Marxism does not seem to be able to escape from ideas about contingent ruptures with all-embracing structures. According to Badiou, the Idea of Communism is an egalitarian rupture with business-as-usual capitalism that has had two major experimental failures, in nineteenth-century socialism and historical Communism. Rather than regarding these as learning processes within an emancipatory dynamic, Badiou thinks of incarnations of the egalitarian ideal as radically contingent and therefore entirely different.

This is reminiscent of existentialist philosophy, with its celebration of the arbitrary decision as the projection of individual intentionality onto collective history. Badiou proposes that "the communist Idea is what constitutes the becoming-political Subject of the individual as … her projection into History" (Badiou 2010: 237). Indeed, in an Althusserian vocabulary, "the communist Idea is the imaginary operation whereby an individual subjectivation projects a fragment of the political real into the symbolic narrative of History … [that is] the Idea is … ideological" (*ibid*.: 240). The spectre that haunts this entire conceptualization is that of arbitrariness, linked to political voluntarism (hence the celebrations of Mao and Lenin as figures of heroic political willpower).

Summary of key points

The radical democratic critique of Leninism

- Laclau and Mouffe argue that Marxism–Leninism depended on a series of classical assumptions about society – the ability of a social group to embody normative universality, the reducibility of ideologico-political phenomena to economic developments, the centrality of the state to the achievement of a rational society – that have now been falsified.
- They propose that in the evolution of Marxism, Gramsci's notion of ideological hegemony provides the way out, by thinking about politics in terms of the formation of collective subjects based on ideological hegemony. The left failed to realize this and articulate its project to the New Social Movements in the 1970s and 1980s, and therefore paid the price for its fixation on class.

Discourse, hegemony and antagonism

- Laclau and Mouffe analyse politics in terms of the creation of discursive formations, a concept that unites the Gramscian idea of a historic bloc with a post-structuralist theory of discourse as the creation of chains of equivalence and difference in the articulation of socio-political identities.

- They propose that hegemony means the creation of a collective subject whose worldview defines what can be imagined in society, through the installation of that collective subject's defining master signifier in the empty place of political power.
- Nonetheless, no hegemony is total, because every collective subject is defined by its opposition to a social antagonist, with the consequence that political conflict is a permanent feature of social life.

New concepts of political strategy

- For Laclau and Mouffe, the implication is that the left must become radically democratic, seeking to develop an egalitarian politics whose strategic aim is left-wing hegemony (as defined above), rather than the elimination of the social antagonist.
- Concepts of democratic citizenship as active participation in political movements and democratic politics as the permanent contestation of social relations, together with an embrace of the idea of the Democratic Revolution of Modernity, are the way, for Laclau and Mouffe, to avoid relapse into the "Jacobin temptation" of Marxist–Leninist politics.
- For other post-Marxists, marginal subversion, permanent protest and moments of radical rupture provide points of entry for left-wing politics into a contemporary landscape dominated by an ideological belief in the technocratic management of social problems that effectively tries to eliminate real politics altogether.

Žižek's return to Lenin

- Žižek's analysis suggests that this sort of left-wing participation in democratic politics, without any strategic objective of transforming society and revolutionizing the state, really evidences an unconscious attachment to the permanence of capitalism.
- His alternative is to conceptualize social antagonism on Hegelian lines as a master–slave dialectic, something that leads him eventually to propose new forms of universality and a revolutionary orientation to the state, expressed through calls to "return to Lenin".

Further reading

Readers wishing to follow up Western Marxism in more depth should begin with the most comprehensive work, Martin Jay's *Marxism and Totality* (1984). Perry Anderson's *Considerations on Western Marxism* (1979) remains a classic short work and Göran Therborn's *From Marxism to Post-Marxism* (2009) brings the story up to date with his impressive survey. Alex Callinicos's *Marxism and Philosophy* (1986) is an excellent critical study of the major schools of Marxism from a perspective sympathetic to both Classical and Analytical currents. Alvin Gouldner's *The Two Marxisms* (1980) makes a pertinent distinction between "scientific" and "critical" Marxism similar to the difference between scientific socialism and social philosophy operating in this book. Leslek Kolakowski's *Main Currents of Marxism* (1978) is a three-volume survey with a vast amount of valuable information, unfortunately animated by the spirit of positivist demolition of Marxism. David McLellan's *Marxism after Marx* (2007) is a major social history of the Marxist movement in terms of the communist politics of working-class organizations, tracing Marxist doctrinal evolution from nineteenth-century Europe, through Russia and China, to the developing world in the post-war era. His *Karl Marx: His Life and Thought* (1973) is an excellent introduction to Marx himself. In *Marxism and History* (1998), S. H. Rigby provides sympathetic overview of Marxist historical research from a non-Marxist perspective, while Paul Blackledge, in *Reflections on the Marxist Theory of History* (2006), provides the Marxist perspective.

Ernest Mandel's *Late Capitalism* (1975) and Michel Aglietta's *A Theory of Capitalist Regulation* (1979) are places to begin reading about

Marxist political economy today. (There are some more specialized references in Chapter 1.) Giovanni Arrighi's *The Long Twentieth Century* (1994), Ellen Wood's *Empire of Capital* (2003), Immanuel Wallerstein's *The World We Are Entering, 2000–2050* (2002) and David Harvey's *The Enigma of Capital and the Crises of Capitalism* (2010) bring these positions up to date. Beyond that, I strongly recommend that the reader look into Regulation Theory, especially Michel Aglietta, Bob Jessop and Alain Lipietz, as one of the most serious and interesting research programmes in political economy around.

Robert Wolff's *Understanding Rawls* (1977) makes a number of penetrating criticisms of modern political liberalism, as does C. B. Macpherson in *The Rise and Fall of Economic Justice* (1987). G. A. Cohen's *Rescuing Justice* (2008) is probably the most impressive egalitarian reply to Rawls. Moishe Postone, in *Time, Labor and Social Domination* (1996), develops a critique of capitalism based on a conception of human flourishing drawn from Marx's *Grundrisse*. Ellen Wood's *Democracy against Capitalism* (1995) represents everything that is best in contemporary post-classical Marxism; I interpret her contribution as a theory of the civic virtue of political participation, with radical consequences. Alex Callinicos's *Equality* (2000) is a spirited Marxist rejoinder to liberalism, defending egalitarianism from a non-market socialist perspective. Habermas's *Between Facts and Norms* (1996) is an impressive effort to articulate a political republicanism that incorporates the best of liberalism without accepting its atomistic conception of human existence. David Ingram's *Habermas: Introduction and Analysis* (2010) is an excellent critical introduction to the most recent elements of this complex theory. Honneth's *Das Recht der Freiheit – Grundriss einer demokratischen Sittlichkeit* [*The Right to Freedom: Foundations of a Democratic Form of Ethical Life*] (2011) is an important new contribution to Marxist-influenced theories of social justice, arguing on dialectical lines for the solidaristic and egalitarian implications of norms that have historically developed within capitalism.

References

Adorno, Theodor 1967. "Sociology and Psychology (Part Two)". *New Left Review* 1(47): 79–97.

Adorno, Theodor 1973. *Negative Dialectics*. London: Routledge.

Adorno, Theodor 1987. "Late Capitalism or Industrial Society?". In *Modern German Sociology*, Volker Meja, Dieter Misgeld *et al.* (eds), 33–56. New York: Columbia University Press.

Adorno, Theodor 1998. *Quasi una Fantasia: Essays on Modern Music*. London: Verso.

Adorno, Theodor 2005. *Minima Moralia: Reflections from Damaged Life*. London: Verso.

Adorno, Theodor 2007a. "Commitment". In *Aesthetics and Politics*, Fredric Jameson (ed.), 177–95. London: Verso.

Adorno, Theodor 2007b. *Philosophy of Modern Music*. London: Continuum.

Adorno, Theodor 2007c. "Reconciliation under Duress". In *Aesthetics and Politics*, Fredric Jameson (ed.), 151–76. London: Verso.

Adorno, Theodor & Max Horkheimer 2002. *Dialectic of Enlightenment: Philosophical Fragments*. Stanford, CA: Stanford University Press.

Adorno, Theodor, Else Frenkel-Brunswick, *et al.* 1964. *The Authoritarian Personality*. New York: Wiley.

Aglietta, Michel 1979. *A Theory of Capitalist Regulation: The US Experience*. London: Verso.

Althusser, Louis 1969. *For Marx*. London: New Left Books.

Althusser, Louis 1971. *Lenin and Philosophy and Other Essays*. London: New Left Books.

Althusser, Louis 1976. *Essays in Self-Criticism*. London: New Left Books.

Althusser, Louis & Étienne Balibar 1970. *Reading Capital*. London: New Left Books.

Amin, Samir 1974. *Accumulation on a World Scale: A Critique of the Economics of Underdevelopment*. New York: Monthly Review Press.

Anderson, Perry 1974a. *Lineages of the Absolutist State*. London: New Left Books.

Anderson, Perry 1974b. *Passages from Antiquity to Feudalism*. London: New Left Books.

Anderson, Perry 1976. "The Antinomies of Antonio Gramsci". *New Left Review* (100): 5–78.

Anderson, Perry 1979. *Considerations on Western Marxism*. London: New Left Books.

Antonian, Armen 1987. *Toward a Theory of Eurocommunism: The Relationship of Eurocommunism to Eurosocialism*. New York: Greenwood Press.

Arato, Andrew & Paul Breines 1979. *The Young Lukács and the Origins of Western Marxism*. London: Pluto Press.

Arato, Andrew & Jean Cohen 1992. *Civil Society and Political Theory*. Cambridge, MA: MIT Press.

Aronson, Ronald 1995. *After Marxism*. New York: Guilford Press.

Arrighi, Giovanni 1994. *The Long Twentieth Century: Money, Power and the Origins of Our Times*. London: Verso.

Badiou, Alain 1992. *Manifesto for Philosophy*. Albany, NY: SUNY Press.

Badiou, Alain 2005. *Being and Event*. London: Continuum.

Badiou, Alain 2010. *The Communist Hypothesis*. London: Verso.

Balibar, Étienne 1995. *The Philosophy of Marx*. London: Verso.

Barrett, Michèle 1980. *Women's Oppression Today: Problems in Marxist-Feminist Analysis*. London: Verso.

Barrett, Michèle 1993. "Althusser's Marx, Althusser's Lacan". In *The Althusserian Legacy*, E. Ann Kaplan & Michael Sprinker (eds), 169–81. London: Verso.

Benhabib, Seyla 1986. *Critique, Norm and Utopia: A Study of the Normative Foundations of Critical Theory*. New York: Columbia University Press.

Benhabib, Seyla 1995. "The Debate Over Women in Moral Theory Revisited". In *Feminists Read Habermas: Gendering the Subject of Discourse*, Johanna Meehan (ed.), 181–213. London: Routledge.

Benjamin, Walter 1973. "The Work of Art in the Age of Mechanical Reproduction". In *Illuminations*, Hannah Arendt (ed.), 219–54. London: Jonathan Cape.

Benton, Ted 1984. *The Rise and Fall of Structuralist Marxism: Althusser and His Influence*. Basingstoke: Macmillan.

Bernstein, J. M. 1995. *Recovering Ethical Life: Jürgen Habermas and the Future of Critical Theory*. London: Routledge.

Bobbio, Norberto 1996. *Left and Right: The Significance of a Political Distinction*. Cambridge: Polity.

Boggs, Carl 1976. *Gramsci's Marxism*. London: Pluto Press.

Boggs, Carl 1982. *The Impasse of European Communism*. Boulder, CO: Westview Press.

Bois, Guy 1984. *The Crisis of Feudalism: Economy and Society in Eastern Normandy 1300–1550*. Cambridge: Cambridge University Press.

Boltanski, Luc, Eve Chiapello, *et al.* 2007. *The New Spirit of Capitalism*. London: Verso.

Boucher, Geoff 2004. "The Antinomies of Slavoj Žižek". *Telos: A Quarterly Journal of Critical Thought* **129**: 150–72.

Boucher, Geoff 2010. "An Inversion of Radical Democracy: The Republic of Virtue in Žižek's Revolutionary Politics". *International Journal of Žižek Studies* **4**(2): 1–25.

Boucher, Geoff & Matthew Sharpe 2010. *Žižek and Politics: A Critical Introduction.* Edinburgh: Edinburgh University Press.

Buchanan, Allen 1982. *Marx and Justice: The Radical Critique of Liberalism.* Totowa, NJ: Rowman & Littlefield.

Buci-Glucksmann, Christine 1980. *Gramsci and the State.* London: Lawrence & Wishart.

Burston, Daniel 1991. *The Legacy of Erich Fromm.* Cambridge, MA: Harvard University Press.

Butler, Judith 1995. "Conscience Doth Make Subjects of Us All". *Yale French Studies* **88**: 6–26.

Butler, Judith 1997a. *Excitable Speech: A Politics of the Performative.* London: Routledge.

Butler, Judith 1997b. *The Psychic Life of Power: Theories in Subjection.* Stanford, CA: Stanford University Press.

Butler, Judith 1999. *Gender Trouble: Feminism and the Subversion of Identity.* London: Routledge.

Callinicos, Alex 1976. *Althusser's Marxism.* London: Pluto Press.

Callinicos, Alex 1988. *Making History: Agency, Structure and Change in Social Theory.* Ithaca, NY: Cornell University Press.

Callinicos, Alex 2000. *Equality.* Cambridge: Polity.

Carrillo, Santiago 1978. *"Eurocommunism" and the State.* Westport, CT: Lawrence Hill.

Carver, Terrell 1983. *Marx and Engels: The Intellectual Relationship.* Brighton: Wheatsheaf.

Chang, Jung & Jon Halliday 2005. *Mao: The Unknown Story.* New York: Knopf.

Chodos, Howard 2007. "Marxism and Socialism". In *Twentieth-Century Marxism: A Global Introduction*, Daryl Glaser & David Walker (eds), 177–95. Abingdon: Routledge.

Claudin, Fernando 1978. *Eurocommunism and Socialism.* London: New Left Books.

Cohen, Gerald 1978. *Karl Marx's Theory of History: A Defense.* Princeton, NJ: Princeton University Press.

Cohen, Gerald 2008. *Rescuing Justice and Equality.* Cambridge, MA: Harvard University Press.

Davies, R. W. 1995. "Forced Labour Under Stalin: The Archive Revelations". *New Left Review* **214**: 62–80.

de Ste Croix, Geoffrey E. M. 1981. *The Class Struggle in the Ancient Greek World.* Ithaca, NY: Cornell University Press.

Deranty, Jean-Philippe 2009. *Beyond Communication: A Critical Study of Axel Honneth's Social Philosophy.* Leiden: Brill.

Derrida, Jacques 1994. *Spectres of Marx: The State of the Debt, the Work of Mourning and the New International.* London: Routledge.

Draper, Hal 1972. "Marx and Engels on Women's Liberation". In *Female Liberation: History and Current Politics*, Roberta Salper (ed.), 83–107. New York: Alfred Knopf.

Draper, Hal 1977. *Karl Marx's Theory of Revolution, Volume 2: The Politics of Social Classes.* New York: Monthly Review Press.

Elliott, Gregory 1987. *Althusser: The Detour of Theory.* London: Verso.

Elster, Jon 1985. *Making Sense of Marx*. Cambridge: Cambridge University Press.

Elster, Jon 1986. *An Introduction to Karl Marx*. Cambridge: Cambridge University Press.

Engels, Friedrich 1950a. "Introduction to *Dialectics of Nature*". In *Marx–Engels Selected Works*, Friedrich Engels & Karl Marx (eds), 57–73. London: Lawrence & Wishart.

Engels, Friedrich 1950b. "Letter to Bloch, 21–22 September 1890". In *Marx–Engels Selected Works*, Friedrich Engels & Karl Marx (eds), 443–4. London: Lawrence & Wishart.

Engels, Friedrich 1950c. "Ludwig Feuerbach and the End of Classical German Philosophy". In *Marx–Engels Selected Works*, Friedrich Engels & Karl Marx (eds), 324–64. London: Lawrence & Wishart.

Engels, Friedrich 1950d. "Socialism: Utopian and Scientific". In *Marx–Engels Selected Works*, Friedrich Engels & Karl Marx (eds), 86–142. London: Lawrence & Wishart.

Feenberg, Andrew 1981. *Lukács, Marx and the Sources of Critical Theory*. Oxford: Martin Robertson.

Feenberg, Andrew 2005. *Heidegger and Marcuse: The Catastrophe and Redemption of History*. London: Routledge.

Frank, Pierre 1979. *The Fourth International: The Long March of the Trotskyists*. London: Ink Links.

Fraser, Nancy 1995. "What's Critical about Critical Theory?". In *Feminists Read Habermas: Gendering the Subject of Discourse*, Johanna Meehan (ed.), 21–55. London: Routledge.

Freud, Sigmund 2001a. *The Standard Edition of the Complete Psychological Works of Sigmund Freud, Volume XIV (1914–1916): On the History of the Psycho-Analytic Movement, Papers on Metapsychology and Other Works*. London: Vintage.

Freud, Sigmund 2001b. *The Standard Edition of the Complete Psychological Works of Sigmund Freud, Volume XIX (1923–1925): The Ego and the Id and Other Works*. London: Vintage.

Freud, Sigmund 2001c. *The Standard Edition of the Complete Psychological Works of Sigmund Freud, Volume XXI (1927–1931): The Future of an Illusion, Civilization and its Discontents, and Other Works*. London: Vintage.

Fromm, Erich 1966. *Marx's Concept of Man*. New York: Frederick Ungar.

Geras, Norman 1983. *Marx and Human Nature: The Refutation of a Legend*. London: Verso.

Geras, Norman 1985. "The Controversy about Marx and Justice". *New Left Review* 1(150): 47–85.

Geras, Norman 1990. *Discourses of Extremity: Radical Ethics and Post-Marxist Extravagances*. London: Verso.

Gramsci, Antonio 1971. *Selections from the Prison Notebooks*. London: Lawrence & Wishart.

Habermas, Jürgen 1970. *Toward a Rational Society: Student Protest, Science and Politics*. Boston, MA: Beacon Press.

Habermas, Jürgen 1972. *Knowledge and Human Interests*. London: Heinemann.

Habermas, Jürgen 1973. *Theory and Practice*. Boston, MA: Beacon Press.

Habermas, Jürgen 1975. *Legitimation Crisis*. Boston, MA: Beacon Press.

Habermas, Jürgen 1979a. *Communication and the Evolution of Society*. London: Heinemann.

Habermas, Jürgen 1979b. "Consciousness-Raising or Redemptive Criticism: The Contemporaneity of Walter Benjamin". *New German Critique* (17): 30–59.

Habermas, Jürgen 1984. *The Theory of Communicative Action: Reason and the Rationalisation of Society*. Boston, MA: Beacon Press.

Habermas, Jürgen 1987a. *The Philosophical Discourse of Modernity: Twelve Lectures*. Cambridge: Polity.

Habermas, Jürgen 1987b. *The Theory of Communicative Action: System and Life-world*. Boston, MA: Beacon Press.

Habermas, Jürgen 1989. "The Tasks of a Critical Theory of Society". In *Critical Theory and Society: A Reader*, Douglas Kellner & Stephen Eric Bronner (eds), 292–312. New York: Routledge.

Habermas, Jürgen 1991a. "A Reply". In *Communicative Action*, Axel Honneth & Hans Joas (eds), 214–64. Cambridge, MA: MIT Press.

Habermas, Jürgen 1991b. *The Structural Transformation of the Public Sphere: An Inquiry into a Category of Bourgeois Society*. Cambridge, MA: MIT Press.

Habermas, Jürgen 1992. "Concluding Remarks". In *Habermas and the Public Sphere*, Craig Calhoun (ed.), 464–9. Cambridge, MA: MIT Press.

Habermas, Jürgen 1996. *Between Facts and Norms: Contribution to a Discourse Theory of Law and Democracy*. Cambridge, MA: MIT Press.

Habermas, Jürgen 1999. *Moral Consciousness and Communicative Action*. Cambridge, MA: MIT Press.

Hall, Stuart and Martin Jacques (eds) 1983. *The Politics of Thatcherism*. London: Lawrence & Wishart in association with *Marxism Today*.

Hallward, Peter 2003. *Badiou: A Subject to Truth*. Minneapolis, MN: University of Minnesota Press.

Hardt, Michael and Antonio Negri 2000. *Empire*. Cambridge, MA: Harvard University Press.

Haug, Wolfgang 1986. *Critique of Commodity Aesthetics: Appearance, Sexuality and Advertising in Capitalist Society*. Cambridge: Polity.

Hegel, G. W. F. 1956. *The Philosophy of History*. New York: Dover.

Hegel, G. W. F. 1977. *Hegel's Phenomenology of Spirit*. Oxford: Oxford University Press.

Held, David 1980. *Introduction to Critical Theory*. Berkeley, CA: University of California Press.

Hindess, Barry & Paul Hirst 1975. *Pre-Capitalist Modes of Production*. London: Routledge & Kegan Paul.

Hirst, Paul 1976. "Althusser's Theory of Ideology". *Economy and Society* 5(4): 385–411.

Honneth, Axel 1991. *The Critique of Power: Reflective Stages in a Critical Social Theory*. Cambridge, MA: MIT Press.

Honneth, Axel 1995. *The Struggle for Recognition: The Moral Grammar of Social Conflicts*. Cambridge: Polity.

Honneth, Axel 2003. "Redistribution as Recognition: A Response to Nancy Fraser". In *Redistribution or Recognition? A Political-Philosophical Exchange*, Nancy Fraser & Axel Honneth (eds), 110–97. London: Verso.

Horkheimer, Max 1974. *Eclipse of Reason*. New York: Seabury Press.

Horkheimer, Max 1982. *Critical Theory: Selected Essays*. New York: Continuum.

Hunley, J. D. 1991. *The Life and Thought of Friedrich Engels: A Reinterpretation*. New Haven, CT: Yale University Press.

Ingram, David 1987. *Habermas and the Dialectic of Reason*. New Haven, CT: Yale University Press.

Itō, Makoto 1988. *The Basic Theory of Capitalism: The Forms and Substance of the Capitalist Economy*. Basingstoke: Macmillan.

Jacoby, Russell 1986. *The Repression of Psychoanalysis: Otto Fenichel and the Political Freudians*. Chicago, IL: University of Chicago Press.

Jameson, Fredric 1981. *The Political Unconscious: Narrative as a Socially Symbolic Act*. Ithaca, NY: Cornell University Press.

Jay, Martin 1973. *The Dialectical Imagination*. Boston, MA: Little, Brown.

Jay, Martin 1984. *Marxism and Totality: The Adventures of a Concept from Lukács to Habermas*. Berkeley, CA and Los Angeles, CA: University of California Press.

Jessop, Bob 1985. *Nicos Poulantzas: Marxist Theory and Political Strategy*. Basingstoke: Macmillan.

Kadvany, John 2011. *Imré Lakatos and the Guises of Reason*. Durham, NC: Duke University Press.

Kellner, Douglas 1984. *Herbert Marcuse and the Crisis of Marxism*. Basingstoke: Macmillan.

Kellner, Douglas 1989. *Critical Theory, Marxism and Modernity*. Baltimore, MD: Johns Hopkins University Press.

Laclau, Ernesto 1977. *Politics and Ideology in Marxist Theory*. London: New Left Books.

Laclau, Ernesto 1990. *New Reflections on the Revolution of Our Time*. London: Verso.

Laclau, Ernesto 2000. "Constructing Universality". In *Contingency, Hegemony, Universality: Contemporary Dialogues on the Left*, Judith Butler, Ernesto Laclau et al. (eds), 281–307. London: Verso.

Laclau, Ernesto & Chantal Mouffe 1985. *Hegemony and Socialist Strategy: Toward a Radical Democratic Politics*. London: Verso.

Laclau, Ernesto & Chantal Mouffe 1987. "Post-Marxism without Apologies". *New Left Review* **163**: 40–82.

Lakatos, Imré 1978. *The Methodology of Scientific Research Programmes*. Cambridge: Cambridge University Press.

Larrain, Jorge 1979. *The Concept of Ideology*. London: Hutchinson.

Lecourt, Dominique 1975. *Marxism and Epistemology: Bachelard, Canguilhem and Foucault*. London: New Left Books.

Lefort, Claude 1988. *Democracy and Political Theory*. Cambridge: Polity.

Lenin, Vladimir Ilych 1977a. *Selected Works in Three Volumes. Volume 1*. Moscow: Progress Publishers.

Lenin, Vladimir Ilych 1977b. *Selected Works in Three Volumes. Volume 2*. Moscow: Progress Publishers.

Lenin, Vladimir Ilych 1977c. *Selected Works in Three Volumes. Volume 3*. Moscow: Progress Publishers.

Levine, Norman 1975. *The Tragic Deception: Marx contra Engels*. Oxford: Clio Press.

Lévi-Strauss, Claude 1968. *Structural Anthropology*. London: Routledge.

Lukács, György 1963. *Die Eigenart des Ästhetischen*. Neuwied: Luchterhand.

Lukács, György 1970a. *Writer and Critic and Other Essays*. London: Merlin.

Lukács, György 1970b. *Lenin: A Study on the Unity of his Thought*. London: New Left Books.

Lukács, György 1971a. *History and Class Consciousness*. London: Merlin.

Lukács, György 1971b. *The Theory of the Novel*. London: Merlin.

Lukács, György 1972. *Political Writings, 1919–1929*. London: Merlin.

Lukács, György 1975. *The Young Hegel: Studies in the Relations Between Dialectics and Economics*. Cambridge, MA: MIT Press.

Lukács, György 2007. "Realism in the Balance". In *Aesthetics and Politics*, Fredric Jameson (ed.), 28–59. London: Verso.

Mandel, Ernest 1978a. *Late Capitalism*. London: Verso.

Mandel, Ernest 1978b. *The Second Slump: A Marxist Analysis of Recession in the Seventies*. London: Verso.

Mandel, Ernest 1986. *The Meaning of the Second World War*. London: Verso.

Mandel, Ernest 1995. *Long Waves of Capitalist Development: A Marxist Interpretation*. London: Verso.

Marcuse, Herbert 1964. *One-Dimensional Man: Studies in the Ideology of Advanced Industrial Society*. Boston, MA: Beacon Press.

Marcuse, Herbert 1966. *Eros and Civilization*, 2nd edn. Boston, MA: Beacon Press.

Marcuse, Herbert 1968. *Negations: Essays in Critical Theory*. Harmondsworth: Penguin.

Marcuse, Herbert 1969. *An Essay on Liberation*. London: Allen Lane.

Marcuse, Herbert 1972. *Counter-revolution and Revolt*. London: Allen Lane.

Marcuse, Herbert 1999. *Reason and Revolution*. Amherst, NY: Humanity Books.

Marx, Karl 1973. *Grundrisse*. Harmondsworth: Penguin.

Marx, Karl & Friedrich Engels 1953. *Marx–Engels Selected Correspondence*. Moscow: Foreign Languages Publishing House.

May, Todd & Jeff Love 2008. "From Universality to Equality: Badiou's Critique of Rancière". *Symposium: Canadian Journal of Continental Philosophy* 12(2): 51–69.

McCarthy, Thomas 1996. *The Critical Theory of Jürgen Habermas*. Cambridge, MA: MIT Press.

Miklitsch, Robert 1995. "The Rhetoric of Post-Marxism: Discourse and Institutionality in Laclau and Mouffe, Resnick and Wolff". *Social Text* 45(14:4): 167–96.

Mouffe, Chantal 1992a. "Preface: Democratic Politics Today". In *Dimensions of Radical Democracy: Pluralism, Citizenship, Community*, Chantal Mouffe (ed.), 1–14. London: Verso.

Mouffe, Chantal 1992b. *The Return of the Political*. London: Verso.

Napolitano, Georgio 1977. *The Italian Road to Socialism*. Westport, CT: Lawrence Hill.

Neumann, Franz 1942. *Behemoth: The Structure and Practice of National Socialism*. London: Gollancz/Left Book Club.

Offe, Claus 1984. *Contradictions of the Welfare State*. Cambridge, MA: MIT Press.

Offe, Claus 1985. *Disorganized Capitalism*. Cambridge, MA: MIT Press.

Palmer, Bryan 1990. *Descent into Discourse: The Reification of Language and the Writing of Social History*. Philadelphia, PA: Temple University Press.

Peffer, Rodney 1990. *Marxism, Morality and Justice*. Princeton, NJ: Princeton University Press.

Picone, Paul 1978. "Introduction". In *The Essential Frankfurt School Reader*, Andrew Arato & Eike Gebhardt (eds), ix–xxi. New York: Urizen Books.

Popper, Karl 1940. "What Is Dialectic?". *Mind* **49**: 403–26.

Popper, Karl 1964. *The Poverty of Historicism*. New York: Harper.

Poulantzas, Nicos 1973. *Political Power and Social Classes*. London: New Left Books.

Poulantzas, Nicos 1975. *Classes in Contemporary Capitalism*. London: New Left Books.

Poulantzas, Nicos 1978. *State, Power, Socialism*. London: New Left Books.

Przeworski, Adam 1985. *Capitalism and Social Democracy*. Cambridge: Cambridge University Press.

Rancière, Jacques 1995. *On the Shores of Politics*. London: Verso.

Rancière, Jacques 1999. *Disagreement*. Minneapolis, MN: University of Minnesota Press.

Rancière, Jacques 2006. *The Politics of Aesthetics: The Distribution of the Sensible*. London: Continuum.

Rawls, John 2003. *A Theory of Justice: Revised Edition*. Cambridge, MA: Harvard University Press.

Reiman, Jeffrey 1991. "Moral Philosophy: The Critique of Capitalism and the Problem of Ideology". In *The Cambridge Companion to Marx*, Terrell Carver (ed.), 143–67. Cambridge: Cambridge University Press.

Resch, Robert 1992. *Althusser and the Renewal of Marxist Social Theory*. Berkeley, CA: University of California Press.

Rickert, John 1986. "The Fromm–Marcuse Debate Revisited". *Theory and Society* **15**(3): 351–400.

Rigby, S. H. 1998. *Marxism and History: A Critical Introduction*. Manchester: Manchester University Press.

Roberts, Marcus 1996. *Analytical Marxism: A Critique*. London: Verso.

Roemer, John 1982a. *A General Theory of Exploitation and Class*. Cambridge, MA: Harvard University Press.

Roemer, John 1982b. "New Directions in the Marxian Theory of Exploitation and Class". *Politics and Society* **11**(3): 253–87.

Roemer, John 1988. *Free to Lose: An Introduction to Marxist Economic Theory*. Cambridge, MA: Harvard University Press.

Roemer, John 1993. "Can There Be Socialism after Communism?". In *Market Socialism*, Pranab Bardhan & John Roemer (eds), 89–107. Oxford: Oxford University Press.

Roemer, John 1994. *A Future for Socialism*. London: Verso.

Rosdolsky, Roman 1977. *The Making of Marx's Capital*. London: Pluto Press.

Sayers, Sean 1998. *Marxism and Human Nature*. London: Routledge.

Schmidt, Alfred 1971. *The Concept of Nature in Marx*. London: New Left Books.

Schoolman, Morton 1980. *The Imaginary Witness: The Critical Theory of Herbert Marcuse*. New York: Free Press.

Shu-Tse, P'eng 1980. *The Chinese Communist Party in Power*. New York: Monad Press.

Sim, Stuart 1998. "Spectres and Nostalgia: Post-*Marxism*/*Post*-Marxism". In *Post-Marxism: A Reader*, Stuart Sim (ed.), 1–15. Edinburgh: Edinburgh University Press.

Sinnerbrink, Robert 2007. *Understanding Hegelianism*. Stocksfield: Acumen.

Sitton, John 1996. *Recent Marxian Theory: Class Formation and Social Conflict in Contemporary Capitalism*. Albany, NY: SUNY Press.

Sitton, John 2003. *Habermas and Contemporary Society*. London: Palgrave Macmillan.

Slater, Phil 1977. *Origin and Significance of the Frankfurt School: A Marxist Perspective*. London: Routledge & Kegan Paul.

Smith, Tony 1989. *The Logic of Marx's Capital: Replies to Hegelian Objections*. Albany, NY: SUNY Press.

Sraffa, Piero 1975. *Production of Commodities by Means of Commodities: Prelude to a Critique of Economic Theory*. Cambridge: Cambridge University Press.

Stalin, Joseph 1943. *Problems of Leninism*. Moscow: Foreign Languages Publishing House.

Tar, Zoltan 1977. *The Frankfurt School: The Critical Theories of Theodor Adorno and Max Horkheimer*. New York: John Wiley.

Therborn, Göran 1980. *The Power of Ideology and the Ideology of Power*. London: New Left Books.

Trotsky, Leon 1970. *The Third International after Lenin*. New York: Pathfinder Press.

Trotsky, Leon 1972. *The Revolution Betrayed: What Is the Soviet Union and Where Is It Going?* New York: Pathfinder Press.

Tse-Tung, Mao 1967–69. *Selected Works of Mao Tse-Tung in Four Volumes*. Peking: Foreign Languages Press.

Uchida, Hiroshi 1988. *Marx's Grundrisse and Hegel's Logic*. London: Routledge.

Vogel, Lise 1983. *Marxism and the Oppression of Women: Toward a Unitary Theory*. London: Pluto Press.

Wallerstein, Immanuel 1990. "Antisystemic Movements: History and Dilemmas". In *Transforming the Revolution*, Samir Amin, Giovanni Arrighi *et al.* (eds), 13–53. New York: Monthly Review Press.

Wallerstein, Immanuel (ed.) 2002. *The World We Are Entering, 2000–2050*. Amsterdam: Dutch University Press.

Weber, Henri 1978. "Eurocommunism, Socialism and Democracy". *New Left Review* **110**: 3–14.

Wiggershaus, Rolf 1994. *The Frankfurt School: Its History, Theories, and Political Significance*. Cambridge: Polity.

Wittfogel, Karl 1957. *Oriental Despotism*. New Haven, CT: Yale University Press.

Wood, Ellen 1986. *The Retreat From Class: A New "True" Socialism*. London: Verso.

Wood, Ellen 1990. "Rational Choice Marxism: Is the Game Worth the Candle?". *New Left Review* **1**(177): 41–88.

Wood, Ellen 1995. *Democracy Against Capitalism: Renewing Historical Materialism*. Cambridge: Cambridge University Press.

Wright, Erik Olin 1979. *Class Structure and Income Determination*. New York: Academic Press.

Wright, Erik Olin 1985. *Classes*. London: Verso.

Wright, Erik Olin, Elliott Sober *et al.* 1992. *Reconstructing Marxism: Essays on Explanation and the Theory of History.* London: Verso.

Zeleny, Jindrich 1980. *The Logic of Marx.* Oxford: Blackwell.

Žižek, Slavoj 1989. *The Sublime Object of Ideology.* London: Verso.

Žižek, Slavoj 1990. "Beyond Discourse Analysis". In *New Reflections on the Revolution of Our Time,* Ernesto Laclau (ed.), 249–60. London: Verso.

Žižek, Slavoj 1991. *For They Know Not What They Do.* London: Verso.

Žižek, Slavoj 1993. *Tarrying with the Negative: Kant, Hegel and the Critique of Ideology.* London: Verso.

Žižek, Slavoj 1994. *The Metastases of Enjoyment: Six Essays on Woman and Causality.* London: Verso.

Žižek, Slavoj 1999. *The Ticklish Subject: The Absent Centre of Political Ontology.* London: Verso.

Žižek, Slavoj 2000. "Class Struggle or Postmodernism? Yes, Please!". In *Contingency, Hegemony, Universality: Contemporary Dialogues on the Left,* Judith Butler, Ernesto Laclau *et al.* (eds), 90–135. London: Verso.

Žižek, Slavoj 2002. *Welcome to the Desert of the Real.* London: Verso.

Žižek, Slavoj 2004. "Ethical Socialism? No Thanks! Reply to Boucher". *Telos: A Quarterly Journal of Critical Thought* **129**: 173–89.

Žižek, Slavoj 2005. *Iraq: The Borrowed Kettle.* London: Verso.

Žižek, Slavoj 2008a. *In Defense of Lost Causes.* London: Verso.

Žižek, Slavoj 2008b. *Violence: Six Sideways Reflections.* London: Profile Books.

Žižek, Slavoj 2009. *First as Tragedy, Then as Farce.* London: Verso.

Žižek, Slavoj 2010. *Living in the End Times.* London: Verso.

Index

commodity   25, 27, 82
communicative action   195–200
communicative reason   196, 197
communism   4–5, 9, 38, 41–2, 43–4,
    46, 60, 69, 75–6, 78, 177, 240,
    242
    as historical Communism   1, 48,
        71, 73–4, 75, 77, 157, 171, 216
    as Eurocommunism   133, 155–7,
        222
Communist party   18, 72–4, 78, 79,
    80, 90, 99

Darwin, Charles   48, 50, 56, 78
dialectic   5, 9, 10, 14–19, 23, 41, 45,
    48, 50–51, 53, 80, 81, 86, 90–91,
    100, 103–4, 107–8, 110, 116–18,
    120, 121–5, 127, 131, 133, 139,
    161–2, 185, 188, 200, 236–7, 243
dictatorship of the bourgeoisie   2, 36,
    103, 110, 124, 133, 183
    as capitalist state   5, 12, 17, 37–8,
        44, 46, 58, 73, 78, 83, 89–90,
        94, 95–7, 99, 104, 110–12, 121,
        124, 128, 159, 180, 183, 185,
        187, 191, 203–4, 205, 207, 211,
        219, 221, 227, 229, 232,
    as nation state   35–8, 68–9, 138,
        145–50, 151–2, 156, 213, 234,
        243
    see also   parliamentary democracy
dictatorship of the proletariat   1, 4, 37,
    70, 156, 171, 240
    as socialist state   1, 3, 41, 46, 67,
        69, 73
    as social republic   37, 41
    as workers' state   69, 74, 75, 77, 78
    see also   participatory democracy
division of labour   21–3, 25, 33–5, 42,
    98, 108, 109, 126, 135, 138, 153,
    154, 185

Elster, Jon   162, 163, 166–9, 173, 174,
    176, 179
Engels, Friedrich   3, 5, 6, 9, 16, 18, 19,
    21, 30, 32, 33–5, 36, 41, 47, 48–52,

61, 62, 65, 66–7, 78, 98, 110, 143,
    172, 188
Enlightenment   13, 14, 17, 44, 104,
    109, 119–24, 128, 184–6, 188–9,
    203
exchange value   24–6, 39, 110
exploitation   5, 23–4, 28, 29, 30, 31,
    35–9, 41–2, 44, 45, 60–61, 68,
    134–5, 152, 154, 168, 169–73,
    175, 180, 198, 207, 224

falling rate of profit   28, 30, 45, 167,
    168, 191
family   15, 31, 33–5, 104, 108, 113,
    115, 149, 151, 153–5, 159, 209,
    210–11
feudalism   7, 8, 9, 30–32, 58, 59, 61,
    62–4, 68, 93–4, 116, 135
Feuerbach, Ludwig   17, 19–20, 50
Fraser, Nancy   208, 209
freedom   2, 5, 13, 14–17, 21, 23, 27,
    39–40, 40–43, 81–2, 106, 109,
    123–4, 125, 153, 175, 208
French Revolution   17, 226
    and Jacobins   218, 226, 227, 228,
        240
Freud, Sigmund   106, 108, 109–10,
    112–15, 118, 120, 122, 123, 125,
    128, 148
Fromm, Erich   103, 110, 113–14,
functionalism   39, 57, 119, 132,
    134–5, 137–8, 145, 146, 148, 151,
    154–5, 158, 162–6, 168, 180, 186,
    200, 204, 210

game theory   161
Geras, Norman   20, 43, 216, 225
Gramsci, Antonio   4, 79, 89–101, 106,
    151, 218, 219, 220

Habermas, Jürgen   10, 11, 41,
    183–209, 210
Hegel, G. W. F.   9–10, 13, 14–20, 21,
    24, 30, 38, 45, 51, 78–82, 84–7,
    89, 91–2, 104, 107, 109, 123,
    126, 133–4, 139, 147, 162,